LARRIMAH

When Caroline Graham and Kylie Stevenson first met in a regional Queensland newsroom, neither of them imagined that thirteen years later they'd be sharing a room in a tiny outback town embroiled in a murder mystery. Before co-writing this book, they made the 2018 Walkley Award–winning podcast *Lost in Larrimah*. In the process, they have eaten more meat pies and pub schnitzels than they should have.

Kylie Stevenson has 20 years' experience as a journalist, her work appearing in *The Guardian*, *The Australian*, the *Weekend Australian Magazine*, the *Saturday Paper* and numerous health, lifestyle and travel publications. She has spent the last 14 years working in the Northern Territory, eight of them at the iconic, croc-obsessed *NT News*. She is currently undertaking a Doctorate of Creative Arts at the University of Wollongong, and to fund this folly she continues freelance writing. Kylie lives on Larrakia country in Darwin with her husband Michael, son Eddie and their dog Walter.

Caroline Graham has worked as a newspaper reporter and magazine writer, and has taught journalism at Bond University for more than a decade. She is the co-author of *Writing Feature Stories: How to research and write articles—from listicles to longform*, has a PhD in creative writing and has written for a range of publications, including the *Weekend Australian*, *The Guardian* and the *Daily Mercury*. Her short fiction and creative non-fiction has been published by *Day One* and Text. She lives on Yugambeh country on the Gold Coast and nothing makes her feel more smug than when someone congratulates her on her morning ocean swim in winter. It isn't even that cold on the Gold Coast.

LARRIMAH

A MISSING MAN, AN EYELESS CROC, AND AN OUTBACK TOWN OF ~~12~~ 11 PEOPLE WHO MOSTLY HATE EACH OTHER

CAROLINE GRAHAM & KYLIE STEVENSON

ALLEN&UNWIN
SYDNEY · MELBOURNE · AUCKLAND · LONDON

First published in 2021

Allen & Unwin
83 Alexander Street
Crows Nest NSW 2065
Australia
Phone: (61 2) 8425 0100
Email: info@allenandunwin.com
Web: www.allenandunwin.com

A catalogue record for this book is available from the National Library of Australia

ISBN 978 1 76087 783 5

Inside cover image: NTLIS (aerial photo of Larrimah)
Maps by Mika Tabata
Set in 13/16 pt Arno Pro by Post Pre-press Group, Australia
Printed in Australia by McPherson's Printing Group

10 9 8 7 6 5 4 3 2 1

*For Larrimah, a town that isn't good and isn't ours
but that we love, earnestly.*

Contents

We acknowledge the traditional owners of the lands we have visited in telling this story, including the Wubalawun people of the Larrimah area. They are the first and rightful storytellers and keepers of knowledge of our land.

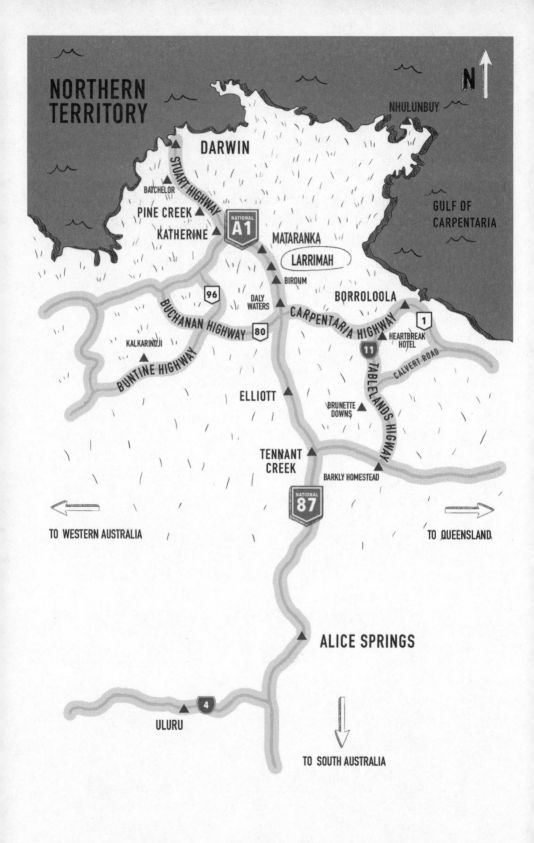

LARRIMAH

FRAN'S DEVONSHIRE TEA HOUSE

LARRIMAH PINK PANTHER HOTEL

PADDY'S HOUSE ▶

STUART HIGHWAY

LARRIMAH MUSEUM

REPLICA RAILWAY PLATFORM ◀

TOWN ROAD

SITE OF GREEN PARK (CARAVAN PARK AND FUEL STATION DESTROYED BY FIRE) ◀

RUBBISH DUMP ◀

TO GORRIE AIRFIELD 11KM NORTH

TO BIRDUM 11KM SOUTH

N

Disclaimer

They say not to let the truth get in the way of a good story, but it very much got in the way of this one. It turns out it's impossible to fact-check who killed whose pet buffalo two decades ago, so we apologise for any errors. If you take out everything we couldn't pin down, this is really just a book about how hot the outback is. That's pretty much the only thing we could prove. Believe us when we tell you: we really tried.

Prologue

If she'd known what would come later, Fran Hodgetts probably wouldn't have bothered with the haircut.

It was an ordinary December morning. The sun had just come up, but the Stuart Highway was already shimmering in the heat. Without the grey nomads and backpackers who usually filled its lanes in the dry season, the highway sat quiet. The wet season is not the time to visit Larrimah—the thermometer hovers around 40 degrees Celsius and the humidity just about kills you. Last night, a big downpour had dumped 33 millimetres on the town and, this morning, the air had thickened in its wake.

Without any tourists, business was slow at Fran's outback Devonshire teahouse. In the dry season, she was flat out brewing tea, baking scones and cooking buffalo and crocodile pies. She'd recently been inspired to add waffles topped with camel mince to the menu. But with the big rains due, there just wasn't the demand. At this time of year, sometimes she'd only sell a coffee a week. Sometimes it was one a month. Still, she tried to keep the gates open—mostly for the company. If no one were around, she'd cook batches of pies and scones and freeze them for the busy times. That was the usual pattern of things.

But today, Fran was taking the day off.

She stood in her bathroom applying eyeliner and pencilling in her eyebrows, knowing full well sweat would distort her efforts before she made it out the front door. It was about seven thirty and she had to hit the road soon if she was going to make her hair-dressing appointment in Katherine at nine thirty. She grabbed her handbag and hurried downstairs to her car, only to be interrupted by her gardener's large frame loping across the yard.

'Look at that,' he called. Owen Laurie had been in Larrimah a few months, tending Fran's bougainvillea and expansive lawn in exchange for a room for him and his dog. He was an old bushie and mostly kept to himself, but he was a good worker.

'Look at all those coppas,' Owen said, pointing towards Paddy Moriarty's house, directly across the highway. Fran nodded. The police had been there yesterday too, crawling over the old road-house Paddy lived in, like ants on a nest. She knew what this was about—she'd suspected Paddy of drug dealing for years. Someone who had been mates with him told her Paddy sold dope, kept it hidden under his floorboards. The drug bust she'd been waiting for had arrived.

She was eager to pay the cops a visit to tell them what she knew. But first, the haircut.

Larrimah is stranded halfway between Mataranka and Daly Waters, in what's called Never Never country. Katherine, 180 kilometres away, is the closest major town—but calling it major is probably overstating it. The book *Sh*t Towns of Australia* says Katherine is 'basically a tarted-up gulag masquerading as civilisation', which seems a little unfair. It does have a Woolworths, a McDonald's and at least five bottle shops, which is a lot more than what's available in Larrimah. The closest thing to a shop here is a dusty shelf at the pub, which at last count held seventeen cans, most of them tinned asparagus.

But the dearth of local produce in Larrimah is fair enough; demand isn't high when you're catering to a population of about a dozen. And, so, regular trips to Katherine for supplies and services are a necessary ordeal for Larrimah's handful of residents, and with a speed limit of 130 kilometres per hour the journey along the Stuart Highway, known as The Track to locals, goes quickly. Fran was only ten minutes away from her Katherine appointment when the police pulled her over.

'You're Fran?' the officer asked.

'Yeah.' Fran wasn't fazed that he knew her name. She was well known in these parts. Anyone who'd driven along her stretch of The Track had encountered her teahouse and homemade pies—or, at the very least, the signs pointing to them. The business had landed her in *Lonely Planet* guidebooks and on several travel programs. She was also a bit of a character—mid-seventies, so short she barely reached most people's shoulders, and built like a kindly grandmother whose soft appearance was at odds with her penchant for the F-word.

The officer leaned in. 'We want you to go up to the head office in Katherine and make a statement.'

'Well, that's where I'm going. I seen you had a drug bust over the road.'

'No,' the officer said. 'Paddy's missing.'

Fran was shocked. 'Nah.'

'Yeah, he's missing.'

The officer told her Paddy's dog was missing, too.

There was a moment of silence as Fran digested the news.

'Well, I never murdered him,' she said.

It was a joke, something she said in the spur of the moment. But, as she conceded later, it turned out not to be that funny.

Fran had travelled almost two hours, so she kept her appointment. At that stage, Paddy's disappearance wasn't considered suspicious. He was only missing. Police just needed to know if Fran had seen him or knew where he might be.

When the haircut was finished, Fran made her way to the police station, ready to tell her story. She hadn't seen Paddy since 12 December, four days before he disappeared. She remembered it well because it wasn't even midday, but it was scorching—the hottest day of the year. She had been in her bedroom packing a bag for a trip to Darwin, and when she looked out the window, she saw a figure on the road, struggling with something heavy. She squinted, and as the silhouette got closer, she realised it was Paddy dragging a dead kangaroo across the highway by its tail. His dog, Kellie, was by his side. He threw the kangaroo somewhere between Fran's driveway and bedroom. Then he looked up at her, smiled, and walked away. That was the last time she saw Paddy, she told officers.

The police interview was the beginning of a nightmare for Fran. The hullabaloo soon moved over the road, from Paddy's place to hers. In the coming weeks, she gave police eighty-one pages of statements. Owen, her gardener, was questioned, too. Search teams went through everything—Fran's personal effects, her business papers. They went through the whole house five times. They took her receipts away. They drained her septic tank, emptied and searched the incinerator, combed through the shed. They unpacked her freezers, turning up a $7000 wad of cash.

Pretty soon, the story travelled. Reporters started turning up at her house. She appeared on *A Current Affair* and Leigh Sales interviewed her on *7.30*. She got a publicity manager. Fame became infamy, and before long there was no pleasure in being recognised. People were driving past her teahouse shouting, 'Murderer!'

Mark Twain once said that a lie can gallop halfway around the world before the truth has time to pull its britches on, and maybe that's what happened to Larrimah. It wasn't that the story got twisted into lies, exactly, it's just that it was already such a strange, tall tale: a dying town, a missing man, his missing dog, a deadly landscape. Alcohol. Enemies. Sinkholes. And a setting so tiny and remote that it seemed tantalisingly contained. Like an outback Agatha Christie. Then, under the heat of the media spotlight, the story grew. The whole thing became mythic. Bigger than the truth. Or, at least, bigger than *a* truth.

Which is how we ended up in Larrimah.

Before we set off to write a book about Larrimah and Paddy, we told ourselves we weren't like all the others—the Hollywood producers, documentary makers and shock jocks, caught up in telling what might be the best Australian story that ever really happened. We were different, we thought, because one of us had met Paddy. We already knew most of the people in town and our interest in Larrimah predated the disappearance. We'd been obsessed with the place for ages—nattering about it at barbecues and pitching stories about the town's history to media outlets and gifting souvenir Larrimah stubby coolers to our long-suffering friends and family.

But maybe that's a lie, too. Something we said to make ourselves feel better. In the end, we got caught up in the story. And the myth.

What we do know is this: back in 2017, Paddy Moriarty was not the only one doing a disappearing act. The town of Larrimah—and maybe the outback itself—was balancing on some kind of knife's edge and we wanted there to be a record of it before it slipped off the map. We needed to find out what the hell happened to the almost ghost town of Larrimah *and* what happened to Paddy. Because it's impossible to tease the two stories apart. They're like two whodunnits, twisted together.

PART ONE

The disappearing man

Three months after the disappearance.

1

A pink pub, a blind croc and an empty bar stool

It's almost 500 kilometres from Darwin to Larrimah and people say there's not a lot to see, but we see plenty. Sixty-eight termite mounds dressed up like people—one in a Santa hat, another in soggy old jocks. One dead pig. Eighteen dead wallabies and two live ones. A broken-down car with all its wheels stolen. Dozens of roadside memorials.

We speed past a tree with hundreds of shoes tied to it, signs about alcohol restrictions, flood markers stranded in the dust, lots of questionable accommodation facilities all calling themselves 'resorts'. The scrub on one side of the highway is burnt black, like someone has tried to match it to the bitumen. Scavenger birds pick at roadkill.

We've seen no one else driving south, and only a handful of cars travelling north. At one point, the odometer stops working, and then it starts going backwards. Somewhere between Mataranka and Larrimah, a whirly-whirly appears, like an angry god has cast a tiny dusty tornado into our path. It's hard to pretend it doesn't feel like an omen.

It is 2 April 2018. Paddy's seventy-first birthday would have been three days ago. He's been missing for more than three months.

The town appears like an absurd oasis on the dusty horizon. After a long stretch of scrub, it's an assault of red earth, green palms, magenta bougainvillea. But an oasis is supposed to be an idyllic escape and, up close, Larrimah is not.

We follow some beat-up billboards with Pink Panthers on them—mostly hand-painted, and not always perfectly proportioned—directing traffic towards the pub, although the town's handful of streets present very little opportunity for a wrong turn. Plus, the pub—commonly known as the Pink Panther—is easy to find because it's painted bright pink and has a giant beer bottle out the front.

If it's possible for a place to look hungover, the Larrimah Hotel does. It's clear something wild happened here—some huge, eras-long party. But it's also obvious the party is over, and the after-effects are showing. Everything is haggard.

For the past twenty years, Larrimah has been one of those few-and-far-between places on the highway that people either sped past or briefly stretched their legs in. But in World War II, thousands of soldiers were stationed here. The region had a picture theatre, a bakery, an ice factory, a railway station and a racecourse, and people reckon part of the war in the Pacific was directed from the verandah of the pub. There was a time when Larrimah *mattered*.

Once the war ended, Larrimah ticked on as a wild, lawless frontier town—a transport hub, the end of the railway line, where people passing through met for beers that turned into days-long benders. At one point, there were three venues with liquor licences and often the pub was so busy you couldn't get a parking spot.

Today, there is no such problem. We are the only car pulled up in front of a couple of oversized Pink Panther sculptures. One is headless, flying a gyrocopter, and the other is reclining in a deckchair.

There must be a line between a town and a not-town, but deciding where to draw it is tricky. When you google the smallest town in Australia, Cooladdi comes up. It's in north-west Queensland and has three residents, but on closer inspection, it turns out they're all related and run the local roadhouse, so it's really more of a family business than a town. Betoota, in south-west Queensland, has tried to claim the honour, too, but its population has been zero since the owner of the pub died in 2004, which puts it firmly in ghost-town territory. Across the ditch, in New Zealand, a place called Cass says it's one of the only one-man towns in the world. But really, when you're down to one, you're more of a hermit than a municipality.

With only twelve people—actually, eleven now—Larrimah is technically a hamlet. It has a handful of houses, an unmanned museum, a teahouse, a few sheds and, of course, the pub.

We cross the verandah of the Larrimah Hotel, past more stuffed Pink Panthers and old trinkets, and find ourselves face to face with Paddy Moriarty. He's wearing a faded cap and a huge grin, which even his lush moustache can't hide. He was known around these parts as a great storyteller; he was such a fixture that people called him the town concierge. But we don't get the jolly welcome he's known for. It's only his face on a laminated sign under a huge headline: 'Missing. What happened to Paddy?'

The police poster has all the grim details. Full name: Patrick (Paddy) Moriarty. Approximately 178 centimetres tall. Black and grey hair. Age seventy. Last sighted at dusk on Saturday, 16 December 2017, when he left the Larrimah Hotel on his quad bike with his dog, Kellie. She's pictured on the sign, too—the red-and-brown kelpie looks young, friendly, with her tongue sticking out.

'Hey, you girls need a hand?'

We spin around.

A man has appeared behind the bar, drinking a tinnie. We haven't met him before, but we recognise him from the news stories about Paddy. His name's Richard Simpson and we know he works at the pub. He's got a long beard, he's wearing a singlet with armholes so long and looping he might as well be shirtless, and his skin is so weathered you can't make out the tattoo on his bicep.

But however rough Richard looks, he's friendly. When we introduce ourselves as the latest mob of press to turn up, he shakes his scruffy head and is gracious about it. In lots of towns, buying a beer is the fastest way to prove you're not an arsehole, so that's what we do. Richard looks a bit relieved and cracks another for himself.

The pace is slow in Larrimah, and we ease into conversation. Where we're from, what we're doing. Small talk about the town. This is Richard's fourth stint at the pub—he loves it. Says the place gets under your skin. But he admits it's an acquired taste.

'If you want five star, you know, clean with no dust, don't stop at Larrimah, go somewhere else. Simple as that,' he says. 'We don't need you coming in and whingeing at us 'cos we're just going to take the piss out of you for it. It's a country pub, you know. It's one of the last ones left.'

We take that as our cue to finish up our beers and ask for the room keys.

'You're in room nine—the executive suite,' he says, then steers us through the pub's courtyard.

The afternoon is thick with the sound of birdsong, made louder by the absence of any other noise. The courtyard is crowded with dozens of bird cages and plastic tables and chairs, shaded by sweet-smelling Rangoon creeper and a huge African mahogany. About ten paces from our bedroom door, we encounter the first of the pub's three crocodiles: golden, at least a metre long, and missing its eyeballs. His name is Ray Charles but everyone calls him Ray-Ray.

'He's got a genetic abnormality,' Richard says. 'Not that there's anything abnormal about genetics.' He starts addressing the reptile. 'Still just a little fella, aren't you, mate? You old snaggletooth.'

As we unlock the room, there is a long, low rumble behind us. The crocodile is purring.

It turns out, our room is called the 'executive suite' because it has two beds and the luxury of a toaster, in which some spiders have made a home. Everything is clean, but the hotel is fighting a losing battle against nature. An army of ants have taken over the en suite and the stench of bore water is overpowering. It smells like rotten eggs and the shower runs hot, even when you only turn on the cold tap. The only window is blocked off by an aviary of birds, casting a dimness over everything.

As daylight fades, the weight of why we are here begins to feel heavier. Paddy's disappearance has heightened existing tensions in the town. Some residents are talking about leaving, and no one is young—health concerns are creeping up on people, and Larrimah is a long way from the nearest hospital. The place is slipping closer to the edge of extinction by the day.

It's not just Larrimah. The outback is full of tiny towns struggling to survive and as they start to drop off the map, their stories, histories and ways of life disappear with them. You can almost see it happening, in slow motion.

Outside, dusk thrums with noises: birds, insects, the wheeze of the ancient box air-conditioner. We are a long way from anywhere, and Larrimah has no phone reception. It's full of things that can kill you: spiders, snakes, crocodiles. Maybe people.

Stories are usually sprawling, murky things. They start in one place and trickle out like rivers into creeks, branching into unexpected territories. But there's something contained about this one. We can draw a boundary around it. The town is 800 metres end to end, with eleven people. Someone must know what happened here.

Richard Simpson. Barry Sharpe. Karen and Mark Rayner. Lenny Hodson. Barry Burke. Fran Hodgetts. Bill Hodgetts. Karl and Bobbie

Roth. Owen Laurie. This is the list of people we need to speak to. A roll call of Larrimah's population when Paddy went missing.

And there's an obvious place to start. In a town this size, being the publican is a little bit like being the mayor. So, the next morning, we go to find Barry Sharpe.

Barry's khaki-clad figure is perched on a stool in the bar, a cup of tea in front of him. It's only 9 am, but he looks utterly exhausted— like he's already put in a hard day and it's wrung the energy right out of him.

'Oh,' he says, looking up when we arrive at his table. 'Want a cuppa?' His northern Australian accent is dense, words rolling into one another. He shuffles out the back and returns holding a couple of chipped mugs with Lipton teabags floating in them.

We settle onto some bar stools beside three human-sized stuffed Pink Panthers riding a triple tandem bike. Barry tells us he's fixed it to the wall because people always tried to ride it after a few beers. We ask if he's ever ridden it.

'Oh yeah. When I was half bloody drunk.' He laughs. Barry has a wonderful laugh. It's a soft and scratchy sound that sneaks up, even on him.

Barry is almost seventy-six and exactly the person you'd cast to play an ageing outback pub owner in a movie. He's not rough, exactly, but he probably has a few outlaw tendencies. His grey whiskers are always hiding a wry smile, and his khaki shirt is cut off at the sleeves, exposing weather-beaten arms. His limbs are thin but his stomach bulges a little from a publican's diet of booze and parmies.

Barry's spent a lifetime in the bush doing ludicrous things: wrangling snakes for antivenin and catching crocs, back when that kind of thing was allowed. He and his ex, Ann Kanters, relocated here from Dunedoo, in New South Wales. 'I just turned up one day, came in for a drink and I never left,' he tells us. 'That was twenty-eight years ago.'

They took over the Larrimah Hotel when the previous manager left in 2002. By this point, they'd already been in town for a while and were involved with the town's volunteer community group, the Larrimah Progress Association.

Barry set up a zoo up the back of the pub, over the years accumulating a pair of emus, some rescued wallabies, a colony of squirrel gliders, a handful of snakes and about five hundred birds. As well as Ray (the crocodile with no eyeballs), he has a freshie called Aggro and a saltie named Sneaky Sam, who he bought when he was just 30 centimetres long and could be kept in a tank at the bar. Now Sam measures 3.5 metres and lives right down the back of the pub in a pond the size of a small swimming pool, potentially because it once was a small swimming pool.

Barry's other passion is history; in particular, the area's history. He's surrounded himself with it in the pub. The war years, the rail, the trucking years, the cattle stations, the region's Aboriginal history—the town's most important eras are all recognised in an eclectic mix of bullets, old crossing signs, numberplates and saddles.

There's no good way to ask someone how their best mate might have been murdered. But Larrimah's the kind of place where things that would stay unsaid elsewhere quickly rise to the surface of a conversation.

Around us, two TVs murmur, both tuned to the ABC. The tin roof creaks in the morning heat. A lazy pedestal fan does its best to beat back the rising temperature. And, although we haven't exactly asked, the story starts to slip out.

2

An esky race, 600,000 mealworms and an uncollected mower

The Sunday began as every other day in Larrimah did: with the chirping of birds—the 'dawn service' as Barry called it—and the sound of donkey hooves disappearing into the scrub. The truckies who'd parked up and slept in the siding overnight had cleared out at first light. The Greyhound bus on its way to Alice Springs paused briefly near the entrance to the Larrimah Hotel. No one got on, no one got off.

It wasn't even mid-morning and sweat patches were already forming in the armpits of Barry's khaki shirt. It had been a bad build-up, although the build-up was always bad. A season of hideous in-between, the time of year when everyone went a little mad waiting for the wet. 'Going troppo', they called it.

Having dished out food to his hundreds of hungry pets, Barry unlocked the pub, made himself a cuppa and melted into a bar stool. He turned the ABC news up loud on the two televisions, but he was only half paying attention. He hadn't been feeling great for a while. The cancer medication was knocking him around.

Richard was up early, too. He'd fed his three antisocial American staffies, chained up under one of the huts in the camping area, then joined his boss in the bar. He rolled a cigarette and sipped from his mug of Nescafé, his straggly, grey beard brushing against the dusty table as he bent to light the smoke. In between serving beers last night, Richard had been boozing with some country folk who were travelling through—welcome company during the off-season. He could have been forgiven for sleeping late in his air-conditioned donga out the back, but the ability to back up after a heavy night on the grog was expected in this part of the world. Drinking skills weren't something to be ashamed of around here; in fact, they were cause to erect the five-metre-tall concrete statue of a beer bottle out front. The Larrimah Hotel claims it once had the honour of selling the most Darwin Stubbies—a two-litre beer that is no longer in production, as it had to be consumed at pace to avoid growing warm. So, to congratulate itself, the pub had built a tribute.

Barry and Richard slumped lethargically in the stagnant air, puncturing the ABC with the usual small talk about what needed doing: things like raking the leaves in the courtyard, restocking the bar fridges, cleaning out the toilet block. They cursed the sparse clouds overhead that had dumped a few inches on the town in a furious downpour a few nights before, but since then had been empty promises that closed in the heat and humidity.

It was probably before 11 am when Richard shuffled along the crowded sliver of space behind the bar and cracked open a drink. He was known to take advantage of his position in charge of the beer fridge, drinking the occasional 'staffy'. On a slow day, like today, it was likely he'd drink more than he sold. Barry turned a blind eye. The pub had always been a bit this way—attracting the kind of employees who'd help themselves. One of Barry's mates had worked there five times and never left on good terms. Still, Richard worked hard and Barry needed the help. He checked his watch: it was almost time for 'church' and Paddy should be here soon.

In Larrimah, days moved slowly, as if the town were wading through syrup, but 'church'—what they called ABC's premier weekly rural news program, Landline—was one of the only consistent time-markers; something to rely on. For years, Paddy and Barry had slipped into the bar after midday on a Sunday and watched the tele together. But on 17 December 2017, Paddy was a no-show.

Barry wasn't really surprised. He'd known Paddy for well over a decade, since before he moved to town, which was plenty long enough to appreciate his propensity for a good time. Paddy had been in fine form at the pub the evening before. He'd upgraded his daily eight mid-strength beers to ten and had left with a bit of a wobbly boot on. He was drunk, but not drunk-drunk. He wasn't Paddy-drunk.

He'd also stayed a little longer than usual, lured by the limelight that came with the fresh ears of tourists, a new audience for his well-worn tales. He might have told the yarn about the shootout he was involved in at Heartbreak Hotel, the place he also told people part of his job was looking after escorts, or all the shenanigans he got up to as a young man working as a ringer on Brunette Downs, or perhaps he'd have boasted about how he could crack two whips at once. There's a chance he might have talked about his neighbour, Fran, who he called the Bush Pig, and how she was always accusing him of poisoning her plants.

Around dusk, Paddy had pulled up stumps. 'Right, this is my last can, this is my last supper,' he said, as he drained his beer. 'Yeah, I'm full, mate, I'm off.' And then he'd jumped on his red Honda quad bike with Kellie, the red-and-brown kelpie-cross he'd adopted six weeks before, and headed home.

Given that it had been a big night, Barry wasn't overly concerned when Paddy didn't show up for 'church'. But Paddy had mentioned he wanted to borrow the pub's mower, so when he didn't show up at all, it was a bit weird.

By Monday, Barry was starting to worry. Paddy should have been at the pub by 9 am. He wasn't a paid employee, but he fronted up every weekday morning to help with whatever needed doing: cleaning the toilets, chopping wood in the cooler months, doing a spot of gardening. Paddy was retired and it was something to do, plus Barry was a mate. It'd been going on a while before someone suggested Paddy take home a case of beer each week for his troubles. And now, he'd missed work and he hadn't collected that bloody mower. Maybe he was sick.

It was only 300 metres to Paddy's place. Barry crossed the highway and went round the back, past the sign discouraging people from buying pies at Fran's Devonshire teahouse and the shelter out front that used to house petrol bowsers, back when it had been the Top of the Town Roadhouse.

'Paddy?' he called. There was a besser block holding the back door shut. Paddy was probably out—he only really used the back door. But just in case there was some sort of problem, Barry kicked the block aside and walked through the house. 'Paddy. You here?'

The place was empty and Paddy's cap and key card were on the kitchen table. Kellie wasn't around, either—maybe Paddy had taken her out for a walk. Except they always went early in the morning, and Paddy wouldn't have gone into the impossible sunshine without his hat.

Still, none of it was cause for panic. There was a chance one of Paddy's mates had stopped in and taken him and Kellie somewhere for the day. That happened occasionally. But as Barry headed back across the highway to the pink pub and resumed his seat at the bar, his unease was building. Something felt off.

A group of tourists wanders in and follows the hum of the drinks fridge to its source and Barry gets up to serve them. It's an Irish guy with his parents and girlfriend, on their way down the Stuart Highway to Alice Springs. They see our microphones and ask whether we're here about the missing guy but they have enough tact not to put the question to Barry. Instead, they quiz him about a bottled snake perched on the bar. The reptile is swimming in a yellow liquid that has become so thick over time that its dead eyes look bulgy.

'It's a taipan, from Innisfail,' Barry tells them. 'A coppa come through here and he ended up giving us that.'

The group picks out some souvenirs—furry pink stubby holders—then asks if they can take their drinks over the road and look around the museum. We decide to clear out, too, conscious of the fact that a bunch of microphones and an open murder investigation might be bad for Barry's business.

Karen and Mark Rayner are some of Paddy's best mates in Larrimah. They used to manage the pub for Barry but now they're running a mechanic business out of an old workshop. We set out to visit them.

One of the paradoxes of Larrimah is its size; somehow, it's big and small at the same time. There's not much here but everything is spread out and the barren patches between properties feel vast. We should be able to tally up the roads and the houses, but every time we try, we become stuck trying to pinpoint the difference between a road and a dirt track, or a shed and a house. Even counting residents is tricky, because some people only live here part-time or temporarily.

Karen and Mark are on the southern side of town, so we strike out towards the old railway houses. We're not even 100 metres from the pub when our city thongs start to melt on our feet.

Even though there's no one around, as we walk, we whisper. Sound is another of Larrimah's contradictions. It's not exactly quiet—there are road trains thundering past and the flies and insects and birds are like a carpet of noise you never quite escape. But under all that, it feels silent. The crunch of the gravel under our feet is so loud we're sure the whole town knows where we are.

We pass the tiny museum, surrounded by World War II relics, and a high-set house that's seen better days. The town had plans of making it into a writers' house, somewhere creatives could retreat to sweat out a book, but that hasn't happened yet. Last we heard, Barry was using the downstairs toilet to store a tombstone.

Barry had given us directions to Karen and Mark but it was really just a half-nod in an ambiguous direction. We're running out of buildings and we still haven't found them. We pause beside a small white house with chest-high grass and a hand-painted sign on the gate: 'Pensioner Keep Out'. It's hard to tell whether pensioners are banned, or whether there's a pensioner inside keeping everyone away. Either way, it doesn't look like somewhere the Rayners would live.

Finally, a tractor zooms out of a nearby property and we're spared the embarrassment of having to return to the pub and admit we'd somehow got lost in this hamlet.

Achieving Princess Diana hair in the outback is a feat worthy of mention, especially because even Princess Di didn't pull it off. When she and her family landed in Alice Springs in 1983, *The Age* described Diana as wearing 'something less than a smile'— she was uneasy and glum, probably because she was wearing an aquamarine silk gown and white stockings and it was about one million degrees. But when Karen Rayner appears, her Princess Di hair is perfect and she's beaming. She's in denim shorts and a fluorescent singlet; she's so tall and lean she makes Larrimah-casual look elegant and she's somehow managed to find the only mascara robust enough for the outback elements. At forty-seven, she's the youngest person in town.

'Don't worry about the dogs, they're always crazy,' she calls as we approach. A Maltese-cross-Shih Tzu and a kelpie zoom around us. Since leaving the pub and zoo around six months ago, Karen has been accumulating her own wildlife collection—four rescued wallaroos, a pair of bunnies (who quickly became thirteen), two squirrel gliders, two dogs and two blue-tongued lizards.

'Come on, I'll show you Norman,' Karen says, leading us over to a pen beside the workshop.

A cow moos delightedly when he sees us. The Rayners adopted him as a poddy calf after his mum was hit by a car. If Karen's hair warrants a mention, so does Norman's. He is the Fergie to Karen's Diana and his auburn locks are impossibly shiny.

'Norman gets a wash once a week with shampoo and conditioner,' Karen says. 'He's the most spoiled calf around.'

When we ask what he's washed with, it's like Karen's been waiting for the question. 'Schwarzkopf, of course. Do you want a cuppa? I'll call Mark down from the tractor.'

The property Karen and Mark live on is Lot 51, but they call it Area 51, because they're kind of the aliens in Larrimah. They're the newest and youngest in town.

We pull up seats in the shade of an outdoor kitchen and dining room, which the Rayners have set up beside their caravan. They're staying here while they renovate one of the town's old rail-houses. It's an impressive temporary set-up, with a sink, fridge, kettle, microwave and wi-fi, all sheltered under a tin roof. There's also an air-conditioned donga, which we assume is where they're sleeping.

'No, that's where the mealworms are,' Karen tells us. 'Six hundred thousand of them.'

Karen breeds mealworms for pet shops in Darwin and Adelaide. When they're the right size, she'll box them up and send them on Greyhound buses, and they'll eventually become food for reptiles and birds. It's an unusual business, but the outback is renowned for implausible entrepreneurialism; people must be creative to get around the limits of heat and distance.

Mark arrives just as the kettle finishes boiling. His pale skin has been darkened by the layer of dust kicked up by the tractor. He was probably once ginger, but he's sixty-three and age has softened his hair with grey.

The Rayners first passed through Larrimah in 2015 on their way to Western Australia. They'd exchanged their Brisbane home for a life on the road, and of all the towns they stopped in, Larrimah made an impression—mainly because the pub owned a crocodile and Karen was afflicted with the same animal addiction as Barry. But they were due to start jobs in Broome, so they continued on their way.

About six months later, they limped back into town. Mark had torn his Achilles tendon and they had decided to head back to Queensland. But within a couple of days the Rayners had agreed to stick around and manage the pub.

In their former lives, Karen had worked in jewellery stores and trained as a chef and Mark held middle-management positions in the engineering industry. But at the Pink Panther they were serving beer, cooking up schnitzels and dealing with a different kind of clientele: brutes who'd pass through at 8 am and demand a beer. And then there were the locals.

'The culture of Larrimah is kind of a real eye-opener,' Mark says.

Still, they got into the spirit of running an outback pub, holding what was (probably) the Territory's first ride-on esky race in 2016, which drew dozens of people from all over—the photos are fantastic. Most of the ride-on eskies were decked out with flags or painted pink in honour of the pub; one bloke even made his into an elaborate train replica. Paddy kept it simple: a blue esky, a set of wheels and handlebars, a cold beer and his signature good hat. Nobody really remembers who won, but everyone partied until 2 am.

Karen and Mark grew close to Paddy during their time at the pub, and Karen sometimes cooked him meals, which he'd receive with praise and wonder. They'd watch cooking shows and Irish dancing together. Karen describes him as one of the only good people in town.

'Paddy was always laughing and always first to offer a hand and he never, ever expected anything for anything he did for you,' she says. 'He always made everyone feel welcome at the pub. People would come to Larrimah to see Paddy and they always left with a laugh.'

'You always looked forward to seeing Paddy,' Mark adds. 'He'd always brighten your day.'

So when word leaked out across town that Paddy hadn't been seen for a few days, they were worried. Karen says, 'I got this really bad feeling that something terrible had happened.'

Richard's phone call came on a Monday, and his gravelly tone suggested he wasn't ringing for a chat. Plus, he and Karen weren't on great terms, so the fact he was calling at all was unusual. 'Hey, I'm doing a welfare check. Have you seen Paddy?'

Welfare checks weren't uncommon in a town where almost everyone was on the other side of seventy, so Mark wasn't alarmed.

'Not for a few days,' he said. Paddy had come by late last week, with Kellie in tow, to collect his swag. The Rayners saw a bit less of him now they weren't working at the pub every day. In fact, Karen had stopped going to the pub altogether because she'd had a run-in with Richard.

It wasn't until that evening, when Mark went over to the pub to grab their mail, that the gravity of the situation became clear.

'What do you mean they haven't seen him or Kellie since Saturday?' asked Karen when Mark got back home and relayed the news. Forty-eight hours was a long time for Paddy not to be around.

The worry intensified overnight. So, on Tuesday morning, Karen and Mark went over to Paddy's. They wanted to make sure he hadn't fallen or had a heart attack, or been bitten by a snake or got stuck tinkering under his four-wheel drive. If any of those things had happened, he'd be lucky to survive in this heat. It'd been more than 40 degrees the last few days.

From outside, everything appeared in order. Except Paddy wasn't there. His car and quad bike were, though. The quad was exactly where he always parked it, with his sunglasses resting neatly on the handlebars.

Karen and Mark checked everywhere they could think of: under and inside cars, down the back of his property, all along the verandah, around bushes. He wasn't in the obvious places, so even the unlikely places seemed plausible. Finally, they reported back to Barry and he called the police at 4 pm. He asked to be patched through to Chalkie— Sergeant Thomas Chalk—the cop he knew at Mataranka. An operator in Darwin took a message and said someone would get back to him.

By Wednesday, the worry was palpable. The police hadn't returned Barry's call so Karen and Mark went back to Paddy's place. They knew he walked Kellie on the dump road so they zigzagged along it, keeping less than a metre between them so they wouldn't miss him if he'd fallen. They checked 20 metres either side of the track, in case he'd tumbled down a ditch. They had a second look around his backyard. They peeked into his shed. They called out Paddy's and Kellie's names over and over, but only the silence answered.

They'd been at it for nearly five hours in the 45-degree heat and Mark was getting sunstroke. The thought that Paddy might have been in the elements for days made them both feel sick.

'Do you think we should look in his house?' Mark finally asked.

There was a long pause. Paddy was a private person—he wouldn't want them poking around his things. Plus, Barry had already been inside. But what if Barry had missed something?

'Yeah, if he's not around,' Karen said. 'Yeah.'

They inhaled their fears and kicked back the besser block Barry had replaced at the back door. Already, they knew they wouldn't find Paddy. He only ever came and went through the back door and he couldn't be inside if the brick was blocking the door from the outside.

Paddy was a meticulous man, especially for an old bachelor. Everything had a place and everything was in place. The first thing Karen noticed was Paddy's good hat sitting on top of an esky. It was a pale, well-worn cowboy hat with a brown band that had leaked and stained the material around it. Paddy wouldn't go anywhere without his good hat. He was quite bald but almost no one knew that because he was so rarely seen bare-headed. If Paddy had planned a trip or gone off with a mate or to a party, the hat would have been the first thing he'd have grabbed. Either that or his everyday cap—but that was on the table, too, along with his keys, bank card, glasses and some food in a clear container, as if ready to be heated up.

Wherever Paddy was, he hadn't planned on being gone long.

Karen also noticed a distinct odour—'Old man smell', she called it—as she approached the bedroom. Paddy's bed had a slight impression in it, as if it had been laid on but not in. They checked underneath to make sure he hadn't rolled off. The light and fan were on.

Karen cautiously stepped down the hall to the bathroom. If she were right, if Paddy hadn't intended to be away, his medication would confirm that. Paddy had had bypass surgery a while ago and he couldn't go anywhere without the pills. The medication was on the sink, beside his toothbrush and toothpaste. Everything looked like he might walk back in at any moment and ask them what on earth they were doing sneaking around his place.

An awful feeling washed through Karen, as if someone had turned up the volume under her skin. Something terrible had happened. She just knew it. They had to get out of there. They shouldn't touch anything.

The only person they could think of who Paddy might spontaneously have left with was Ray Aylett, who lived at Elliott, 240 kilometres south. He and Paddy had been mates for twenty years. Karen and Mark didn't have his number, but Elliott is the sort of small town where you can call up the shop and someone will run a message over for you.

'I hear you've got Paddy kidnapped there or something,' Mark said, when he got through to Ray.

Ray had no idea what he was talking about—he hadn't seen Paddy in weeks.

Mark and Karen had a moment of reverse-claustrophobia, the sense of the enormity of the landscape around them. If Paddy were out there, somewhere in the scrub, they needed to find him, now—and they couldn't do it alone. Mark wondered about sending up his drone to *survey the area from above, but it seemed such an insignificant gesture. A tiny machine, trying to scan the infinite.*

So instead, they hurried back to the pub and urged Barry to call the police again. The whole time, they could feel their own too-fast heartbeats, a drum roll for the bad news they suspected would come next.

3

Some dingo scalps, a stolen piano accordion and a desperate search through the wretched Never Never

The sun has been pummelling us all day over at Karen and Mark's but by dusk it's lost its ferocity and transformed into something beautiful. The sky is awash with pinks, softer than the pub but no less luminous, and the birds return from their day out bush and settle noisily in the trees.

When we walk into the Pink Panther, there's a trio of Chinese tourists huddled by the bar—young women who look puzzled about where they've ended up for the night. We strike up a conversation. We imagine that, coming from China, it must be strange to visit a town of eleven people.

There's a moment of confusion.

'Eh?' They translate between themselves but incredulity is a universal language.

'Eleven people?'

'Eleven people here? Only eleven people?'

They gasp, almost in unison. One of the women starts counting heads in the pub. 'One. Two. Three. Four.'

We all laugh; there's something funny about seeing the disbelief live, but it's a reaction people have had to this place and this story, over and over. Larrimah's size is the thing that people seem to keep coming back to; it's the reason the story has travelled so far. It frames the case in such rigid terms, like a locked-room mystery, with a pool of suspects so shallow that any armchair detective can surely solve it.

But for people here, this isn't a story and Paddy isn't a character. Later, as the bar clears out, Richard grows sombre.

'I've been pretty good the last few weeks, but since you came to town . . . At half past three this morning I woke up, couldn't get back to sleep,' he tells us. 'I was just thinking about Paddy, trying to remember everything again. Going through it and thinking, "Where the fuck are you, mate? What's happened here?"'

He continues collecting glasses, packing away beer coolers, wiping condensation from the bar tables as he talks to us. Richard is fifty-one and full of contradictions: he's the type of guy who refers to a woman he knows as 'Vinegar Tits', but goes to great lengths to tell us how much he loves his mum and his six older sisters.

In twenty-two years of stopping in at Larrimah, Richard has witnessed the town's slow crumble up close. When he first pulled into town in the late nineties, it was 2 am and a man called Siddo was running the pub. It was full of swags—patrons simply rolled out their beds on the floor next to the bar once they finished drinking—and when Richard picked his way through them to ask for a bottle of rum, Siddo told him: 'Son, you can have two.' It was Richard's kind of place. Now he's four work-stints deep, and each time he comes back, more people have moved on and everyone who's still around is a bit less interested in a big night on the grog.

Richard's most recent return was prompted by a quad-bike accident. He'd broken his back and leg and needed somewhere to put himself back together. He stops short of saying Larrimah saved him, but it pulled him out of a hole and he's sentimental about the place. '[Larrimah] is way better than the bullshit therapy I've done,' he tells us. 'Spent a small fortune. It gets to a point where all they do is feed you more opiates, and they're no good for your body.' He lights a rollie and takes a puff. 'It's a good place to be healing. It's warm, and there's beer.' But the town isn't the same with Paddy gone, Richard tells us. It's like the disappearance is a domino that set in motion a whole suite of other changes.

'One of the hardest things is people coming in and making jokes about it all,' he says. 'It's really offensive and it's wrong. Because we know in our hearts that Paddy's come to mischief somewhere.'

It's been particularly hard on Barry. It's one of the reasons he's selling the pub, Richard tells us. We'd known the Pink Panther was for sale, but there's something about hearing it aloud that feels like a punch. It's the right decision for Barry—he's too old and sick, it's too much work and it's also too awful, without Paddy. But the sale of the Pink Panther puts the whole town in jeopardy. If no one steps up and buys it, Larrimah could disappear, too.

'Barry should live at least another twelve months, that would be nice to see,' Richard says. 'If we can sell this pub then he can actually get something for himself. If he decides he's had enough, he can just walk away.'

In the meantime, Richard knows that telling Paddy's story keeps his friend's memory alive and puts pressure on the police to find answers. But that doesn't mean it's easy.

'Just the idea of him being not in a grave somewhere, you know. That's just not right. And knowing that he wanted to live to be one hundred, knowing his state of mind. It's difficult to reconcile, especially when I believe I have a pretty clear, confident idea of what's happened.'

There's an accusation lurking underneath Richard's last statement, and we can feel Paddy's absence, pulling at the fabric of the town. It's made everyone a bit edgy, Richard says. Suspicious. Aware of blow-ins parking in odd places or of what their neighbours are doing.

'I'll be honest with you, I now lock my door. I don't need to because I've got three dogs who'll tear you apart if you're silly enough to open the door up, even. I've spent so many years travelling around, being in such dangerous places at times. I've always felt pretty confident in my own abilities. But yeah. For some reason I do actually lock the door of a night-time now.'

Since the disappearance, Richard's also changed his attitude towards police.

'Normally under any given circumstances if a coppa asked me a question, I'd tell them to fuck off,' he tells us. 'I do not deal with coppas at all. But this is Paddy. It's not about me or Sharpie; it's not about Larrimah. It's about Paddy.'

Even when Larrimah was busy enough for its own police station, the kind of incidents reported here could be pretty odd. A stolen pair of pants. The theft of a piano accordion. Bad meals at the pub. No beer at the pub. Bestiality. Homesickness. Constipation.

The town got its own police station in 1958—in those days, the staple law-enforcement duties were cattle duffing and road accidents. Large mobs of cows went missing with alarming regularity, usually pilfered by the station over the fence, which says something of the town's neighbourly relations, even then. When they weren't tending to bovine burglary or car wrecks, the single constable and Aboriginal tracker were dealing with non-suspicious deaths, domestic abuse, petty crime, fuel theft, drunkenness, people bogged in blacksoil and the occasional stolen set of buffalo horns. In the early years, there was also a lot of time devoted to disposing of dingo scalps, part of a culling program in which people could take them to the local cop shop for a cash reward.

The Larrimah police station closed in 1981. After the trains stopped running, there wasn't enough troublemaking to justify a local station. Residents petitioned to keep it open, but it's hard to wrangle many signatures in what was then a town of twenty-odd people. And so Larrimah, and several other bush stations, were consumed by the Mataranka police station—which means, nowadays, a three-person team enforces the law across

50,000 square kilometres. The area, roughly the size of Switzerland, is area known as the Never Never.

It's a Saturday when we roll into Mataranka, 75 kilometres north of Larrimah, and, except for the sound of traffic on the Stuart Highway, it's utterly quiet. There are only a handful of shops, most of them closed, and the only figures in sight are a few statues from Jeannie Gunn's classic Australian novel *We of the Never Never* standing around the park.

The Never Never is a slippery term; it's hard to get a definitive answer on where it came from, but it has become a catch-all for the bleak nothingness of the Australian interior, which tends to kill people. Colonial journalist A.J. Boyd dedicates a whole soliloquy (in *Old Colonials*, 1882) to the question: 'What on earth is to be done in this wretched Never-never country?', and the phrase also pops up in poet Barcroft Boake's cheerless ode to dead blokes in the bush. 'Out on the wastes of the Never Never—That's where the dead men lie!'

We can only assume that when Mataranka adopted the title 'Capital of the Never Never' they had Jeannie Gunn's more romantic interpretation in mind: '. . . we who have lived in it, and loved it, and left it, know our hearts can Never-Never rest away from it', she wrote. That's why she gets the park full of statues, despite the book's problematic descriptions of Indigenous Australians. A likeness of her, defying the elements in a long-sleeved blue dress with too many layers, stares sternly at the police building across the road.

The station is a boxy red-brick affair that looks more like a public toilet block. Back when police job descriptions included 'leper escort duty', they used to have corrugated iron cells out the back—but they were so hot it wasn't really possible to lock anyone up there so they just let prisoners wander the unfenced yard, like some kind of penal honour system.

We pull up outside and are immediately attacked by two sprinklers. Damp and embarrassed, we knock on the side door and Sergeant Thomas Chalk pokes his head out. He's in his thirties, dark-haired. He looks like the kind of guy who'd play in the local touch footy side and organise the barbecue after—an affable personality at odds with the hostility of the drab interview room he leads us to.

Sergeant Chalk has been in Mataranka for four years; for him, it's not a tour-of-duty in the bush to earn himself a better posting in a capital city. This *is* the better posting. He grew up on cattle stations across the Top End and has been a police officer for thirteen years; apart from a brief stint at the college in Darwin, all of his service has been in bush stations. 'I hope I'll never police Darwin,' he tells us.

The dingo scalp duties might be long gone, but, much like those before him, Sergeant Chalk finds himself on the front line of the Northern Territory's two biggest issues: domestic violence and alcohol. Alcohol consumption rates in the Territory are the highest per capita in Australia, with equally high rates of alcohol-fuelled violence and crime. Booze-related crime accounts for $75.9 million worth of police time each year and, according to Australian Bureau of Statistics 2017 data, the Territory has the nation's highest rate of family and domestic violence–related offences.

For people like Sergeant Chalk, who aren't just reading those figures in a report or seeing them in a news story, it can be awful. But working in such a challenging environment can also be rewarding, he tells us. He cares about his community. He wants to make a difference. And he has a theory on how to do it. 'I always say to the people I work with, "Your mouth is by far your best tool. Stand there and talk to people."'

Because of this approach, despite his Switzerland-sized beat, Sergeant Chalk is on a first-name basis with pretty much everyone. Including Paddy.

Sergeant Chalk was on a peace-keeping mission at an Indigenous funeral 220 kilometres away from Larrimah in Minyerri, navigating the complexities of grief and large crowds during the culturally important weeks-long sorry business. Just as things were wrapping up, a message to call Barry came through so he called the publican.

'Paddy's missing.' It wasn't a question, or a plea. It was a statement. And if he hadn't been so familiar with the laid-back cadence of Barry's voice, Sergeant Chalk could easily have missed the seriousness of it.

Despite Barry's apparent composure, Sergeant Chalk heard alarm bells in every fact he relayed. Gone. Since Saturday. No sign of him. His car still parked outside his place. Sergeant Chalk's first thought was that maybe the old man had died in or around his home. That sort of thing happened every now and then, especially in far-flung towns where old bushies lived alone without family nearby. And Paddy had health issues.

Sergeant Chalk's second thought was of Joanne Anderson, a 37-year-old Aboriginal woman who'd gone missing from Mataranka three years earlier. She'd never been found. It still bothered him that, despite an extensive search effort, he'd never got to the bottom of what happened to her. He told Barry he'd be right there.

The moment he set foot inside Paddy's back door, Sergeant Chalk knew the old Irishman wasn't there, dead or injured. Given the time of year and the heat, there was no way the house was hiding a decomposing body. But it was hiding something, because there was no sign of what might have happened to its owner. No obvious evidence of a disturbance.

The kitchen chair was partly pushed in, as if Paddy had just stood up. The fridges were still on, stocked with beer and food. There was a container of dim sims on the table, as if Paddy were about to heat them up, alongside his cap, keys and key card. His calendar had the days crossed off until the fifteenth. It was as if some fairies had picked Paddy up and just taken him away. And, even stranger, it seemed like they'd taken Kellie, too. Her collar and dog bowl were also on the table.

Over at the pub, Sergeant Chalk questioned Barry and Richard. Paddy's car and quad bike were at his place, but could some friends have picked him up?

'Paddy wouldn't have gone away without letting us know,' the two men told him. He sometimes visited a guy called Terry in Queensland at Christmas, but he hadn't planned on going this year. And anyway, they'd called a few of his mates. No one had seen him.

'Even if some long-legged blonde came through who was filthy rich and fell in love with him on the spot, by now he'd have rung up for bragging rights,' Richard said. 'He wouldn't do that, anyway. He'd have rung up to say I'm gonna have to do those toilets on my own for a bit.'

Sergeant Chalk called his boss, who mobilised the Territory Response Group (TRG), an elite group of NT police responsible for counter-terrorism, bomb response, close personal protection and land search and rescue. The next morning, tactical police in camo gear spilled out into the bush, uniformed officers from Darwin door-knocked and stopped cars on the highway. Search and rescue teams on motorbikes rode the fence lines. Volunteers walked shoulder to shoulder through the scrub. A helicopter zigzagged overhead. It was the most action the town had seen since the war had ended.

'It would be one of the biggest searches I've ever seen,' Sergeant Chalk tells us, and he's seen plenty of them. He spent the next few days in Larrimah, even though, once the situation escalated, he wasn't running the show anymore. As a local, his input was important. He knew the place and he knew the people. He knew Paddy.

We ask about Sergeant Chalk's impressions of Paddy and his answer is tinged with sadness. 'Paddy was just an old Territorian from what I knew of him. He spent a large portion of his life here. I formed the opinion that . . . he'd sort of see out his days [in Larrimah]. I never thought it would be so soon.'

As we finish up and walk back out into the brilliant sunshine, dodging the sprinkler on the way to the car, we can't help thinking about how impossible it is for police to avoid dealing with people they know in this part of the world. How often must you be called to an accident, an assault, a murder, where you know the victim—or, perhaps, the perpetrator? Of course, that's an occupational hazard for any small-town cop, and other professions aren't immune, even journalists. But the Northern Territory is particularly tangled. The population is small, about 245,000, and scattered over 1.4 million square kilometres. The communities bundled into little pockets are tightly woven. Although the threads between them are long, they're also strong. Because of that, Sergeant Chalk wasn't the only one searching for a man he knew.

When Mataranka Fire and Emergency Response Group Captain Des Barritt's phone had rung, his stomach dropped. A missing person was never great news but then he was told the name. It was his mate, Paddy.

Des was in Larrimah a lot. He loved it. When he did visit, he'd sit in the pub and have a yarn to Paddy and Barry, and whoever else happened to be around. He'd lived in the area for forty years and when Katherine, where he used to live, got a McDonald's he'd moved to Mataranka. He always said if the fast-food giant ever came to Mataranka, he'd clear out and move to Larrimah.

By the time Des got the call, Paddy had been missing ninety-six hours and he knew the chances of finding the old Irishman alive were slim.

There was always a chance of survival, an ember of hope fed by a steady string of against-the-odds tales. The media was full of them. There was Rod Ansell, the grazier-cum-buffalo hunter the Crocodile Dundee character was based on. In 1977 his boat was sunk and he lasted fifty-six days in remote western Northern Territory with nothing much but a rifle, eating wild cattle and buffalo meat and drinking their blood. James Scott survived forty-three days lost in the Himalayas subsisting on melted snow, a caterpillar and two chocolate bars. And Robert Bogucki endured the same timeframe—forty-three days in a red-hot expanse of Western Australia's Great Sandy Desert. Somehow, he made it out alive. Extraordinary things happen, sometimes.

But Des also knew all the stories without happy endings, and it was a much longer list. Families and tourists and hikers who'd made one mistake—got lost or bogged or dehydrated—that had proved fatal.

Gathered in the shade with the other volunteers, Des listened to the bleak brief: there was little or no chance Paddy was lost. The most likely scenario was a medical episode. Paddy had ischaemic heart disease and coronary artery disease. He'd had surgery a while back and was on medication. He was a strong candidate for a heart attack. Check either side of the tracks, they were told, in case he'd stumbled off course and his body lay somewhere obscured by the scrub. Keep an eye out for the dog.

Already cloaked in a layer of sweat that seeped through his long sleeves and soaked into his socks, Des and the others formed a line, shoulder to shoulder, and started the slow march from Paddy's back door. The plan was to follow his route to the dump, where he walked Kellie: a broad, flat track, one bulldozer blade wide and three footy fields long. They'd barely gone beyond the back step when a black whip snake shot out of the unkempt tangle of grass.

A helicopter looped overhead, the thump of the rotors providing a beat to walk to. As the day wore on, searchers on either side of Des began to wither in the heat. In bigger places, volunteers would be swapped out so they could have a break, but out here there was no one to tag-team. Sweat outpaced Des's water consumption, no matter how much he drank. Thursday was long, and then they were called back to do it all again on Friday. And Saturday.

They searched up to 300 metres off the tracks. Followed the old railway line, out towards a ghost town called Birdum, 11 kilometres away. Ventured out to old World War II sites and checked among the debris. Followed the near-dry creeks and poked around on the *riverbanks. If it hadn't been so desperate it might have been inter-esting—the landscape offering up its history and secrets. Volunteers started to talk about sinkholes—the area was supposedly pockmarked with them—but Des and the others didn't find any.*

They checked for caves; the Katherine region is known for cave systems, deep enough to make the perfect hide-out. In the sixties, a man called Larry Boy went on the run after murdering his estranged wife and attacking her lover with a tomahawk. He'd been found cowering in a cave somewhere near Elsey Station, in Mataranka, forty days later.

The possibilities felt infinite—in landscape like this, a search could literally go on forever. Des and the others could feel themselves doing it: stretching out hope. Not so much for finding Paddy alive, but for finding a body. It'd be messy and unpleasant, but at least they'd be able to lay him to rest. If they just went those few extra kilometres, those few extra hours, well, that might make all the difference. Paddy could be just over that rise, around that bend.

When Des tells us of those days spent scouring the bush looking for his friend, we imagine ourselves in his shoes, marching to that dreadful probability. How do you go home at the end of a search when the person is still out there? Paddy was a mate; how do you stop?

Des is a tall, lanky cowboy who has spent decades bouncing between teaching in remote schools and working as a ringer on remote stations—pragmatism comes naturally to him. 'We really did our darndest to find him,' he says. 'But there was no way he was going to be alive.'

A survival expert, Dr Paul Luckin, had done the grim calcu-lations. If Paddy had been injured, fallen ill or become lost, he could only have survived forty-eight to seventy-two hours. Best-case scenario, he'd have been dead before he was even reported missing. The timeframe for survival had well and truly expired.

The outback has a way of swallowing bodies. The whereabouts of ten-week-old baby Azaria Chamberlain, taken by a dingo at Uluru in 1980, has never been discovered. The body of British backpacker Peter Falconio, murdered by Bradley John Murdoch at Barrow Creek in 2001, remains hidden in the outback, too. Both were the subject of some of Australia's biggest search operations.

So, just to be sure, the search for Paddy Moriarty lasted one more day after Dr Luckin's calculations. Police double- and triple-checked everything, until they were confident they'd done all they could. Convinced, now, that something else was going on, the search parties packed up. And in came the Major Crimes squad.

4

A half-liquefied chicken, a pop band attacked by termites and the word 'murder'

Detective Sergeant Matt Allen had just stepped off a plane in Darwin after celebrating his fortieth birthday on the Gold Coast when the message came through: Missing person in Larrimah, foul play suspected, Major Crimes needed there. Now.

He didn't even unpack. He just threw his bag into his car, picked up a couple of other detectives and started driving. Six o'clock the following morning, he and a team of four detectives and the three Mataranka officers were in Larrimah.

Detective Sergeant Allen had twenty years' experience as a police officer in the Northern Territory. As a younger man he'd studied business at university and had plans to combine his qualifications with his love of sport, perhaps by becoming an agent. Then, when he was nineteen, he'd been assaulted. A group of guys jumped him and his girlfriend at Surfers Paradise and he wound up in hospital with a broken jaw. The whole process of making a statement to police and putting together a comfit of the perpetrators felt interesting. And, not long after, he'd seen an ad in the paper featuring a LandCruiser with a swag on top. The NT police force was recruiting. He'd been on a family trip to the Northern Territory as a child, and he'd loved the outback. So, using his winnings from a footy tipping competition, he'd bought an airfare to Darwin and signed up. His first posting was Alice Springs, then he did stints at Yuendumu, Kulgera and Papunya.

Even though he'd worked remote before, Larrimah came as a shock. There was no CCTV and no mobile reception, so the usual methods of tracking people's movements weren't available. The town didn't even have a fuel station.

Detective Sergeant Allen didn't know it, but at one point there'd been three servos in Larrimah. One had been at the pub, but it got rid of its bowsers ages ago. Another had been sold off and converted into Paddy's house. And the last one had been attached to a caravan park called Green Park, but it had burnt down a decade ago. Now, the town seemed like it had no purpose, a place that had sprung up out of the bush suddenly and unexpectedly as if part of a practical joke.

The officers involved in the search had briefed Detective Sergeant Allen on the hot, fruitless days spent looking for Paddy, but he wanted to look for himself so he went up in a chopper and surveyed the savannah woodland. The visibility took him by surprise—the tiny town and vast, empty spaces beyond were laid out before him in high resolution. He could see the concrete slabs of old World War II buildings dotted across the landscape, and fence lines distinguishing paddock from scrub. Cattle grazing. Wallabies jumping. There was no way the air searches could have missed a man and his dog. If the dog were alive, it would have bolted at the sound of the chopper. If Paddy were alive, he'd have waved to get their attention. And if they were both dead, searchers would have seen the bodies against the featureless backdrop.

But if he were honest with himself, Detective Sergeant Allen hadn't expected to see Paddy or his dog. The more he'd thought about it, the less a medical episode made sense. The thing Detective Sergeant Allen kept tripping up on was Kellie. The dog. A heart attack or a snake bite or dehydration—even a sinkhole—could take a man's life out here. But a man *and* his dog? Unlikely. And if Paddy had somehow died, the dog might have stayed with him for a time, but then it would have come back to town looking for food. So where was the dog?

Police had already established Paddy's bank accounts hadn't been accessed, his passport not used. No plane or bus tickets had been booked in his name. Detective Sergeant Allen was convinced. Someone did this. This was a murder investigation.

So, back on the ground, he began pursuing leads.

Officers at Paddy's place had discovered a barbecued chicken from a Katherine supermarket in the microwave. Half-liquefied in the heat by the time they got to it, they could still make out the date stamp on the packaging: 16 December. The last day Paddy had been seen alive. And since Paddy hadn't been to Katherine the day he disappeared, the chicken had come from someone else—possibly the last person to see the old man alive. Detective Sergeant Allen began looking for them.

He also started tracing a two-tone Mitsubishi Delica van that a few people had seen hanging around Larrimah since early December, which didn't belong to anyone in town and had disappeared a few days after Paddy did. Detective Sergeant Allen put a call-out through the media for anyone who might have information on the car.

Police did a thorough background check on Paddy: where was his family, did he owe anyone money, did he have a criminal history? A lot of the personal details were difficult to establish—Detective Sergeant Allen learned that Paddy had stored all his documents in a donga out the back that had burnt down in a suspicious fire years earlier. His past had gone up in flames.

Then Detective Sergeant Allen and the other officers started door-knocking residents, asking basic questions—where people were last Saturday, what they were doing, did they have any visitors? It was a struggle. Because what police were looking for was hard to come by in Larrimah: specificity. Particularly when it came to times and dates and names. Just eight days had passed but it was like an unbridgeable gulf. Heat and booze and the sameness of each day blurred memories to oblivion.

The next day Detective Sergeant Allen sat people down for long, formal interviews. Still, even the most basic details were impossible to establish. Barry and Richard had seen Paddy before he left the *pub and disappeared into thin air, but between the pair of them they had virtually no memory of who else had been around, what Paddy had been wearing, who he had been talking to. They wanted to help; Detective Sergeant Allen could see that. But they had nothing. In fact, both men had insisted Paddy was last there on Friday night, that they hadn't seen him on Saturday 16 December at all. Detective Sergeant Allen told them that was impossible: Paddy's bank records and the date stamp on the chicken found in his microwave proved otherwise. The blur of days baffled the police officer.*

Then, at the end of the interview with Barry, Detective Sergeant Allen took his fingerprints and asked him to sign and date the form.

'What's the date today?' Barry had asked.

Detective Sergeant Allen was incredulous.

'It's bloody Christmas Day, Barry.'

'You don't understand until you go there,' Detective Sergeant Allen tells us. 'You need to drive there, get out of the car, look around, to really appreciate what it's like.'

We know what he means. It's one to describe Larrimah to someone, but it's quite another to be there. To plant your sweaty feet in the red soil and get your head around the geography, the climate, the infrastructure. You can tell someone about a twelve-foot Pink Panther in a deckchair, but until they're standing in its shade, listening to the blind croc over the fence purr, it's kind of difficult to appreciate the weirdness of it all.

For Detective Sergeant Allen, it wasn't just the town that was confounding, it was also the people. On Christmas Day, when they'd gone door to door, it was one strange thing after another, he said. One man lived in a shed full of junk. Another lived in a caravan at the back of the pub next to the emu enclosure. Another did his police interview in a pair of old undies, until the female officer eventually insisted he put on some pants. And everyone was candid. Rather than downplaying their personal dislikes for a probably dead man, they just said whatever came into their heads. One man admitted he wanted to punch Paddy sometimes. One woman flatly said she hated him.

Detective Sergeant Allen says that as each interview progressed, as they pushed for details, more than a decade's worth of strangeness started spilling out. Who hated who. Who had ruined the town. Who had shot whose pet buffalo and eaten it. Who stole whose meat pie recipe. The detectives heard all of it. And, suddenly, it was all relevant.

'Unique personalities,' Detective Sergeant Allen says tactfully. 'Relationships were good and bad between all of them. Unique is the word. Most unique place I've come across.'

Lenny Hodson has referred to his house as a shed, but we still aren't prepared for what awaits us. Lots of people live in converted dongas and garages in the north, but shed is probably too generous a term for the ramshackle tin structure we find ourselves lurking outside of.

There are a lot of problems with living in a shed—the heat, the rats, the absence of a bathroom. But for us, it's a simple matter of politeness. It's hard to know how to get someone's attention when they don't have a door to knock on.

We call out to announce ourselves.

A voice floats back. 'I'm in here. Come in.'

Lenny is sitting on a low camp stretcher he uses as a bed. The concrete floor around him is jammed with boxes housing haphazard collections. There's a caravan in one corner, another outside. Near his feet is a stack of records, the packets in flakes. The top one is *Homemade*, by The Osmonds, but the faces of the five band members have been snacked on by white ants.

'My next-door neighbour got me that,' he says, noticing us

staring longingly at a huge fan. It's turned off, even though Lenny appears to have collected all the heat in Larrimah under one tin roof. 'I'm not game to turn it on. Might blow me away.'

Lenny is eighty-two, which, according to everyone else in Larrimah, is too old to be doing the things he does. Too old to be slashing the grass around the railway in the midday heat. Too old to be buying a bomb of a car interstate and driving it thousands of kilometres cross-country, or crawling underneath it to fix it up. Too old to be sleeping in his swag on the side of the road because he's too cheap to get a motel. Too old to be chasing wild pigs down the railway line in the section car. And definitely too old to be out in 47-degree heat searching for a missing man. But he is happily oblivious to anyone's opinions.

'I'm glad you came. There's a book around here somewhere I wanted to show you.'

He hauls himself up, and fishes around—among kitchen appliances and souvenir mugs—and emerges with a hardcover called *Iron Roads in the Outback: The Legendary Commonwealth Railways.* There, on page 140, is a photo of Lenny with the little section car he used to drive up and down the old railway tracks to Birdum, the town that was once the head of the rail.

Larrimah only exists because of Birdum, 11 kilometres south— which in turn only exists because of a series of stuff-ups. Back at the turn of the last century, Australia got swept up in a grand plan to run a railway line right through the nation's dead heart, from Darwin to Adelaide. It was a big investment—almost a million pounds—and they were in a hurry. Sometimes there were thousands of labourers frantically laying one kilometre of track a day. They started building at both ends of the country, planning to meet in the middle. The Adelaide to Alice leg went off without a hitch but the Darwin to Alice line took longer. It had only been pegged to go to Daly Waters, but then, in 1929, the country ran out of money and a panicked bureaucrat in search of a penny-saver made a call to stop building the transcontinental rail. 'Just quit, wherever you are,' they said.

Unfortunately, where they were was Birdum—a blacksoil wasteland in the middle of nowhere—which meant that there was still a terrible 900-kilometre gap in central Australia between the two railways, and Birdum became the accidental railhead for the northern section of the railway.

It wasn't until 2004, when The Ghan extended its luxury train service all the way to Darwin, that the 121-year dream of a north–south transcontinental passenger railway was finally fulfilled, although it was on a new track about an hour west of the original rail.

Apparently, there's not much left at Birdum now. Larrimah salvaged anything that could be used to further its own development and the rest has been eaten by termites. But we're still keen to see it.

'Lots of history in Birdum,' Lenny says. 'I'll give you a ride if you want.'

We're tempted, until we realise what he means.

A lift with Lenny in the vehicle he's pictured with in the book would be one thing, but time has not been kind to the section car, or the railway. Or Lenny. He still takes the section car for the occasional illegal run down the line to Birdum, even though the old girl has rusted into something that's mostly a shelter for death adders, and the rickety train track is overrun with long grass and termite mounds.

'We started taking passengers on it, until somebody tried to stop us because they reckoned it was too dangerous and we didn't have any liability insurance,' Lenny says.

He's not sure who the party-pooper was, but we wonder whether maybe they had a point. Is it possible to derail the car? we ask.

'Oh yeah, it's easy.' Lenny willingly divulges his accident history. 'First time I derailed it I hit an ant bed; couldn't see it. Put me off the rails. The second time was a stone on the track. The next time I had passengers on the trolley...'

We stop him there. Clearly, neither he nor the section car can be trusted. It's a shame, because trains are the bookends of Lenny's life. His stepfather drove a steam train during the war, and Lenny worked as a trainee fireman shovelling coal on the steam trains near Newcastle. He also did a stint as a tram conductor in Sydney. Then, his train-loving life was derailed by other interests. He did national service for ninety days and joined the army reserves. He worked for the side-shows, travelling the country running electric racehorses and mirror mazes. He drove trucks interstate. He got married and had three daughters. And then, about twenty years ago on a holiday north with some mates, he called in at Larrimah.

As he tells the story, we immediately realise that everyone has given us the wrong headline about Lenny. His defining feature isn't his age—it's his thriftiness.

The reason Lenny chose Larrimah was the free power at the caravan park, then he'd come back a few years later on the promise of a $5 room. At some point, Barry said Lenny could set up his caravan down at the workshop and stay there for free. Then, when Karen and Mark bought the workshop from Barry, Lenny moved up to the shed. It's owned by a Pommie bloke, who also lets Lenny stay for next to no cost, and the guy who lived there before him happened to leave around $900 in power credits, so he gets that for nothing too.

Larrimah is a spendthrift's dream. But, beyond that, Lenny doesn't have much to say about the town.

'I don't know much about the place, even though I've lived here for fourteen years,' he says. 'Actually, there's nothing here. Nothing really to talk about. It's just a spot on the map with houses and people.'

And not very many of those, we add.

'No. And there's one less now.'

Lenny would be quite happy to leave it there—it's not that he's evasive, he just exudes a level of nonchalance we've never encountered. For example, he does not care how we spell his name—Lenny, Lennie, Len. It makes no difference. He hates his name, he says, his parents made a mistake.

Still, we push for more detail about Paddy and he, nonchalantly, obliges.

He and Paddy were mates, even though they'd had their differences. 'I'd put him out on the lawn a few times,' is how Lenny puts it. We take in his age-wasted limbs and pot belly, the bung knee that barely resembles a knee, and wonder just how that might have looked. But their disagreements had always been over something trivial and they'd be back to being drinking buddies again the next day.

When Lenny learned Paddy hadn't been seen for a few days, he rushed over to Paddy's place in his ute. Paddy had been talking about getting someone to spot him as he took a kangaroo jack out from under a truck, in case it fell. Maybe Paddy was trapped under his car. But everything at Paddy's was normal, there was no sign of the Irishman. Lenny went for a bit of a drive up the back, out to the dump and along the back roads. He found nothing.

Then, before police showed up, Lenny skipped town.

'It must have looked a bit suspicious.' He laughs. But Lenny goes south often. This time, he'd driven about 3000 kilometres to Melbourne to get his caravan fixed. Police eventually caught up with him in Victoria, questioned him and cleared him.

'It's just a mystery,' he tells us. 'Though they all have their suspicions.'

Something about the way he says it reminds us of Richard's half-accusation. We ask what relationships are like in town—do people get along, generally?

Lenny just shrugs.

'I don't take any notice of that,' he says. 'I talk to everybody.

Probably got into trouble for it a couple of times. Doesn't worry me. I class everybody as a friend.'

If we're looking for details, though, we could try next door, he says. 'My neighbour, Cookie, he's been here a long time.' Cookie knows something of the town, Lenny says, and its history. He knows a bit about the trouble here, too.

5

A dead donkey, fifty shades of biscuit and the problem with pies

We haven't met Cookie, but we've heard about him. He doesn't come to the pub, because of some accusations involving the misappropriation of Mars bars.

'He got caught thieving, stealing chocolates out of the fridge and stuff,' Richard had told us. 'Out the side door, which is why the side door's always locked now. They caught him, dressed him down, made him empty his pockets, took all the chocolates off him.'

Cookie also comes with a heavy language warning. His house has been described as a white elephant—he's poured years of money and hard work into renovations. When he has appeared on the news to be interviewed about Paddy's disappearance, the caption across the bottom where a job title usually appears just says 'hermit'. And he openly admitted to not getting on with Paddy. Since we're already in the neighbourhood, we figure we might as well drop in.

We find him out the back of his house, cleaning his car wearing only a pair of sagging undies and a damp blue singlet. He invites us straight in for a cuppa, and we expect he will duck into the bedroom and put on some pants. He does not.

Instead, he gets straight into the business of telling us everything. He's candid, to a fault, even though the kettle hasn't boiled, we haven't explained why we're here and we haven't asked any questions.

'Yeah, well, there's not much going on around here. I mean old Paddy went missing. They reckon he's been bumped off.'

We ask if he was mates with Paddy.

'No. Well, on and off. I've threatened to punch him in the head a few times. I just sort of keep away from them because it's not really my scene and I got blamed for doing things I never done. And one thing led to another. I got barred from the pub for something I never done. So I thought, "Stick it up your arse, brus, I don't want nothing to do with it." And I just got away from it all, you know. What do you girls have, milk and sugar?'

Cookie's real name is Barry Burke, but no one calls him that. We assume that he's nicknamed after a biscuit but, apparently, it's because he used to stand in front of the mirror combing his hair like Kookie Byrnes—the guy who played dance-show host Vince Fontaine in *Grease*, and who also had a hit song in 1959 called 'Kookie, Kookie (Lend Me Your Comb)'.

Larrimah Cookie also sports a thick head of hair, but it's been grey for a while. Despite his choice of attire, he moves with the confidence of a man who's both wearing pants and used to a level of success with women. When we ask his age, he tells us he's seventy. No, seventeen. Wait, seventy-two. He followed a friend's cousin up here for a holiday about forty years ago and then ended up staying in the north, working as a tour guide, then driving trucks, side-tippers and loaders out bush.

But when we explain that we're here to ask about Larrimah and its history, he brushes us off. All Cookie wants to talk about is his home renovation. It's like he's been waiting for the crew of *The Block* to walk in for years, and he's realised we are as close to that dream coming true as he's going to get. So he takes us through his custom kitchen, shows us the depth of his pantry, points out the wall colour (Biscuit) and the skirting boards (Half Biscuit), and chats nonstop about the $9000 genuine Italian leather lounge he fell in love with in Alice Springs, which changes colour in the sunlight.

The Block really should come and do a feature on Cookie, because the story of his reno is a triumph of one man over heat, distance and stink beetles, which he had to remove by the bucket-load. And his place is—sincerely—gorgeous. He's retained the old railway house's original floorboards and installed a mahogany tree as an architectural feature.

But the logistics of tackling a full gut-job reno 500 kilometres from the nearest Bunnings have been challenging. 'I've been waiting on a tin of putty to come up from Alice Springs for three weeks. It's a nightmare.'

He's made it work by convincing truckie mates to drop things in on their way through and hijacking the occasional plasterer (his sister's daughter's boyfriend's brother) to come do some work for him. 'I used to be a heavy smoker and drinker and one had to go so I could finish this house, so I gave up smoking to keep drinking,' he says. 'They do say you have to have liquid in your body.'

He ushers us through room after room, limping on a strapped knee—he's waiting for news about a replacement.

'A lot of people think I've spent too much money on it but I haven't really. I don't think I have anyhow. Because if you want something to look nice, you have to be prepared to do what you want to do, you know?'

Anyway, he tells us, he doesn't care what people in town say about the house. Because Larrimah is full of arseholes. That's also what he told police when they came around asking questions.

Most people faced with what was rapidly turning into a murder inves-tigation wouldn't begin by telling the police how much they hated the bloke who was missing. But Cookie was not like most people. For a start, he wasn't wearing pants.

He'd been out bush when he'd heard the news about Paddy. Not long after he got back into town, some cops appeared on his verandah with questions. He did his best to help—not that he knew much. A side effect of being banned from the pub was that, typically, information took a while to reach him.

'Did you have anything to do with knocking him off?' the police asked. They probably didn't ask it quite like that, but that's how Cookie remembered it.

Cookie was characteristically candid. 'Sometimes I've felt like it, don't worry about that. I'll be honest with you. I felt like breaking the guy's neck, sometimes, but it never happened.'

According to Cookie, Paddy was the kind of bloke who'd cause trouble in an empty house—he was also the reason Cookie had been exiled from the pub.

'They reckon I stole Mars bars and all this shit and I've got sugar diabetes,' Cookie told police. 'Why would I want to sit here and eat Mars bars when I've got sugar diabetes? That's why I don't have sugar in my tea, I've just gotta watch what I eat around here.'

Cookie said Paddy lied to everyone about the Mars bar thefts. And he lied about other things. He told everyone he'd been a ringer at Brunette Downs, but Cookie had heard from a few people that Paddy was only the cowboy gardener. Paddy used to edit himself into other people's stories, too. Once, Lenny had accidentally set fire to a tree, which then crushed Cookie's car, and Paddy claimed to have been there—even though he'd been spotted in Katherine that day. He was always telling tall tales, Cookie said. They'd had confrontations about it.

'I said, "You're a lying arsehole, Paddy, that's all you are." I said, "Don't tell me any more lies, Paddy." I said, "I'll finish up smacking you in the head."'

But there's a big difference between wanting to do something and doing it. On 16 December 2017, Cookie was out of town so he was quickly ruled out of the investigation.

He did have some theories about what might have happened, though. Paddy had probably been knocked off, he told the police, and the wild pigs would have got into him.

'There's not many pigs around here,' the cops said.

'There bloody is, further out,' Cookie replied. He said it with the certainty of a man who'd encountered a lot of animal yarns over the years.

Cookie doesn't feel weird about living in a town with a potential murderer, but he's not renovating the house for himself. He plans to sell up, which will leave the town short another resident. His motivation for leaving is 'because of people's attitudes'. That, and he's got a girlfriend back home in Tasmania.

'She's a bloody good woman,' he tells us. Moving her to Larrimah is out of the question, apparently. She came up to stay once, but it didn't go well.

'She couldn't hack it.' Cookie laughs. 'She said, "How the bloody hell do you live here?" She didn't like it much because she couldn't go to the shops. So I've been trying to get this place finished and on the market 'cos we're not getting any younger. I just want to go home and spend a bit of time with her and bloody go places. And I'm sick of it here. They're a bunch of lying arseholes.'

Over a second cup of tea, Cookie starts to fill us in on his list of local grudges: it's approximately half as long as our list of town residents.

Take Barry, for example, over at the pub. Being one of two Barrys in a town of a dozen people has thrown up problems and, on more than one occasion, Cookie's mail has been opened by the other Barry. Presumably, this is accidental, but Cookie's not so sure.

'He steamed a couple of my letters open,' Cookie says. Barry also ripped open some mail—apparently thinking it belonged to him. 'I said, "Well, how did he get Barry Sharpe out of Barry Burke?

You tell him to fucking leave my mail alone or I'll rip his head off."
I was pissed off with him, hey.'

Cookie also blames Barry for shutting down the town's cricket matches, and his contempt extends to Richard. But he's not offside with the whole town—he drops in on Lenny for a cuppa and would do just about anything for Karl and Bobbie Roth (including mowing their lawn for them, in his undies). He and Bill Hodgetts go to Katherine together sometimes and stop for a beer on the way home.

We ask who else he's mates with in Larrimah. There's a long silence.

'No one.' It isn't a sad answer, or a mean one. Cookie just says it like it's obvious.

What about Fran, we wonder. Are you friends with her?
More silence.

'No, she's taboo to me. Have you been over there yet?' he asks. We confess we haven't. 'Well, I dread the day you go over there. We used to be friends, years ago. When you do go, have a look at that pergola out the back of her shop: I built that for her. Never got no thanks, no nothing for it. She's getting to be bad news lately. She charges sixteen dollars, seventeen dollars for a pie. And anyone who pays that amount of money for a pie has got rocks in their head. 'Cos she makes them and then freezes them. And then she puts them in the microwave . . . You know what stuff's like in the microwave,' Cookie goes on, looking to us for confirmation. 'You pick a pie up and the arse falls out of it and you finish up getting scalded with hot meat. I've had one pie off her, she gave it to me after working for a week on the pergola. It wasn't even real good. I didn't like it.'

Cookie tells us there used to be another pie-maker in town. Dianne Rogers—Bobbie Roth's daughter. She's long since left, but when she lived in Larrimah Di ran the pub before Barry and Ann, then she bought the caravan park, known as Green Park, and expanded the menu.

'Di used to make the best pies and pasties and sausages rolls here. Just one of her pasties and pies were a meal. She had bloody everything in them. Geez, they were beautiful. They were beautiful.'

And just like that, Cookie's face softens with the memory of pies past.

We knew the pies would come up, of course. For people who've seen the story of Paddy's disappearance in the news, the pies are the most salient of all the case details, the image that seems to have stuck in the public imagination. If there's anything the public likes more than a pie with mushy peas and extra tomato sauce, it's a pie war.

It's not easy to pin down the details, and we're planning to try to get to the bottom of it while we're here. But in broad brushstrokes, the crux of the historical pastry hostility is this: Fran was working as a cook at the pub and, as she tells it in the media, she put the town on the map with her specialty pies. Eventually she went out on her own, established the teahouse, and strengthened her baked-goods empire, selling pies to stations and businesses in Katherine, as well as travellers going up and down the Stuart.

Even though Larrimah is tiny, at one point it was home to four businesses. When Di began selling homemade pies at Green Park, it was an abrupt end to Fran's stranglehold on the market, turning Larrimah into a pastry-oligopoly. When Barry took over the pub, he got in on the action, too. Things escalated. Pie-eating clientele are hard to come by in the middle of nowhere, and the obvious way to attract them was with signs. There are stories of billboards being taken down, painted over, moved. People started poaching each other's customers. Fran made complaints about Di to the Department of Health. By the time Paddy moved to town, it was a full-scale war and he wanted in on it. He erected a sign out the front of his house directing people towards the pies at the pub and started telling tourists pulling up outside the teahouse that they'd get sick if they ate there. 'Fran has the worst pies,' he famously told the ABC in 2011. 'I used to go over there and the dog wouldn't eat me pie.'

From a distance, it sounds ridiculous, squabbling over something as trivial as a pie. But now we're in town, we can see up close how hard it is to eke out a living from this forsaken landscape. A few dozen pie sales a week might be the difference between keeping the lights and ovens on over the wet season. In a place where industry is hard to come by, pies aren't just good money—they're one of the only ways to make a buck.

There's a point in the afternoon when we realise Cookie's pretty much interviewing himself. We're not the least bit disappointed. There are some diversions to talk about the glory days of the trucking industry, Italian weddings and the kangaroos out the back, which he calls 'mobile backhoes'. The stories never seem to have an ending and part-way through one incredible tale we find ourselves dragged—completely willingly—into an entirely different one. At one point, Cookie spends close to ten minutes regaling us with a series of escalating snake stories, beginning with a few pythons and some king browns over at Lenny's shed, and working up to the time he and some bloke called Neil saw a snake the girth of Cookie's mahogany tree and as long as the highway is wide.

'Taipans are the worst ones because if they bite you they go straight for the nervous system and they paralyse you,' he says. 'Once you hit the nervous system you're buggered—you can't walk, you can't talk, you can't do nothing. They just sit there and hoe into you.'

It's yet more evidence of how treacherous the landscape is but nobody in the search party mentioned taipans; we ask Cookie if they travel this far north.

'You get taipans up here, shit yeah, it's all blacksoil country.'

We wonder, aloud, whether that's something that could have happened to Paddy.

'No, if it had've been a snake, he'd have got to the pub or rung up. A snake bite won't kill you straightaway. Usually you just wrap it up, like with a piece of cloth or something. Some people say you should suck it but they reckon if you've got bad teeth the venom gets into your teeth and you're buggered then, because you're dead. He never goes anywhere without his hat, anyhow.'

It's getting late, and Cookie's supposed to be getting ready to go to the doctor tomorrow.

We wish him luck with the house and ask flat out: what does he think happened to Paddy?

There's the slimmest of pauses.

'They've got a couple of suspects in town . . . but it's like the old saying, you've gotta prove it, haven't you? You've gotta prove what they've done.'

We knew the accusations would come up—anyone following the case would know about Fran: the pie lady over the road who'd had years of trouble with the missing man. She'd given media interviews in which she was frank about how much she hated Paddy, and colourful in her language. 'I'll take an oath on my life going to Katherine and back that I know nothing about the disappearance of Paddy Moriarty,' she told ABC journalist Leigh Sales. When *A Current Affair* dropped in, she confessed that she hated Paddy's guts. 'But I'm not a fucking killer, I'm too busy to do that.'

Like a bushfire, the whole thing went from ember to inferno quickly. Suddenly everyone had a theory. After a while, it didn't matter whether there was any truth to it. The story that an eccentric septuagenarian pie-maker had knocked off her neighbour had generated a mythic life of its own.

Everyone in town knew Fran and Paddy weren't on good terms, and Barry tells us what he thinks happened between them. The story starts light-hearted, full of Barry's characteristic suspenseful pauses and scratchy laughter. There were a lot of pranks, he tells us. The pair of them, Fran and Paddy, would rile each other up and then Paddy would come over to the pub and everyone would crack a beer and laugh about it.

'I do know that Paddy had thrown a kangaroo under her window, probably more than once. If there was a dead kangaroo on the road, he'd throw it over her fence. One time, a donkey got run over. Paddy went and cut its penis off and threw that up her driveway.' Barry laughs so much it becomes a wheeze and it takes him a few attempts before he gets the next sentence out. 'And from then on Fran's pies were called donkey dick pies.'

Paddy gave Fran the nickname the 'Bush Pig', Barry tells us. 'And he used to call it to her, to her face. He would say of a morning, when there were customers pulled up on his side of the road, he'd say, "Don't go over there. She's going to rob you blind. You can't eat the food, you're gonna be sick." He'd say, "She's just a dirty old bush pig, don't go near her." And a lot of them wouldn't. You can see how that would irritate you.'

There's a long silence; we don't know how to fill it. Paddy was pretty mean to Fran.

'Yeah,' Barry agrees. 'But he was a larrikin. He'd come back here some days and say the things he'd done and we just couldn't stop laughing.' Barry concedes, looking back now, it's not that funny.

Richard agrees; he'd also witnessed the tension between Fran and Paddy up close. But it wasn't the only friction between Paddy and his neighbours. Fran also had a live-in gardener called Owen.

'Him and Owen had a barney about a week before he went missing,' Richard tells us. 'Owen threatened the dog, Paddy threatened Owen.'

It was just on dawn, a few days before Paddy went missing. Richard had come down to the space between the campground and the highway to run his three staffies, like he did every day. They were proper bush dogs and not the nicest, so he kept them on chains for the rest of the day. As they enjoyed their moment of freedom, Richard sat and sipped his coffee, watching the peachy arc of the sun grow bigger on the horizon. It was a peaceful time of day; the temperature was still tolerable, the handful of tourists were sleeping and it was mostly quiet except for the birdsong.

Then he heard barking. It sounded like Kellie, that flighty new kelpie of Paddy's. She was only a pup and was always barking, so, at first, he didn't pay much attention. But then the yelling started and Richard's dogs took off up the road towards the commotion.

'Shit.' Richard put his coffee down and called them back. Once he'd got them to heel, he looked through the dappled light up the highway and saw Kellie on the road outside Fran's place, Paddy coming up behind her. Richard watched as his mate stopped in the middle of the road, hand on his hip, like he always did when he was trying to make a point. He could see he was shouting, but he couldn't make out the words. And he could hear someone shouting back.

From where he sat, Richard couldn't see the other person, but he was certain the second voice wasn't Fran's. Her voice was unmistakable and this one was deeper, more even. It had to be Owen.

For three months, Owen had been working as a gardener for Fran and living in the building they called the doll's house or the bungalow—a sort of granny flat in Fran's yard. But Richard would have been hard-pressed to recognise the bloke, even if he'd walked into the pub and ordered a beer. Owen had pretty much stayed on Fran's property the whole time he'd been there. To Richard, he was just a tall, feature-less shadow in the distance.

Their only interaction had been a few weeks beforehand. Richard used to walk his dogs on the dirt track between the back of the pub and Fran's place, where they wouldn't encounter anyone. But one day another dog had come hurtling towards them. In the distance, Richard could see Owen. He was sure the dog belonged to him and that he'd set it on Richard's dogs but he couldn't be bothered with an argument, so he'd just stopped taking his dogs that way.

Now, he listened to the confrontation between the mysterious gardener and Paddy. It was all over in less than a minute. Richard sat back down to finish his coffee and had a little chuckle to himself. At the pub later that day, when Paddy fronted up for beers, Richard would have to ask him what the hell had happened.

6

A suspicious croc, a drained septic tank and a landscape full of secrets

Within a week of Paddy's disappearance, detectives had come to the firm conclusion he had met with foul play. They'd worked several leads: the barbecue chicken had come from some interstate travellers who'd given the leftovers to Paddy for his dog—they didn't know anything; Paddy was originally from Ireland but didn't seem to have any close family there and he appeared on no birth certificate for any Australian children; the Mitsubishi Delica that had been spotted in town around the time of Paddy's disappearance seemed to be an innocent traveller who'd camped on the side of the road for a few days. So far, everything was a dead end. So, two days after Christmas 2017—eleven days after Paddy had last been seen—another group of searchers arrived in Larrimah. They were still looking for a body but, this time, they were looking for something else: evidence.

Sergeant Meacham King stood in Fran's backyard watching the contents of her septic tank spill out onto the lawn. The smell of sun-heated human waste was overpowering, especially when combined with a black smog of blowflies. But it was a job that had to be done. Dr Luckin, the survivability expert, had told Sergeant King that if someone had thrown a body into a cesspit, decomposing fat would probably float to the surface and they'd be able to smell it from outside. Dr Luckin wasn't sure; he'd

never been asked that before. So they'd decided to pump the septic tank out just in case.

'What is that?' Sergeant King asked, moving in closer. There was something different coming out, something that wasn't the same as all the other sludge.

'Sorry!' he heard someone shout. 'I accidentally used the toilet.'

Shit, thought Sergeant King. Shit. Shit. Shit. Then Fran's voice called out from the house: 'Do you blokes want a pie?' Sergeant King politely declined.

With two decades in the Northern Territory Police Force and 150 searches under his belt, Sergeant King was used to the grisly task of looking for bodies. It wasn't a glamorous job. Sometimes you found a human head stuffed into a termite mound. Sometimes you had to watch as human body parts were pulled from the stomach of a crocodile. But Sergeant King loved his job. It was rewarding when his team came to a resolution, even if the person they were looking for was no longer alive. And people were usually pleased when he showed up because they knew he was there to help.

As the day in Larrimah wore on, though, Fran became less pleased about Sergeant King's presence. By the time they scraped out her incinerator, she wasn't offering snacks anymore. 'Get her out of here,' Sergeant King told one of the officers. When they finished with the pie shop, detectives put her and Owen in there while they searched her home and Owen's accommodation, and both their cars. None of it turned up anything. Nothing pleasant came from her sewer either, but also nothing suspicious. It was time to fan out and search the rest of the town.

Before they set off into the malevolent bush on the second day, Sergeant King phoned a friend. Senior Sergeant Jim Whitehead in Queensland was the godfather of search and rescue in Australia. He'd been doing it for thirty-one years; he literally wrote the manual on search and rescue. Sergeant King wanted his input.

'Whoever took him would have struggled to manhandle him so they're not going to go far,' Senior Sergeant Whitehead said. 'If they pulled off the side of a road, they might drive up a dirt track, get the body out and drag it fifteen metres and then dig—they're not going to want to drag it a long way. If there are fence lines, they're not going to drag him through barbed wire, so search up to those.'

Sergeant King told Senior Sergeant Whitehead about the bunkers and gun pits scattered around the bush. And the sinkholes.

'Search all of them,' Senior Sergeant Whitehead said. 'What about crocs?'

Unlikely, Sergeant King told him. Paddy went missing early in the wet season and the only potential croc habitats, a couple of creeks that flowed into the Roper, were dry at the time. They'd already checked the pens of the resident crocs. Sneaky Sam—the only one big enough to be suspicious—was in the clear. Check the creeks anyway, Senior Sergeant Whitehead advised. Someone might have buried a body in the soft soil of the banks.

Over the next three days, Sergeant King put some of his officers on motorbikes and quad bikes and told them to go out along the tracks and fence lines. He assembled his remaining seven officers and a dozen Northern Territory Emergency Services volunteers into lines and sent them out into the bush, shoulder to shoulder. Larrimah is mostly hard, rocky ground, so wherever they encountered soft ground or depressions in the earth that might have recently been tampered with, they stabbed them with pokers. They didn't turn up anything. They waded through a shallow dam, conscious that stirring the water could bring a body to the surface. Nothing floated to the top.

They also had to keep in mind that a body might not look much like a body after a couple of weeks in the heat and rain, and then there was the wildlife. People who've spent time in the bush tell you varying things about wildlife and dead bodies. Most say if pigs or dogs come across a body they will quickly pick it to pieces, devouring almost everything, but that there will still be something left—usually fragments of bones scattered about. But some will tell you about the time they saw some pigs take down a cow and tear it to pieces, and that twenty-four hours later there wasn't a scrap left. Or they'll tell you about an old recluse in Tennant Creek whose own pet dogs ate him in 2001, leaving almost nothing behind.

Police weren't only looking for remains. They were looking for anything man-made: a cigarette butt, an item of clothing, evidence of a dog, a weapon. Anything that might offer even a small hint as to what had happened to Paddy Moriarty.

On 30 December, exhausted from the heat, Sergeant King called an end to the search. They hadn't found anything. As they packed up and readied for the drive back to Darwin, he took in the shrubby panorama before him. He was confident they hadn't missed a body. Their efforts had been extensive. They'd covered dozens of kilometres a day. But maybe that wasn't far enough. Sergeant King remembered something Senior Sergeant Whitehead said when he'd first spoken to him.

'If someone did cross a fence line, past the barbed wire, how far would they go?' Sergeant King had asked.

'If someone was going to go to that much effort, he could be anywhere.'

Anywhere is a big word, but one Sergeant King refuses to be over-whelmed by. By the time we sit down with him he's had time to turn over all the possible scenarios in his mind. To go back over the evidence search and really feel confident that the reason they didn't find Paddy was because he just wasn't there. 'I'm pretty convinced he's met with foul play and whoever's done it has moved the body to a location to hide it,' he tells us. 'I think he's underground.'

Sergeant King has had enough experience with bizarre murders to find the prospect of Paddy being killed over some sort of trivial conflict not all that strange. These things often roll out like a film plot, he says.

'You watch movies where they do something wrong, and they need to cover up because they'll get in trouble. Then to cover that, they do something wrong again and, before you know it, it ends in this horrible, horrible mess. You hear of so many things that could have just been a fight but it escalated to silly stuff because they were worried about getting in trouble. Circumstances quite easily get out of control.' As to who such a fight might have been with, Sergeant King remains tight-lipped. That's for the homicide detectives, he says.

Now, with the search over, he thinks there are only two ways Paddy will be found. The first is by accident. Like someone digging post holes to put in a fence, or Telstra putting in a line underground. 'Or maybe we have a really big wet season and we get a significant amount of water moving around—that might uncover it.' In an isolated town where development is scarce, it might not be likely, but it's possible. During the 2001 search for Peter Falconio, a few bodies were found in remote outback locations—just not Falconio's. And recently, some pig-hunters in rural Darwin stumbled across a human skull and femur, which turned out to be a suicide victim from three years before.

'People have found all sorts of strange things all the time.'

The second way Paddy's body will be found, says Sergeant King, is if someone talks.

7

Camel mince waffles, a roadkill prank and a yearning for a gin and squash

It's difficult to imagine the kind of person courageous enough to combine camel mince and maple syrup. But so far, that's all we've been doing: imagining Fran. It's time to meet her in person.

We follow the heat of the highway north about 200 metres, and as we draw closer to the teahouse, we're confronted with an overkill of peculiar signs. There are at least a dozen of them, all displaying a disregard for the basic principles of sign-writing. Fran has used an erratic combination of upper- and lower-case letters and the words bunch up together to form indecipherable blobs. There's no punctuation other than the hyphens, which break up words in odd spots. But, against all logic, the signs do work—it's impossible to drive past without noticing the teahouse.

We're barely in the front gate when Fran straight-up tells us she doesn't want to talk about Paddy. She's had enough of it, she says. A gutful. Between the police and journalists, she's had people turning up for months asking uncomfortable questions.

Stranded in her driveway, somewhere between an invitation and a fuck off, we absorb as many details as we can. Even though we know what she looks like from media interviews, Fran comes as a shock because, against all the weirdness of her teahouse—collections of stuffed toys, a peacock fountain and the pandemonium of signs—her appearance is utterly ordinary. The only remarkable thing about her is her height. Apart from that, she is the granny you'd pass in the supermarket aisle. She's round and pale with short dyed-blonde hair, and she's wearing a stripey black-and-white shirt.

It's fair enough she doesn't want to talk about Paddy—we half expected it. But we can't really tell the story of Larrimah without input from one of its eleven residents, especially the one who's been here the longest. Would it be okay if we interviewed her about the town and had something to eat? we ask.

'Oh yeah,' she says, suddenly delighted. 'Come on in, I'll tell you all about the history of Larrimah. What did you want? A Devonshire tea?' We agree, because we're not brave enough to eat camel, let alone camel on a waffle.

As she disappears into the kitchen, a tall man with his head down appears from down the back of the property. He strides past without looking up and enters the little bungalow adjacent to the teahouse and closes the door. Owen. It happens so quickly, we don't even have a chance to approach him, so we sit down in the green plastic chairs under the awning and tell ourselves we'll get another opportunity.

It's already feverishly hot. Country music is playing and we can hear the clatter of dishes, the bleep of a microwave coming from inside. We gaze at the chaos of teddy bears arranged in little scenes around the verandah and garden. SpongeBob SquarePants smiles at us from above the kitchen door, Tweety swings in his perch under the verandah, a trio of teddies on the lawn are arranged under a tiny red umbrella reading 'Beware of the Bears'. Every wall is plastered with old newspaper articles and certificates. And if the dozen or so signs outside weren't enough, there are plenty more under the verandah telling customers what they can and can't have. One is a wobbly handwritten manifesto justifying the prices.

We hear the microwave signal it's finished, and soon after Fran emerges from the kitchen and delivers plates to a table that isn't ours. 'I need to sit next to the fan,' she calls over her shoulder as she returns to the kitchen. We move our gear across to the food:

it's one plate each featuring a scone, a sliver of mud cake, a chunk of fruit cake and half a lamington. Fresh, she tells us. Straight out of the freezer. She plonks a couple of mugs of hot water in front of us, the Lipton teabag tags dancing in the breeze of the fan, then sits down with a cup of instant coffee and some biscuits, the crumbs spilling onto her stripy chest. 'Now,' she says. 'The history of Larrimah.'

We know Fran's place used to be the police station, and she points out the old officer's accommodation (her house), the old cells (her sheds), the old office (Owen's granny flat), and the old tracker's quarters (her teahouse). Part of what is now the teahouse kitchen was designed as a courthouse, but they only ever scheduled one trial here and the defendant didn't even turn up.

From there we cover a range of topics. Fran worked in factories in Melbourne and started cooking when she moved to the Territory in 1974 with her then-partner, Bill Hodgetts—the one everyone else calls Billy Lightcan. She and Bill bought the house in Larrimah in 1984 or 1985, and she worked at the pub for nine years before striking out on her own. 'I put my heart and soul into this, as you can see.'

Despite having an 'i' information sign out the front of her place, she's vague about anything outside the categories of personal details or town gossip. 'The Yanks were here in World War II. They built the road. I think it was the Yanks that named Larrimah.' She doesn't sound certain. 'It means meeting place.' She doesn't say in what language it means meeting place, and quickly moves on to another topic.

The conversation flows and it's easy to forget about the accusations levelled at this great-grandmother. But there are little reminders about the enmity that exists in the town. Fran finds regular opportunities to run down Barry Sharpe: he stole money from the Larrimah Progress Association, she says, and when he took over the pub, that's when the town went down the gurgler.

She hasn't been for a drink since. 'Not being rude, but I just don't like him because he used to poach birds.'

She also brings up the pie wars but describes them as 'a bit of a clash, nothing nasty'. 'My pies was the first ones ever to do buffalo and camel and crocodile. I was the first one ever, so even if they put a pie shop across the road, it wouldn't matter because nobody cooks the same.'

We've been talking for twenty-five minutes when she brings up Paddy. 'I did have history but I don't want to get into it,' she says mysteriously. Then she gets into it: 'I did have a big heap of books, all my visitors' books and everything on the history, but Paddy across the road came and pinched them and burnt them all on me.'

It feels like an opening, but ethically it doesn't seem right to ask questions when we've agreed not to talk about the missing man. Plus, we're having quite a pleasant time with Fran—it's like morning tea at Grandma's place, except it's 700 degrees and she's dropping F-bombs regularly. We don't want to misstep and have her kick us out. We haven't finished our Devonshire teas yet, and they cost seventeen dollars each. But it turns out we don't have to push. In the middle of a yarn about one of her television appearances, she swerves and says: 'I get people coming in now asking for Paddy pies, you know?'

From there, Paddy is pretty much all she talks about.

Fran's front gate faces Paddy's place. He'd bought the house on the opposite side of the highway in 2006, and apart from the occasional guest, he'd lived alone. His house is almost hidden behind trees and a shabby bottle-green shade cloth; the skeleton of the old petrol station the only indication there's something in there, though it looks more like something *had* been there rather than *is*.

Fran's and Paddy's houses are both at the north end of town. They're on the outer, as if someone—perhaps the police, when

Fran's teahouse was a station—deliberately decided to live beside town rather than in it.

'I had trouble with him for ten years. Bad trouble,' she tells us. 'Everybody knows that with Paddy. I had him in court in 2016 for poisoning my garden.'

She's talking about a personal violence restraining order she applied for, against Paddy. She also claimed he'd stolen her umbrella, abused her customers, destroyed her furniture, cut the cord to her security cameras and slid a newspaper cut-out of her under her fence, smeared in human faeces. But the judge ultimately dismissed the case because Fran had no proof.

Fran tells us a lot of things about Paddy—he was dealing drugs, she always thought, because there were cars coming and going at all hours and someone had told her he was selling dope. And he used to get into fights with truck drivers who'd pull up out the front of his place, or teahouse customers who'd park on his side of the Stuart.

His disappearance is probably all Fran has thought about for three months; she can't escape it.

'They're driving past saying, "Murderer, murderer, murderer." It's terrible. It's hard.'

She talks and talks, and it's around the 52-minute mark that we interrupt with a question about Paddy. Is it true he threw a dead kangaroo over your fence? we ask.

'Yeah. He done two,' she replies. She's not angry, she's almost laughing—as if she can see the funny side of it, even though it was an ugly inconvenience. 'One under me kitchen window and one under me bedroom. Stinkin' it was. Two big ones under me kitchen window in me shop last year.'

Why was he doing this stuff? we ask.

She shrugs. 'Because he doesn't like me,' she says. 'I've got a good business. Jealous. But anyway, that's beside the point. Come in and I'll show you me kitchen.'

We've only just made it in the doorway when she pivots back to the police investigation. 'I am tough. With what I've been through, *shhheeew*, you've got no idea . . . I was under arrest at Christmas time, you know, house arrest. Detectives said I can't go anywhere, can't do anything, can't feed my dog, they've got to feed it. Wouldn't wish it on my worst enemy. Anyway, everything's quiet now. There has to be an inquest, there'd have to be. We're not worried. We know what we are.'

The shift to 'we' seems to hang in the kitchen. She's talking about Owen. Throughout our whole conversation, whenever she's brought up Paddy, Fran has lowered her voice and gestured to the little hut Owen entered earlier. Now she leans in and whispers: 'I can't talk too much because of him, he gets upset. It's bad, it's very bad.'

We ask what she means when she says he 'gets upset'. Is she frightened of him? Is she in some sort of danger?

'No, no, no, he's an old man,' she insists. 'When it happened he'd been here four months and they—Barry and that—put the knife in and said that I paid him to knock Paddy off.' Her voice fades to a whisper again. 'Which was bullshit. Why would I ruin what I've got here? For that across the road?'

She confides that it's not just Paddy who's brought trouble her way over the years. It's also her ex, Bill.

'Bill Hodgetts ruined my teahouse,' she says. 'He flooded my kitchen here a few times, he cut me security cameras down off the wall. It cost me twenty thousand dollars to get it all renovated.' She peers out the kitchen window. 'He's over in that caravan, he watches me all the time.' From here, there is a clear view to Bill's caravan parked at the side of the pub. He's been there since she kicked him out a few years ago.

It must be difficult, living so close to an ex, we say.

'I know!' she says. 'At least I can see where he is. Not that I want to.'

She tells us they were never married, even though they were together for more than thirty years and share a last name. 'He was a drunk,' she confides. 'He just drinks and drinks and drinks. He had cancer twice, I looked after him. I bought all his clothes, everything, and he treated me like shit so I kicked him out.'

Since then, things haven't been harmonious between them. Fran claims Bill and Paddy even teamed up to target the teahouse, sneaking over and damaging her property whenever she went to Katherine. 'He got Paddy to poison my garden in 2016. He couldn't do it, Bill, because he was going for a property settlement. He got Paddy to do it.'

Fran says the attacks stopped after Owen arrived, but she lives with the guilt of having brought him here. 'I feel awful . . . I give him the job and he's blamed for this. He's a beautiful man. Honest. He doesn't take food or money or wages. All he wanted was a roof over his head for him and his dog . . . He's a lovely man. He's as tough as old boots. Fuck, he's as tough as nails. But he's got a bad heart. And he's off today 'cos he's got pains and they're accusing him, but they can't prove anything 'cos he never done it . . . I'm his witness, I was here, my bedroom windows are open all the time, his bedroom windows are open all the time. He works for me. If he wasn't here, I'd know.'

Besides, the police didn't find anything when they combed Fran's property for answers, she says. 'They done my septic out—found nothing. They done me house out three times—found nothing. They done me incinerators out—found nothing. Done me shed out—found nothing. Until one day they found a hacksaw that had blood on it but it was fuckin' meat blood 'cos Owen cuts meat up for the dogs. So they took that away. We knew it was only turkey and mince.'

Her voice spikes a few octaves higher when she gets deeper into the subject of the police. She claims police tried to blackmail her to dob Owen in. That they locked her in a room with no air-conditioning for four hours to try to get her to confess. That they recorded her without her knowledge.

Fran seamlessly shifts from the murder investigation to a tour of her kitchen. 'This is where I store all my pies and pasties. That's me shepherd's pie. I don't have as many because I'm not doing any more after this, I'm doing the waffle pies.' She explains, in detail, what goes into this new creation (bacon-crusted waffle, camel mince, fried mashed potato, cheese and maple syrup), and how she was inspired by one of the American cooking shows she watches. The whole time she's giving us the recipe, she's also showing us the neatly stacked plastic containers inside her big chest freezer. Then, the smell of something sweet cooking on the stove distracts her. Mango, lemon and ginger jam, she tells us.

As she steers us in beside the stove, she comes full circle back to Paddy and what she thinks happened. 'His dog used to roam and that's what I reckon. He went missing six o'clock at night and that's when the kangaroos are around—they come out in the evening. I reckon the dog's seen a kangaroo and I reckon Paddy's gone after him. Nobody's done anything to him. He's gone. He's gone where little doggies go, you know?'

We don't know. But the kangaroo theory is not entirely implausible.

None of this conversation with Fran has been linear, but from here it's a quietly spoken layer cake of Paddy and the jam she's cooking. She switches so smoothly between the two subjects that it feels as though they belong together.

'He left the pub at six o'clock, see, he had a bad heart. Here, grab a spoon and try that. And he hadn't been seen since. Do you like that? Try that? Imagine that on ice-cream. Or on scones. I use pulp mango, sugar, a lot of pure lemon juice and a big jar of ginger. And pulp it, then cook it up. Then I thicken it with a little bit of cornflour. Do you like that? Take it and you can eat it. Hang on, I'll give you a little bit of ice-cream. Paddy went missing—I'll go get the ice-cream—on the sixteenth. We didn't know he was missing until the twenty-first. That was five days later. And we didn't even know. Nobody rang me. If I hadn't have gone to Katherine I wouldn't have even have known until they came over here. I've got plain—I saw him on the twelfth. I seen him throw the kangaroo under me bedroom. And I'll give you this and you can go and try it and we won't talk about it anymore out there because he'll get cranky. I can't afford—hang on, I've got to have a little bit meself. I've got plain ice-cream there. Here, take a spoon out of there. I do ice-cream in cones, as well. You can take that back for afternoon tea.'

As we walk back out into the furnace of the day, Fran looks directly at the room where Owen is and, in a loud voice, says: 'And that's the history of Larrimah.'

After we hand over all the cash we have, it takes another twenty minutes to get through Fran's gate. On the way, she introduces us to her fluffy white Shih Tzu, Scruffy, insists we take some photos of her peacock water feature, and stops to point out her favourite plants. She is chatty to a fault, but when we ask her if she thinks Owen might talk to us, she lowers her voice again. 'He's very quiet, he won't talk to anyone.' Then she encourages us to admire a magnificent bougainvillea and points out where the wild donkeys have messed with her lawn.

On one hand we're surprised by how open she's been with us, but on the other, it is perhaps understandable. We have been Fran's only customers today. Her hatred of Barry is so intense she has banned herself from the pub and no one else in town talks to her. Even though she claims to be happy with her own company, it must be at least a little lonely when there aren't any tourists.

If Barry sells and moves on, would she go back over to the pub, we ask?

She pauses for a minute, perhaps picturing what that might look like: her sitting on a stool at the Larrimah Hotel after all these years. 'I'm not a person to go all the time, but it'd be nice to know if I feel like a gin and squash, I could go across and have a talk to somebody.'

Back at the hotel, Barry wants to know how the interview went and we take the opportunity to cross-check Fran's allegation: Was there any way Paddy would have been dealing drugs?

Barry shakes his head. 'Paddy never took drugs,' he says. 'Paddy hated drugs. Paddy never even smoked.'

Then he pauses. 'Actually, there was one guy in town who was selling drugs. Marijuana, mainly, but then he started selling ice and he got raided and jailed. He blamed me for dobbing him in, well it wasn't me. Then he blamed Paddy for dobbing him in. I don't think he would have dobbed him in.'

Richard appears; he's keen for an update on our teahouse visit, too. 'Did Owen talk to you?'

Barry waits for the answer, too.

No, we tell them. We saw him, though.

But when they ask us for a description of that shadowy figure who crossed our paths so briefly, we are embarrassingly light on detail. We cannot remember what his hair was like, or what he was wearing, or what age he looked. He is tall. But beyond that, Owen is still a complete mystery.

8

A world war, a maybe-murdered buffalo and Monty the unbeatable lizard

Richard is the first one to tell us about the buffalo. He's out the back feeding a pair of barn owls that look like they've just flown in from Hogwarts. He takes a break to roll a cigarette—when he licks the paper to seal it, little curls of tobacco attach themselves to his beard. He wipes them off.

We're trying to get to the bottom of a rumour about a peacock being fed to a crocodile in an act of revenge, but the story takes a turn, swerving from birds to bovines.

'I don't know much about the peacocks but I do know that the buffalo got shot and eaten,' he says. It was a wild buffalo that Barry had adopted as an attraction for the pub.

So who shot it?

'Karl.'

Karl Roth lives directly across from the pub with his wife Bobbie. We've heard there's some bad blood between them and Barry, but we don't know all the details.

Why would someone shoot a pet buffalo?

Richard laughs as he lights the cigarette and takes a suspenseful drag. 'So they could eat it and could piss off Barry, obviously.'

The way he says *obviously* is a thinly concealed barb. A reminder that we're not from here, and couldn't possibly understand the intricacies of a buffalo feud, if such a thing even happened. And isn't that always the problem with tall tales? Even as you're leaning in, hanging on every word, you're never quite sure if you're in on the joke or whether, maybe, you are the joke.

So we set out to find Barry, to see if he can offer any clarity.

We catch him in the lull of the late morning, joking with Lenny beside the knee-high chalkboard balanced near the door to the Pink Panther. 'Position Vacant: New Owner', it says in soft capitals. 'Enquire within.'

The sales strategy feels a bit half-hearted, even for Barry—a man who uses a plastic cutlery divider covered with a tea towel as the pub's till. After all, how often does a prospective buyer stumble in for a beer and leave with the whole pub? But the decision to put the pub on the market hasn't been an easy one—Barry's sick, he's not getting better, and the pub's a handful.

It doesn't feel right to bring up Barry's declining health with Lenny hovering around, so instead we ask whether it's a good time to talk about the town's history, the buffalo-shooting and how the place fell apart.

'If you're interested in history, I've got some photos around here somewhere,' Barry says. 'Hang on.'

He disappears behind a stack of postcards perched on the bar; one features a cartoon Pink Panther inappropriately fondling a bare-bottomed woman lifting her tennis skirt. There's a lot of shuffling and eventually Barry returns with a weathered shoebox labelled 'Barry's Birdum Photos Etc. Knife'.

'Bit weird to keep your knife with the photos,' Lenny teases.

'I know, that's why I had to put the knife on the label,' Barry says, unfazed. He's equally unfazed to find that the knife is not, in fact, in the box. 'Well, it must be around here somewhere.'

Then he dumps the faded photos onto one of the bar tables and pulls up a stool. After Birdum was abandoned, Larrimah was the railhead for goods and passengers travelling from Darwin by train and one of the priorities for the Larrimah Progress Association (whose mission was to improve the town's prospects) was preserving its rail history. Sometime in the mid-1990s, Barry and the others restored the train station and got the old section car up and running again.

Barry picks up a picture of a train platform, decorated with pots of bright bougainvillea. 'Now this is what our railway station used to look like,' Barry says. 'It was beautiful, mate. A picture. We all worked together on it.'

We lose Barry for a moment as he's pulled back in time; this wasn't always a place where people fought over pies and buffaloes and buffalo pies. Back then, the Larrimah Progress Association was thriving; everyone in town gathered regularly on the Pink Panther's verandah for meetings and beer. After they restored the train station and section car to their former glory, they cleared the railway line so they could get out to Birdum. Then they set about commemorating the region's history with a sort-of-annual Back to Birdum Festival.

Knowing some of the players, it's probably not surprising that the festival revolved around a pub. And as pubs go, it was an important one. The original Birdum Hotel had been built in 1930, and in the war years the Americans rented it and made it their Asia-Pacific headquarters, coordinating their war effort from barstools on the porch. General MacArthur might even have stopped in.

But the Birdum pub was also born in the shadow of death. The badness started on opening night, when the celebration was interrupted by the news that a bloke had shot himself down the road; nine days later, a hotel guest died in their bed. And the deaths kept coming.

'Yeah, there was a murder there,' Barry says, sifting through photos and papers. 'We should have it documented somewhere. His relatives came to one of our Back to Birdum festivals.'

Apparently, the family showed up in Larrimah, all wearing WHO KILLED BILL JACOBSEN? T-shirts. 'The murder's never been solved,' Lenny pipes up.

'You can imagine it'd be pretty easy to get away,' Barry says. 'You'd only have to jump on the train.'

He digs out an article. Jacobsen worked on the rail and his wife, Dolly, ran Birdum's only shop. On 24 January 1936, Dolly found her husband's body less than 100 metres from their home, with a single bullet wound in his head. It must have really weighed on the family, Barry reckons, for eleven of them to show up seventy years later. Dolly had passed away but Bill's daughters came, he tells us. They never got over it.

It meant a lot to people in Larrimah that they turned up for the festival; in a way, the town was commemorating a death, too, albeit of a different kind: Birdum's. The decision to move the railhead to Larrimah had singlehandedly killed the town of Birdum. And if it wasn't enough that they took the terminus, Larrimah also took the pub. The porch, the roof, the timber—everything useful was shifted 11 kilometres north to build the Pink Panther.

So, in memory of the pub their locals had cannibalised, Barry and the others had built a replica pub in Birdum. They'd followed the imprint of the old building, then hung festoon lights, installed a bar fridge, hooked up a generator and built a stage so travelling muso, Bernie, could come and haunt the wilderness with Eagles covers.

'Here's a good photo of the pub,' Barry says.

'Show me,' says Lenny. 'Oh, Barry looks a bit chubby back then, doesn't he?'

They laugh, but there's something sad about the picture—this frozen evidence of how good they'd all had it. The duplicate pub is lit up against the nothingness of the Birdum bush. Paddy and Lenny are grinning; Barry is in the middle, clutching a beer and brandishing a pair of scissors, about to cut the ribbon. The photo is a history within a history; they really did breathe life into the past. A past that really only lasted as long as it did because of World War II.

There's no major, coherent account of the war years in Larrimah, which is a shame because it's pretty much a season of M*A*S*H—except that it was a long way from active conflict, the military hospital spent more time treating scrotal dermatitis than bullet wounds and there were a lot of goannas.

When World War II broke out, someone in the armed services scanned a map of the Top End of Australia in search of a place to plonk several thousand soldiers and a large-scale staging camp. They needed somewhere far enough south to be out of reach of Japanese planes (and bombs), with good transport access. To someone who'd never been there, the railhead at Birdum and the land around it looked perfect.

So, the United States built a staging camp for a few thousand soldiers at Birdum, over the next few years the Aussies settled six thousand five hundred soldiers just north, in what became Larrimah, and the air force stationed another six thousand people just north again, at Gorrie Airfield. The three camps bled together into one huge, temporary outback settlement. Over the course of the war years, three hundred thousand soldiers and five hundred thousand tons of equipment passed through Larrimah and Birdum via the rail. At its peak, one hundred and forty-eight trains a week thundered up and down the tracks.

But if that makes it sound impressive, then it should be noted: it was not.

For example, the region's military hospital was established by Dr Wigg, a captain with one week's army experience. He arrived in Alice Springs, explained what he was supposed to do, and found himself inside a Monty Python sketch.

'I'm off to Larrimah, to build a hospital,' he told people cheerfully.

'You can't go to Larrimah,' they told him. 'There's no hospital there.'

'I know,' he said. 'That's why I'm going. I'm supposed to set one up.'

'No, you aren't permitted to go there. There's no hospital there.'

This circular argument continued until Dr Wigg finally requisitioned a vehicle and headed up the Stuart Highway, which at that stage was a dirt road so terrible it sometimes gave people appendicitis. On arrival, he was confronted with the reality of his situation. When people in Alice had told him there was no hospital in Larrimah, what they should have said was: there was no anything in Larrimah. No permanent sleeping quarters. No cookhouse. No eating facilities. No recreation quarters. No toilets. Just bush, grass and trees. Also, food was scarce and the tents and marquees that were earmarked for Larrimah had been stolen. So Dr Wigg and his men set up their army-issue wood-fire oven next to a nice termite mound and started weaving beds from saplings and snacking on the local wildlife.

As the war unfolded, infrastructure improved. It's incredible, looking back, how the bush in Larrimah, and so many places like it, was colonised over the space of a few wartime years: bitumen roads, electric light and power, sewerage, army stores, garages and refuelling stations, hundreds of miles of plumbing. Decades of progress happened in a sweat-drenched frenzy.

But being stationed in Larrimah was never a luxury gig for soldiers. The area was so hot that men made DIY air-conditioning in the form of wet bloomers (based on the assumption that if your testicles were cool, the rest of you would be cool, too) and were sunburnt through their army uniforms.

For a first-person account, it's hard to go past Clem Coady, an air force sergeant, who remembers his time in the region with something considerably less than fondness. 'Never, never, have I spent a more boring thirteen months,' he wrote in ex-servicemen's journal Reveille (quoted in The Long Arm by Hugh V. Clarke).

Clem describes the way the flies hovered in dark clouds. 'Each man would have his own black shadow swarming around him,' he writes. 'They shared our food, our drink, the very air we breathed. They were in everything. I have seen men raving, foaming at the mouth, jump into slit trenches and try to pull the top in over them. Anything to escape the black hordes.'

Worse, even, was the boredom. As the staging camps grew, so too did the entertainment options, but even then, most of them were pretty shit. You could play volleyball on a dusty, open-air court with a medicine ball on a 48-degree day or, if you were an officer, have a spot of tennis on a court surfaced with crushed-up termite mounds, complete with a homemade net constructed from Women's Weekly magazines. You could sit on a 44-gallon drum (it was BYO 'sore-bum seating') and watch the weekly movie through the pouring wet-season rain. Or you could gamble your earnings on an illegal game of two-up, while a 'cockatoo' stood sentry to make sure you weren't caught. Once, in 1943, there were picnic races held in Mataranka—it wasn't exactly the Melbourne Cup, but was still exciting for a population so bored it was hiding pythons in people's beds for entertainment. But even then, the landscape conspired to make things harder than they had to be. When the horses set off, they kicked up so much dust it was impossible to see who'd won.

Soldiers made their own fun, and for Clem that came in the form of the lizard races. He had a little beauty called Monty who couldn't be beaten. Some other blokes adopted a goanna, and there were pseudo-pet echidnas and birds, too. Invariably, they'd disappear, and the camp would be awash with whispers about who might have eaten them.

In the face of the never-ending ennui, of course, there was the pub, too. There is always, it seems, no matter how far-flung the town and how wretched the landscape, a pub.

The miracles of the war years—the transformation of the nothingness into roads and houses and settlements—disappeared, almost overnight. Within a few months of the war ending, the bush and the termites reclaimed almost all of it.

'There's some good shit in here,' Barry says, as he flips through scrapbooks and loose photos. But history isn't just contained to the shoebox. Barry is sitting a few feet from the bar, surrounded by memorabilia from recent and distant history. There's a wall of empty tinnies, three battered hats, a painting of a parrot dressed as a pirate drinking a cocktail, a backwards Coopers sign with 'Paddy's Corner' scrawled in marker underneath, some stretched T-shirts and some animal skulls. It's a haphazard inventory of Larrimah paraphernalia and all of it feels like a metaphor for life out here. But maybe the most Larrimah thing up there is a bird clock. Instead of numbers, the clock features twelve birds and it's broken; the second hand moves, but it's constantly ticking in the same spot, and the hour and minute hands haven't budged in years. It's permanently stuck at a blackbird to wren.

Barry pauses on a photo of Fran, standing over a plate of food at the pub, squinting into the camera and smiling. 'We were friends once, I suppose,' he says. 'It was a long time ago.'

So what happened? we ask. How did the town end up in a series of feuds?

Barry has a heap of accusations, and they're all a bit slippery. War relics sold on eBay. The buffalo might have been part of it but after so many years of fighting, he's hazy on the details. He's not even sure it was his buffalo; he thinks it belonged to Green Park, the caravan park on the other side of the highway. The Roth family did kill it, though, he says, and then it probably ended up in Fran's pies.

The thing that grates on Barry the most seems to be the theft— or sale, or loss, or disappearance, it's hard to say—of a 100-tonne orange diesel locomotive worth about $17,000. No one can really confirm where the train came from—it seems to have appeared from Western Australia as part of some strange tourism deal, and the Larrimah Progress Association (LPA) may or may not have paid for it. When the train arrived in Larrimah, it was too big for the old tracks and the plans they had to run tourists up the line were shot. So it was left beside the recently restored train platform—still a tourist attraction, just not the one the town had envisioned. After Barry and his ex, Ann Kanters, were ousted from the LPA, the remaining members did some sort of covert deal for it to go to Adelaide River—but then the train mob at Pine Creek swooped in and took it.

Around the same time, the station platform fell into ruin. Barry produces a 24-page laminated document from the bottom of the box. His partner Ann made it, he tells us, to catalogue the restoration and demise of the Rescue Birdum Project. Partway through, there's a large heading: *'The Following Photos Tell The Sad Story—it took just 4 months of neglect and lack of commitment for the previous 2 years voluntary hard work to be destroyed.'* Then, there are ten pages of photos of dead palms and bougainvillea.

We're all staring at a picture of the rusted yellow section car Lenny is so fond of sitting lifeless on overgrown tracks, wondering what the hell went wrong with the tourist venture the LPA worked so hard to build.

What year would it have been when it was all up and running? we ask.

'It would have been . . .' Barry thinks. 'It was before the Destroyers got here. They got here in '98, it was before that.'

We repeat the name back to him, to be sure. The Destroyers?

'Yeah, they came here and destroyed everything.'

Who's that? we ask.

'Two of them live over here at the moment.' He nods at the house on the other side of the road. It wouldn't be 20 metres from the pub: it's a high-set building with a gorgeous garden. It belongs to Karl and Bobbie Roth. 'They came here as a family. The whole family took over everything, destroyed our progress association. The only thing we have left is the filing cabinet.'

Barry tells us the filing cabinet is a sticking point because it contains the town's historical, financial and government documents, and the progress association minutes. He says that when he moved it into the museum, the Destroyers accused him of theft and called the cops. The police decided it was a civil matter and left them to work it out between themselves.

'He'll get it over my dead body,' Barry says, glaring across the road. 'That's our town's history, that's our heritage. And it's not going back to him to be destroyed.'

We try to arrange our faces into something sympathetic but, inside, we're more than curious. Anyone who has ever been on a committee knows that if ever there was a roadmap to the chronology of small-time in-fighting, a series of passive-aggressive minutes is it. We ask if we can peek inside.

'Maybe,' Barry says, casting a languid look towards the chaos behind the bar. 'I'd have to find the key. It's around here somewhere . . .'

9

A town war, a prince with the trots and enough sinkholes to make you nervous

Karl and Bobbie Roth do not look like two people who have destroyed a town. Bobbie is wearing an embroidered blouse, with her hair in a ponytail. And Karl resembles every other man in these parts—greying, faded tattoos, a little larger than he should be, sporting a standard-issue blue singlet.

Plus, they invite us in for tea and biscuits when we turn up unannounced and their house looks like it's been pinched straight from an issue of *Better Homes and Gardens*. Except for the signs, that is. On one, there's a picture of a hand holding a gun saying: 'Never mind the dog. Beware of the owner'. Another has a collection of faux bullet holes: 'Nothing inside is worth dying for'.

We pull up seats at the table in their carport and make small talk. They're used to people just popping in—the Vietnam Veterans ribbon is painted out the front, which means Karl's fellow veterans stop in often. But the small talk doesn't last long because he and Bobbie have a smorgasbord of wild stories—like the one about the time Karl was bitten by Australia's deadliest ambush predator.

'We'd had a disagreement about something,' Bobbie says.

'We'd had a row,' Karl agrees.

'He said to me, "I'm going to catch snakes," and I said, "Good, I hope you get bitten," as he went out the door. And it was about twenty minutes later that the hospital rang and said, "Mrs Roth, your husband is down here, he's been bitten." And I said, "Oh yeah, what with?" and they said, "Death adder." Shit.'

They laugh, in unison. This happened forty years ago in Alice Springs, but even still, we're surprised at how nonchalant they both are about it. The death adder regularly appears in Top 10 Most Dangerous Snake listicles, plus Karl is allergic to antivenin.

'It just felt like a pin-prick, it doesn't hurt,' Karl says. 'Pythons hurt more, and goannas hurt more than that.'

It's a comparison he's qualified to make because once, also in Alice, he was photographing a goanna and it turned on him. 'He grabbed me on the hand and wouldn't let go,' Karl says. 'I sat there for an hour waiting for this thing to let go and, of course, every time you twitched, he'd grab tighter. In the end I had to get the handle of my pocketknife and prise open his jaws.'

'For years and years you could see the scar,' Bobbie says.

After more than four decades of marriage, there is something almost musical about the way they tell stories. Karl's the melody but Bobbie chimes in to add, correct, harmonise.

'We met at the drag races in Darwin in late 1970,' Karl starts.

'Early 1970,' Bobbie says.

'Early 1970, then,' he concedes.

All their memories seem to be shared, stored in each other. It must have been love at first sight, we guess.

'No!' they both say at once.

'I had a beard and I asked her out and she said, "I don't like blokes with beards . . ." and I said, "I don't give a stuff what you like, lady," so I went home and had a shave.'

Karl laughs—it's a hearty sound, and one he makes often.

Since that first shave, they've done a lot together.

'We had dinner with Prince Charles,' Karl tells us, and of course we hound him for the details.

It was during a surprisingly glamorous 25-year stint in Alice Springs. Karl and Bobbie were both working at the museum, doing everything from digging up megafauna to meeting visiting VIPs. It was a good gig; they'd put on their finest clothes, pick up a bottle of scotch and regale everyone with goanna-bite anecdotes. But Prince Charles's 1977 sojourn didn't go according to plan.

'We all got shigella—a really bad bug that gives you stomach infection,' Bobbie says.

'I didn't,' Karl is quick to qualify. 'I'm not a fussy eater but I looked at the plate: aspic jelly. And I said, "I don't like it." But about a hundred people got the shits. That's the only way to put it.'

'We were all in hospital on drips.'

'Except me. But Bobbie was in hospital for about ten days, really ill.'

Prince Charles copped it too—they put him straight on a plane back to England. The poor guy was supposed to be celebrating his twenty-ninth birthday.

'We can honestly say we were with Prince Charles when he got the shits.' Karl does his incredible laugh again.

By 1998, the social calendar in Alice had gotten a bit hectic for the Roths. They wanted a simpler life in a place they could wear shorts and singlets.

Their daughters, Dianne Rogers and Charmaine Roth, had both moved to Larrimah earlier that year and Karl had always had a soft spot for the town. He'd stopped in a lot over the years, and remembers a time his family stayed there a few nights when he was a kid, and he'd crept to the edge of the campground with his sister late at night to listen to the haunting hum of didgeridoos through the bush. It was the first time he'd heard Aboriginal music, and it seared Larrimah in his memory forever.

So, when they heard there was a house for sale there, they packed the car and headed north.

The house in question had been the town's official post office, from when it was built in 1962 until the rail closed in 1976, so it was a piece of history. It was also the town's unofficial grandstand, because it was high-set and had a view down to the oval. But time hadn't been kind to it. It had no windows and the walls and floors were wrecked. Karl and Bobbie pretty much redid everything, then they started on the garden.

Di was leasing the pub and Charmaine was raising her children and running a punctilious School of the Air. Larrimah's population hovered between twenty and twenty-five—busy by today's standards, but quiet enough for a war vet with PTSD. Karl and Bobbie had always been the kind of people who, when they saw something that was broken, tried to fix it. So after they'd fixed the house, they set about fixing the town.

It started with the fire and rescue. The first few times an accident happened on the highway within spitting distance of Larrimah, they went down to the site to see if they could help—the town is at least an hour from the nearest ambulance.

'That happened a couple of times and we just thought if we're going to do it, we might as well do it properly,' Karl says. They contacted the Darwin office and leapt straight into volunteer duty, along with their daughter Charmaine and, later, their grandson Ben. They were using their own vehicles and supplies for almost a decade before anyone in government offered to at least pay for fuel. Eventually, Karl cornered a minister visiting Mataranka and harangued him for a proper fire and rescue truck. He must have been persuasive because one arrived two weeks later.

Together, Karl and Bobbie covered 600 kilometres of road—and all the side routes in between—for eighteen years. They averaged a dozen major accidents a year and umpteen less serious crashes. That's not to mention the bushfires, they say, like it's an afterthought.

'During the dry you might get four or five call-outs a day,' Karl says. 'You might be out all night and then you'd be up and down, all day and all night, checking fires to see what they're doing. It's a pretty hectic two or three months at the start of the dry season.'

On one notable day when Karl was away for knee surgery, Bobbie—who can't weigh much more than fifty kilos—single-handedly put out two bushfires and a road-train fire. Another time, they waited almost six hours for an ambulance at the scene of a car and truck accident just south of Larrimah. A man and a dog had died, there were three injured kids, an injured woman and a driver with half a leg missing and a hole in his throat. They stemmed the bleeding with towels and waited while two different ambulances broke down en route.

What do you do when an accident like that happens? we ask.

'The best you can,' Karl says, almost too quickly.

The Roths also got involved in the Larrimah Progress Association. At first, the group didn't need to discuss much because everyone knew what had to be done. But then cracks started to show. A few people have told us it began when the Roths started going through the association's books and noticed some discrepancies. When they brought the finances up with Barry and Ann, things turned nasty.

Anything the Roths tried to do, Barry and Ann tried to stop. Karl says he dug holes to plant 152 trees; before he could put the saplings in, they reported it to the insurance company as a liability. Barry had the power and water contract and sometimes he'd cut the power to the pub, which Di was running. One time, he invented a story about a problematic water pipe and called his mates at the department to dig up Charmaine's front yard. The complaints and accusations were relentless, and soon the main street of town marked a division between warring factions. Eventually, Di banned Barry and Ann from the pub, and Ann, the LPA vice president, was ousted from her position. The civil war continued, and the biggest casualty was the town.

'They were trying to get the railway to run,' Karl says. 'We got a railway engineer to come down from Darwin to look at it. He said, "No way, it's unsafe, the public liability insurance would kill you. It would cost you thousands and the track's unsafe." They'd already had accidents where the quad car had left the railway line and I didn't want to take the risk of hurting somebody. We have enough bloody problems on the road without a railway, too.'

It seemed wrong to keep a $17,000 train around, decaying in the elements. It couldn't run on the tracks anyway. So they made plans to get rid of it.

'It was a progress association decision,' Karl says. 'It wasn't my decision. Though I must admit I said yes to it and I contacted the Conservation Commission—I think it's Parks and Wildlife nowadays—who owned the engine. I rang up the commissioner and said, "What do you think about it going up to someone who might actually do something with it? It's just sitting out there rusting away." And they said, "Yeah, go for it." Which created a bit of a blue. Ann was in front yelling, "Save my train!" It was pissing down rain.'

Karl laughs, loud enough to confirm that none of it weighs too heavily on him. But relations between the Roths and Barry have been icy ever since; they didn't thaw after Ann's death. Karl and Bobbie don't go to the pub, not even to collect their mail, despite being close enough to see the post arrive each day on the Greyhound. Instead, they make the 150-kilometre round trip to Mataranka. They don't even remember how long it's been since they last had a beer over the road.

'Seven, eight, nine years?' Karl guesses. 'Years ago.'

We've been here for an hour and we haven't asked about Paddy. When the subject does arise, it's in the middle of a series of anecdotes about various local animals. You must have seen a lot of strange things around here, we venture.

'Only Paddy, that's the only really strange thing that's happened,' Karl says.

We ask if Paddy had any enemies.

'I don't know of any that would want that,' Karl says. 'I know one who threatened to a few times, I'm not going to name names. I'll just look up the road.'

There are a lot of strange things about Paddy Moriarty's disappearance, but for Karl and Bobbie one of the initial strange things was that nobody had bothered to tell them about it. The first they heard about it was when some police knocked on the door, wanting to know if they knew where Paddy had gone.

'He might be in Daly Waters on the booze,' Karl offered. 'Or staying with that mate in western Queensland. He used to go there sometimes. Check with Terry over in—what's the name of that pub?'

'Torrens Creek,' Bobbie added.

'Yeah, Torrens Creek pub. He goes over there every now and again.'

The Roths thought that would be the end of it—Paddy would be gone for a couple of days and would come back with a hangover and a bunch of new stories to tell. Except, it turned out, he'd been missing for six days, his car and hat and money were all at home and his dog Kellie was gone, too.

When Karl found that out, he knew something bad had happened. And in that moment, the first thing he thought about was the rain. There'd been a big mob of rain that week, so if there had been tracks or blood or some other sign of what had happened, it would have already been washed away.

Karl and Bobbie knew, better than pretty much anyone else in town, what police were up against—how hard it would be to pry answers from an unforgiving landscape used to keeping secrets. People go missing all the time in the Territory and, over the years, the Roths had volunteered in search parties. In 2014, they'd spent three hot, gruelling days scouring the area around Mataranka for Joanne Anderson, whose husband and family woke up to find she'd vanished without a trace.

And a few years before that, in 2006, 26-year-old New Zealand back-packer Jamie Herdman disappeared somewhere around Daly Waters, 90 kilometres south. His Kombi van—containing his mobile phone, clothes and cash—was found abandoned on the Stuart Highway near the Hi-Way Inn. He'd passed through Larrimah on the way down there; Fran had been one of the last people to see him alive. But when it came to the search for Paddy, Karl had had two knee replacements and it was 42 degrees and 80 per cent humidity—they were in no position to help out and didn't see what difference two more people could possibly make. So, they did the only thing they could: they went to Mataranka to make a statement.

Inevitably, the question of the Roths' relationship with Paddy arose.

'We were on talking terms. He could be a pretty obnoxious shit when he wanted to be if he was half pissed, but most of the time he was all right,' Karl reckoned. 'He'd give you a wave or give you the finger, depending on what mood he was in.'

Police knew that the Roths, because of all their years of fire and rescue service, were local experts on the terrain. So they asked Karl, point-blank: 'You've been in these parts for years, if you wanted to dispose of a body where would you put it?'

'Well, I wouldn't put the bloody thing here,' Karl said. 'Anybody who lives here knows you wouldn't dump a body here, it's too open and the country's too flat. I've lived in the Territory for nearly sixty years and you'd throw him in the car or something and take him a hundred kays down the road . . . If you took it down the highway, you'd put it on a sharp bend or something like that, somewhere nobody would pull up because it's dangerous.'

But Karl told the police he didn't think Paddy would ever be found. 'You only gotta be out there a couple of days and the dogs and the pigs and the hawks and the eagles . . . be gone in a week. Few bones, they're scattered.'

Karl wasn't in the habit of getting in the middle of things, but he knew about the long-standing feud between Fran and Paddy. On the

*balance of things, he didn't think a local would have been able to pull
off a murder. But he was convinced of foul play and, because Paddy's
life was so routine and predictable, that whatever happened had been
carefully planned.*

*'It wasn't just a spur of the moment thing because nothing was
disturbed.'*

It wasn't Paddy's disappearance that changed the town for Karl
and Bobbie—it was something that happened much earlier.
Larrimah hasn't been the same for the Roths since their children and grandchildren packed up and left. Di stuck around
for nine years, then sold Green Park and moved to Queensland.
Charmaine shifted to Katherine a few years later. The Roths
went from being 50 per cent of Larrimah's population to just
the two of them.

Now the family is spread all over the country, and we ask if
they've ever been tempted to follow them—to Darwin, perhaps,
where their grandson, Ben, who they helped raise, now lives. But
Karl hates cities and Bobbie's content here, too.

'Maybe I'll go up to Darwin in a box,' Karl laughs. 'Not that
I'm saying I'm going to die any time soon.'

We're struck again by the level of candour in Larrimah, and
we use it to finally address the buffalo in the room. It seems a bit
rude to ask someone if they're a buffalo-murderer so we keep the
question general: we heard a rumour that *someone* killed and ate
a buffalo, maybe someone's pet buffalo. Is that true?

'No,' Karl says, quickly. Like it's obvious. 'I don't know about
that one.' He laughs. 'That's a new one.'

Bobbie is confused. 'Someone did what?'

So we have to repeat the rumour, which is sounding more
ridiculous by the second. Now that we think of it, Barry thought
the buffalo belonged to Green Park, which would have made it a

Roth buffalo. *Someone* had a pet buffalo and it was killed and then *someone* made it into pies, we say, unsure.

'Nah, crap,' Karl says.

'Barry had two buffaloes, he let them go,' Bobbie says, dutifully trying to get to the bottom of it. 'I don't know where they went. Di had that pet one and the calf and they went to Kalala Station. No, they took the pig.'

Karl starts listing more buffaloes that have called Larrimah home—there are a lot of them. No wonder it's hard to keep track. But he thinks the buffalo we're talking about was let go. It probably followed the creek and ended up at Warloch Ponds or Elsey Station, further north, he suggests.

It seems much nicer to imagine the buffalo-of-questionable-ownership trampling through the Never Never on the way to water. It certainly seems more plausible than it meeting some kind of pastry-wrapped ending. So, we put that rumour to bed.

～～

Larrimah is situated in what people call 'limestone country', which means the area is prone to sinkholes. Limestone dissolves in water, especially groundwater. It happens in secret, at first, underground. Cavities form, gradually creeping closer to the surface, until there isn't enough support for the soil above. When the collapse does come, it's sudden and violent. Nature's trapdoors, they call them.

We know police took the possibility of sinkholes seriously, but they didn't find any. So we check: have the Roths ever seen one?

Karl doesn't miss a beat. 'Yeah, down on Maryfield there's dozens of them, and there's a few over here on Birdum Creek,' he says, referring to two cattle stations in the area. 'It's just a hole in the ground anywhere from this size—' he makes a small space with his hands, about 30 centimetres wide, 'to as big as this house. It's just flat plains then WOOMP, shit, watch out.'

'You fall in,' Bobbie says, from across the table.

We wonder aloud whether that's what might have happened to Paddy. Could a sinkhole really have consumed a man and his dog, without trace?

'Nah, they've got a bottom,' Karl says. 'The only one we couldn't see the bottom of years ago, down on Birdum—we ended up getting a ladder and ropes and going down there and it opened up into some caves. But you can see the bottom of most of them, they're not these fantastically deep pits.'

It's easy to see why foreign dignitaries loved Karl and his ways-to-die-in-the-outback scenarios. We start to get uneasy, though—could we get sinkholed, even in town?

'There probably are caverns,' Karl says. When they were drilling for water here, sometimes the drill would hit a huge hollow, so there are definitely caverns. And there's also plenty of water, the other ingredient for sinkholes. 'We had a tank burst a few years back and it was twenty thousand litres of water—but it only made a puddle about that big.' He gestures with his hands. It's not a big puddle. 'It just goes straight down. So there's plenty of water here.'

We hand back our cups and say thank you for the tea and the stories, then sneak back across to the pub—partly because we're hoping Barry and Richard won't notice that we've been cavorting with the very pleasant enemy, and partly because we're worried that if we don't walk gently, the angry landscape might swallow us up, too.

But it's impossible to do anything quietly in this place of open space and echoes. When we get back, Barry is waiting for us on the porch of the Pink Panther, brandishing the filing cabinet key.

10

A moment of civic glory, an alcoholic donkey and two not-so-undercover cops

The museum used to advertise using the (admittedly lengthy) tagline: 'Can You Beat This!!! Larrimah Museum Has The Longest Opening Hours In The Territory'. This was not due to the volunteers' extraordinary work ethic—it's on account of the place being unmanned. The museum is unlocked from 7 am until whenever the pub closes, and for the price of a gold coin patrons can wander through at their own pace, beer in hand—which is good news for us as it's getting late in the day and we're thirsty. We flick on the panel of old-fashioned light switches, and the air fills with the buzz of fluorescents.

'The history of the Larrimah–Birdum region is a history of irony', the first sign says. 'A history that, in many respects, is a reflection of the history of the Northern Territory itself. It is a history of great promise and unfulfilled expectations.'

Inside the old phone exchange, the museum houses descriptions of all the main eras: the Overland Telegraph (a communications line that connected Darwin with Port Augusta in South Australia, considered the greatest engineering feat of nineteenth-century Australia), World War II, the rail and the trucking years. It's all interspersed with the kind of strange-but-true absurdity we've come to expect from Larrimah. The photos are like an exhibition of tall tales: four soldiers holding an enormous snake; an anthill at least 6 metres high; 2-centimetre long termites that, in the space of a single night, ate a table, lead sheeting and the casing for a battery. There's a photo of a 'ghastly, featherless' white cockatoo called George who became a mascot for soldiers during the war. A camel-powered wagon. Trucks bogged up to their floors. A world-record 21-trailer road train measuring 312 metres in length, complete with 402 tyres.

In one corner, there is also an old-fashioned toilet with—for no reason—a fake human hand inside it.

But we're here to find the town's *unofficial* history, tucked up in a tiny room at the side. The key catches in the lock and the door swings open, revealing a rusty filing cabinet full of civic disputes, hidden under a blanket of cobwebs. What Barry hadn't told us was that there's much more than just the filing cabinet. There are boxes spilling over with documents, shelves lined with dusty trophies, table-sized town plans, mildew-covered photos and the occasional crocodile receipt. It takes a while to piece it all together. It's a bird clock–level chronological disaster—hundreds of sheets of paper, erratically ordered. But eventually the shape of the whole mess starts to emerge, somewhere between the reams of competing progress association minutes and a drawer full of complaint letters.

Anyone who has driven through regional Australia will know that you can tell how good a town is likely to be by how prominently they display their Tidy Town sign. A billboard welcoming you to 'Queensland's Tidiest Town, 1990' before the road signs even suggest a change in speed limit is a sure-fire indication you're in for some gruesome accommodation and zero entertainment options after 6.30 pm. The only thing worse is hitting a sign that says: 'Tidy Town Runner-Up'.

But the awards are, as far as markers of civic pride go, kind of lovely. They give towns a chance to bask in their achievements and encourage them to strive for sustainable futures. The work Barry and the others did for Larrimah resulted in them winning a Tidy Town award in 1998.

The cabinet is full of letters of congratulations and evidence of toasts at the town meetings. On top of repairing the railway to Birdum, the progress association secured tens of thousands of dollars in grants and sponsorship, started a tree-planting initiative, sunk a bore, welcomed three thousand visitors to the new museum, developed a sports and recreation oval and started hosting an annual cricket match called the Irish Ashes, with teams from Borroloola, Katherine, Mataranka and Dunmarra attending.

They also had big plans. They wanted to reopen the racecourse, run campdrafts (a horseback sport based on cattle-working skills) and rodeos, and start up four-wheel-drive bush tours to secret waterholes and bird-watching spots. They imagined nature trails, bush walks and a flora and fauna park, and local cattle station holidays—maybe even a few more residents. The land around the township could be carved up into small-scale hobby farms, they suggested, for melons, sorghum, emus, ostriches and alpacas.

But, as if to foreshadow what was to come, in February 1999 there's a point where the progress association minutes take a turn. 'The secretary wishes to place on record,' the minutes say, 'due to the chairperson failing to keep to the agender [sic] items . . . and the fact that the tape . . . being inaudible because there were screaming children and shouting parents and the members all talking at once . . . items of business may not be in the exact order and some may be missing from the minutes.'

At the following meeting, in March, Karl asks Ann to stop riding her quad bike up and down the side of his house, as he feels she is only doing this to stir up his dog. Then, in May, it really falls apart. Questions arise about the allocation of funds and Ann is deposed as vice president by order of a secret ballot. She refuses to quit, then spends more than a year appealing the decision, writing letters to government ministers and ombudsmen, demanding an independent audit, trying to clear her name. In the minutes, it's alleged she takes the town's spell-checker with her. It's not clear what a 1999-era physical spell-checker even is, but it must have been important or expensive because it gets a lot of attention. Eventually, she returns the device, but it doesn't prevent errors from creeping into the minutes.

Perhaps the best way to imagine what happens next is through the eyes of an out-of-towner named Robby. In June 1999, he asks if he can join the LPA. But some members are sceptical, concerned he might be a slippery slope to outside interference in the town. The official record of the discussion reads: 'Robby G. said that Larrimah is a dying town & needed all the help it can get. Barry said that if Robby joined, that anyone from anywhere could also join.' Eventually, the association decides that people who come to Larrimah every weekend, spend time and money here and have the town's best interests at heart can join. Robby withdraws his membership three months later, though, 'due to tension amongst members'.

It's a story as old as time—repeated in body corporate nightmares, high school P&C fallouts and embroidery club quarrels. One thing gets under someone's skin and suddenly everything is part of the conflict. But in Larrimah, the accusations are as weird as they are rampant. Someone says a resident was drink-driving the train car on Christmas. There's a fight over what to name the two streets in town, and the secretary loses it over some tongue-in-cheek suggestions and quits.

The police are called into town a few times: about harassment, assault, hooning, loutish behaviour and firearms at the pub. Speed bumps are installed covertly. There's a secret Irish Ashes cricket tournament—some of the town, including Ann and Barry, are not invited. Karl takes over as LPA president and his extended family form exactly half of the executive. He starts fielding phone calls about the $17,000 train.

The town conducts a burn-off, and Ann and Barry complain that they weren't given enough time to move Ding Dong, an alcoholic donkey they'd adopted from Barunga.

According to Fran, the mail service is an issue, too, because letters are going missing, or being opened. Everyone agrees. Then someone paints over her teahouse signs and the police investigate. For a while, it's hard for the association to hold meetings because there aren't enough members for a quorum. There are some meetings where the attendees are all from the extended Roth family.

By 2004, there's a new association in town. It's called the Larrimah Development Association, led by Barry. In its first year, it found sixteen people to pay the $20 membership fee (many of them out-of-towners). One of the members is Paddy. They have eleven more members than the Larrimah Progress Association.

Before we slam the drawer closed, we notice a thin folder up the back marked 'Barry's Legal Documents'. We pause, not sure whether we should look inside something so personal. We like Barry.

We like the Roths, too—we like pretty much everyone, and it's beginning to be a problem. We don't want to take sides but it's increasingly obvious we're going to have to. Individually, everyone's version of events seems reasonable but they're all in conflict; you can't make anything coherent out of it all without choosing the most likely reality.

Eventually, we decide to crack open the folder because there is every chance what's inside is not what the label indicates. Maybe the photo-box knife is even in here.

The file houses a lot of mundane documents—things like permits for dangerous poisons. But there is some more substantial legal paperwork.

For example, there are documents related to a time Barry was assaulted at the Pink Panther—he'd mentioned the incident to us earlier. It had happened late one night when a man came into the pub, drunk or high, wanting to buy a bottle of rum and borrow the phone. Barry let him, but when the call dragged on too long he suggested the man wrap it up. The guy started throwing chairs around, then threw Barry around. Characteristically lackadaisical, Barry waited a full day before seeking medical attention and by then he was in agony. The ambulance raced him to Katherine then flew him to Darwin; that night, they cut him open and found a burst intestine.

There are other stories in the too-personal folder. Some make the Roths look bad. There's a witness statement about another assault on Barry, accusing one of the Roths' friends of verbally abusing Ann, threatening to kill Barry and then punching him in the jaw. In the wake of this police report, Barry and Ann are accused of vexatious litigation and banned from the pub, the town's recreation areas and the museum. Later, Barry is trying to carry out his power and water contract by reading the meter for the pub while Di is there and he's served with a trespass notice.

But at the back of the folder are a few things that look pretty bad for Barry. One is a fine for poaching birds and the other is an old assault charge. According to a witness, a trailer had caught fire while the driver was in the pub, which by then Barry and Ann had taken over running. Karl turned up in the SES vehicle and started squirting it with water. Barry arrived and told Karl to get off his land, then accused him of stealing water. There was a scuffle, it got violent and Barry ended up assaulting Karl.

Moths arc around the fluorescents above us, casting shadows on pages we wish we hadn't read. It's well into the evening and everything suddenly feels too late and too close. We came to Larrimah thinking this was a contained story. Eleven people, a handful of houses, a smattering of issues. But somehow, it's as if the tight boundaries around this place, its tininess, only increase the depth of what is contained here. There's a bottomless well of trouble in this town and it's hard to know which parts we have a right to haul to the surface.

Police investigating Paddy's disappearance must have had a similar problem. On one hand, the town's size was an asset; there weren't that many people to interview and their lines of inquiry were necessarily limited. On the other, the town's size was a liability for them, especially coupled with its remoteness.

Criminologist and Bond University Associate Professor Dr Terry Goldsworthy says the Paddy Moriarty investigation is basically a detective's nightmare.

The problem, Dr Goldsworthy tells us, is that this is a circumstantial case. All signs point to foul play, and while it's *possible* to convict a murderer without a body it's both difficult and rare. In Australia, police have only done so a handful of times, and most of the cases are controversial and notorious, including Lindy Chamberlain-Creighton's overturned conviction for the murder of her daughter Azaria (who was taken by a dingo), Keli Lane's conviction for the murder of her newborn baby, Tegan, and Bradley John Murdoch's conviction for the murder of Peter Falconio.

Almost every circumstantial case hangs around a few things: witness statements, forensic evidence and contradictions in the alleged killer's version of events. But in Larrimah, detectives are up against it on all fronts. No witnesses to what happened to Paddy have come forward, the landscape has stolen any forensic evidence and the lack of phone reception or CCTV cameras means it's hard to resurrect a credible version of the past in the courtroom. Out here, the line between something happening and not happening, or maybe happening, is slim. Without a digital footprint to trip someone up or corroborate their story, there's no way to prove the difference.

Other investigative methods were off-limits or hard to execute, too. Dr Goldsworthy says the police wouldn't have been able to pull up in a fake Telstra van to install listening devices in a suspect's house without attracting attention, for example, or send in a bunch of covert officers. One resident told us a great story about how they *did* stumble into a couple of people who might have been undercover cops at the town's only rest stop, a few weeks after Paddy disappeared. 'Nice work,' they told the pair, who were lurking awkwardly. 'You're really blending in.'

Unless you're disguised as a grey nomad, there aren't many places to hide in Larrimah and, even then, you've only got a few hours admiring the museum and taking photos in front of the deckchair Pink Panther before people start asking questions about what you're doing in town. No one sticks around for more than a night here. Not without a good reason.

Police had no choice but to investigate everything—old feuds, long-held grudges, implausible stories. 'We are investigating a— you used the word stoush, we can use the word feud—that's been the subject of an investigation,' Detective Sergeant Matt Allen told us. 'Information in relation to Paddy's background, his relationships to people in the town . . . It's a factor that's very, very relevant to his disappearance. If he has disagreements, that doesn't mean that [someone is] going to kill him over their disagreements, but it's something we need to investigate and we need to investigate it thoroughly.'

So, as we lock the museum door behind us, we commit to a similar philosophy. For now, we'll hear everything out.

11

A bogged camel, an exploding cow and a series of fallings-out

Barry's behind the bar, tapping his fingers, looking nervous.

'Can I get a picture, mate?' It's a grey nomad and it's not Barry he wants a picture of. It's the bar. On the front of it, some long-ago publican has hand-painted: 'We're at Larrimah, the highest bar in the Northern Territory'. Beside it is the longitude and latitude, and the height, 181.04 metres. For some reason, tourists love it. They always want to pose beside it, as if having visited a place with such a low-stakes claim is a remarkable achievement.

What does 'highest bar' even mean? we ask Barry once he's dispatched the nomad to the museum, frostbitten ice-cream in hand. 'Well, it has two meanings,' Barry says. 'One is the altitude, we're at the highest altitude. The other is it's the tallest bar.' Barry places his hand on his chest, like a measuring stick. The bar is tall, but not impressively so, maybe a little higher than average. Apparently, the idea was you could order a beer without having to dismount your horse. We ask if either of the claims—the tallest bar or the highest altitude—are true.

Barry looks surprised. 'I don't know. No one's ever disputed it.'

He goes back to tapping the top of the ambiguously highest bar in the Territory and looking out the front door, as if awaiting an important delivery. 'That buyer was supposed to come today,' he tells us. 'Hasn't shown up. Again.'

Selling an outback pub by chalkboard is a bit like casting a fishing line into a bathtub, but Barry's had a few nibbles. One bloke was keen and said he'd come by; Barry likes him because he knows him, and he'd probably take the animals if he bought the pub, too. But it's been almost a week of promised pop-ins and there's still no sign of the guy. Barry looks beaten.

'I'm sure he'll turn up,' he says, but even he knows he's lying.

We get a drink and log on to the wi-fi. Larrimah is not the highest bar in the Territory, if we're talking altitude. Not by a long shot.

To tell a tale in the Territory is to tell a tall tale; the further inland you go, the harder it is to pick apart fact and fiction. Maybe it's the legacy of so many scumbag-settlers, people whose pasts were pure invention, created when they moved to the outback. But inflating stories seems like a wasted habit out here because nature has already done so much of the exaggeration for you.

When Mark Twain visited Australia in the late 1800s, he described the country as 'curious and strange'—although it's worth mentioning that Australia found Twain equally perplexing. 'His head is like an amazed gum tree,' wrote one reporter in *The Bulletin*. 'His hair gives him the wild expression of a man who has just found a baby's shoe in his soup.'

Twain took in all the weirdness Australia had to offer, and still concluded that the nation's greatest novelty was its story. 'It does not read like history, but like the most beautiful lies,' he wrote after his 1895 visit. 'And all of a fresh new sort, no mouldy old stale ones. It is full of surprises, and adventures, and incongruities, and contradictions, and incredibilities; but they are all true, they all happened.'

Perhaps it is exactly this oddness that keeps people coming to places like Larrimah. Where, for the price of a beer, the bartender will tell you about crop circles or a croc with no eyes, and you can for a moment be part of the outlandishness of it all. Sure, there are a lot of tall tales. But some of the strangest stuff is true.

So, when we hear the rumour about Billy Lightcan, we're equal parts sceptical and hopeful. It's a story so far-fetched that, if it's to be believed, means Bill should not be living in a caravan at the back of a pink pub, behind the emu enclosure. He should be one of the richest men in the country.

We've seen Bill at the pub every day and it's almost impossible to describe the way he looks, because nobody else has ever looked like him. He's strong and tough but his body has been knuckled by illness, which has robbed him of all his flesh. He's all bone and muscle and sinew, covered in tattoos that have shrunk into unrecognisable images. He might well have been handsome once, though, with a neat moustache and brown spiked-up hair.

Each day we've encountered him on the verandah of the pub, drinking and smoking, and we've stopped for brief chats. Now we find him reading a book on the shady side of his caravan, which faces the animal park. It's a position that is in conflict with Fran's claim that her ex watches her and she keeps an eye on him. For that to be possible, he'd have to move around to the other side of the caravan, which is not an inviting prospect. There, the sun's fury cooks you and you're seasoned by the dust from the road trains that drive the dirt track between the pub and the teahouse.

Bill gestures for us to join him under the awning and we survey a series of mismatched chairs, a blue esky, an upturned milk crate and a wheely bin, and then select the seats that look least likely to topple over.

'Would you like a beer?' he asks.

His voice is another thing that's hard to describe—it's like he's speaking through a mouthful of golf balls.

We decline the beer and ask Bill what he's been up to today. If Fran has been watching what Bill is doing, it would not have made very interesting spying. His itinerary for most days includes listening to the radio in his caravan, wandering over to the shower block, then returning to the shade of the awning to read. After dinner he goes to the pub. Occasionally, he jumps in his red ute and drives up to Katherine or Mataranka for supplies. Often, he drives the 20 metres to the pub.

Bill is extraordinarily polite to us. So polite that it's hard to know where to begin. Certainly not with Fran's allegations about him. So we start with what we think is an unintrusive question: how did he get the nickname Billy Lightcan?

'Oh, that,' Bill says, pleasantly. 'I got cirrhosis of the liver at one stage, I nearly died. I had blood coming out me eyes, out me ears, out me nose, out me backside, everything. It scared the shit out of me. So I thought, "I'll drink these light cans, they don't knock me around so much."'

Of course, the health benefits of drinking light beer are questionable when you've consumed so many that the empties line an entire wall at the pub. We tallied them up when we first arrived: 437 cans of XXXX Gold, Carlton Light and Eagle Blue. There are some VB cans in there too, though Bill doesn't say if he broke his diet or if someone else slipped them in there.

We're beginning to adjust to the way Bill's vowels warp together. He wastes no time in explaining the illness that caused the speech impediment, even though we haven't asked.

'I got cancer just after I bought me house,' he says. 'Me jaw has all been made up, me bottom jaw. I've had half me tongue cut off, that's why I don't talk so good. They took the bone out of me hip and made me bottom jaw out of that. I had no feeling in it.' Bill was laid up at home for nearly two years recovering, he tells us, but eventually he got so bored he went back to work and ended up in hospital again. 'The doctors were mad,' he says. 'They said,

"Don't go back to work again, Bill, you've run out of bones we can make a jaw out of.""

Then he takes in our sympathetic faces and assures us he's all right now, even if he's rail-thin. On doctor's orders he eats all the junk food he can, but it makes no difference—he finds it impossible to gain weight.

We move to what we think will be the safer territory of his first years in the north, but stumble straight into another trauma. Along with Fran, Bill moved from Melbourne to Darwin in 1974 and for the first few months they lived in a caravan. One night, Bill was invited to a Christmas party forty minutes out of town at Humpty Doo, and even though he'd heard the rumours of a cyclone approaching, there was barely a breeze at the party so he figured it was a false alarm.

'The next morning I was driving back, there were power poles all over—trees, dead animals, cattle all over the road, trucks overturned,' Bill says. Cyclone Tracy, which killed seventy-one people and left more than half of Darwin's residents homeless and all of them pretty traumatised, had destroyed everything.

Somehow, Bill's caravan survived. 'The annex was gone and it had a lot of dints in it. But the old double-decker bus next door to me—that finished up over the other side of the railway line on the Stuart Highway, upside down. A double-decker bus! And that was right beside me! I couldn't get over it.'

Maybe it's that Larrimah candour, but having covered all this ground within the first few minutes, we give up playing it safe. There are two things we really want to talk about—Paddy, and Bill's family. We heard something about your grandfather, we venture.

Bill smiles.

'Oh yeah, that was Lasseter.'

A qualified ship captain, inventor, carpenter, Mormon, soldier, prospector, journalist, original designer of an arch bridge for Sydney Harbour—Lasseter claimed to be a lot of things. Roughly half of them were true and, of those, roughly half were only half-true. But the only claim that mattered in the end was the one about the reef of gold. The highway of gold. The cave with gold nuggets as thick as 'plums in a pudding'. Whichever way he described it, Harold Bell Lasseter knew it would be irresistible.

With the key detail—the gold—locked in, the story he told people was a simple one. He'd been lost in central Australia thirty years earlier, and as he crawled around on the desert sand, close to death, he'd pulled up a handful of gold nuggets. He was gobsmacked until he looked up, and then he was double-gobsmacked. The glittering rocks stretched 15 miles into the horizon.

Years later, when he started approaching people to fund an expedition to recover the gold, Australia was on a downward slide into the Great Depression. Unemployment and poverty were rising, incomes and profits were plummeting: it was the perfect time to pitch an outback treasure hunt. Some fringe politicians in Sydney who relished the idea of saving the country from economic strife and becoming heroes agreed to bankroll Lasseter, throwing so much money and manpower at him that his journey became the best-equipped mining expedition the country had ever seen.

But soon after Lasseter and his team set off from Alice Springs on 21 July 1930, his companions started to get hints the mission was doomed. Their all-terrain vehicle became hopelessly bogged before they'd even made it out of town. A few days later, when they went to radio in, they realised Lasseter had left the mouthpiece for the two-way behind and they'd be unable to communicate with anyone if they got into trouble.

As they edged further into the desert, expedition leader Fred Blakeley began to have doubts. Lasseter refused to give them exact coordinates of the reef; in fact, he seemed to have no knowledge of the landscape.

Huge landmarks were unfamiliar to him and he claimed to remember things that could not have possibly been around when he'd supposedly been there, thirty years before. He couldn't even make damper, a skill any bushman needed for survival.

After a few weeks, Blakeley and the others had finally had it. Lasseter was a charlatan, they decided. They left him with a young German dingo scalper named Paul Johns, who'd rocked up in the middle of nowhere one day with a few camels. You go find the gold, they told the two men. We're going back to Alice.

Johns and Lasseter forged on through a series of hellish calamities, including three days digging a bogged camel out of the sand with their bare hands. Eventually they got into a scuffle and Johns may or may not have shot Lasseter in the arm. Either way, Johns was out. He took off back to Alice Springs, leaving Lasseter alone in the outback with no food, little water and only a couple of exhausted camels with drooping humps for company.

It took a while, but eventually someone went looking for Lasseter. It was a tracker by the name of Bill Buck, a bushman. Likely he was more interested in finding the gold than the man who'd gone missing looking for the gold but, in either event, he succeeded quickly. Lasseter's body was in a cave, Buck told people when he returned with some dentures and his diary. Some Aboriginal people he had met told Buck they tried to care for Lasseter but he'd died of starvation or dysentery.

Lasseter's death made headlines all over Australia—in part because the location of the gold reef had not died with him. Before he'd set out, Lasseter had stored the coordinates in a bank vault and his financial backers could now go to court to access them. Except, when they got their hands on the document, written in invisible ink, they discovered an indecipherable jumble of numbers that meant nothing. It must have been a blow, and an embarrassing one at that. In retrospect, Lasseter's story bore a remarkable resemblance to several fictional novels, including American writer Harold Bell Wright's The Mine with the Iron Door. This was the man from whom Lasseter had taken his name.

That should have been the end of it. It had all, surely, been a hoax. The duplicity of an accomplished fraudster. But some, including Blakeley, began mounting a case that Lasseter had not, in fact, died. And Buck eventually admitted that the bones he'd found may have belonged to an Aboriginal person. People argued that Lasseter's backers, who needed a death certificate to access the coordinates, had paid Buck to kill him or find fake evidence of his death. People began to wonder if Lasseter had found his gold and shot through.

Gold fever is a curious thing. Many thought Lasseter a liar. But, then again, people are still looking for his gold.

'At school whenever they brought up Lasseter in class, I'd say, "That's my grandfather!" but the teacher would accuse me of lying,' Bill says. 'I'd go home and tell Mum and she'd get all his diaries and march down to the school and go "See, he's not lying!"'

We laugh but we really want to know about the gold reef. Was there ever any gold?

Bill shrugs his thin shoulders. 'Mum had a few of his diaries. He did find gold but Mum just thought it was strange at the time, he wasn't working and all of a sudden this thing came up that he's got to go see the government about launching an expedition. They believed him. Mum reckoned he was full of shit.'

In an alternate universe, where Lasseter found the gold and made it back to civilisation, it's doubtful Bill would have ended up here in Larrimah. As an heir to a gold reef, he wouldn't have given decades of his life over to the gruelling and often unruly business of truck driving.

The Territory has always been a lawless sort of place. In 1898, Banjo Paterson made some judgey (but probably accurate) comments in *The Bulletin* about the Territory's drinking culture: 'They start drinking square gin immediately after breakfast, and keep it up at intervals till midnight. They don't do anything else to speak of, yet they have a curious delusion that they are a very energetic and reckless set of people. But it's all talk and drink.'

He was talking about the state of things in 1898, but he could easily be describing the Larrimah Hotel more recently—with the exception of the gin, of course. We've never seen anyone order anything but beer or rum here—Barry still talks about some blokes in the 1990s who asked for red wine. And if you'd happened through in the 1950s or 1960s, when the town was a major transport hub, connecting road freight to the rail, you'd have seen some wild things.

It's an era mostly full of stories that you can't tell in public but, luckily, someone did. Bob Foster's trucking memoir *Birdum or Bust!* suggests there were four major hazards—potholes, anthills, vegetation and animals. But we'll happily add a fifth: other drivers. It wasn't uncommon for drivers, exhausted from punishing schedules and binge drinking, to intentionally have a snooze on the straight, or to pass the time imbibing a bottle (or case) of rum.

The road was bad—no one had done any work on it since the war, and goods were transported in vehicles you could only call trucks if you were feeling optimistic. They were mostly homemade rigs MacGyvered from cheap, scrounged or stolen ex-army semis. Brakes were considered a luxury but bullbars were not. The worst thing to hit was a buffalo, but a cow exploding on impact came a close second, especially if you had one of those open windscreens and you and all your worldly possessions got sprayed with goop that would quickly rot in the heat. One driver held the record for hitting seven horses at once. Long-haul driving also leaves plenty of time for thinking, and mostly what drivers in that era thought about was how to prank one another. You could turn someone's truck around while they were drinking so they ended up going the wrong way, or hijack a hitchhiker (they called them road parasites) and make them drive part of the way while you had a nap. You could drive for hours with your lights off and suddenly ram someone from behind. Or, if you were the offsider on a route, you could leap onto someone else's truck while your mate drove past straight-faced and lie quietly in the back for a few hours. Then, when the night was at its darkest, you could pop up in the cabin and scare the rum-laced urine out of the driver.

After days with nothing but your thoughts and fears for company, you'd suddenly run into a mate at a pub like Larrimah's—somewhere the long arm of the law might have trouble reaching. Bob Foster remembers convoys of drivers tearing into town, with drivers passing bottles between moving trucks. It was a rough crowd in the 1950s, full of ex-ringers, boundary riders, timber jinker drivers and broken-down diamond drillers. Bob, a truckie himself, describes them as loners: 'Probably not good team players, a resume might note, if you ever had to write one.'

Everyone carried a gun. Established truckies carried several. The preferred form of dispute resolution was the threat of a shootout. 'We had little contact with "normal" people,' Bob says, 'so we received limited feedback on our behaviour.' It's little wonder Larrimah petitioned to get its own police station.

We ask Bill what he remembers of the trucking years—his version is a little later and a little cleaner. There were good times on the road, he says, crisscrossing the country, and in the days before regulation no one minded if drivers fuelled up on grog before, during and after long-haul trips. For truckies, Larrimah wasn't the middle of nowhere, it was the centre of everywhere—a day out of Queensland or Western Australia, a day-and-a-bit from South Australia. Bill stopped here all the time to load freight onto the trains, and it was always a good time.

So when the former police station eventually came up for sale, Bill jumped at the opportunity. He and Fran had been together a while, the children from their previous marriages had grown up, and they'd always talked about settling in Larrimah.

Bill's relationship with the house went way back too—he was once put in the cells for a night, the local cop having picked him up on some drunken misdemeanour he no longer remembers the details of. When he woke the next morning and realised where he was, he panicked.

'I thought, "I'm going to miss the train, it'll be gone. I've still got a load of frozen freight." I'm calling the cop up in the house with his missus, calling him all the names under the sun. I said, "Let me out of here, I've fucking got two trailers of freight there, the train'll be gone." He said, "Bill, settle down, push the door." I pushed the door and it was open. I owed him an apology for that.'

Years later, when he moved into the house, Bill knocked out a couple of walls and made the old cells his shed. He kept the bars, though. They added character.

While he lived there, Bill says almost every cop who'd ever worked there called in at some point to reminisce about their outback policing stint. He was always glad to show them around and sit down and hear their stories. But he had never seen so many cops at once as there had been in those days following Paddy's disappearance.

Bill and Paddy went right back—they had known one another well before they'd come to Larrimah, back when Paddy was in his twenties, fresh off the boat from Ireland and working at one of Australia's biggest cattle stations, Brunette Downs. Paddy was a bit of a scallywag, and they'd had their run-ins over the years, but they were mostly on good terms. Paddy had taken Bill's side in the divorce—some people say

that's what started the rift between Paddy and Fran, but it had been going on for ages before that.

In the beginning, when Paddy moved in over the road, they'd all been friends. Paddy had heart surgery shortly after coming to Larrimah and Fran had even cooked and delivered meals to his door. But around that time, Bill headed off on another long run in the truck, and when he returned a couple of months later, Fran and Paddy hated one another. Bill never got to the bottom of what sparked it. Paddy had always been a bit of a shit-stirrer, but this was something else, and it escalated into outback warfare. Paddy would hurl abuse at Fran; Fran would give it right back. Then Paddy began stopping in on his way to the pub, creeping over the fence and vandalising the teahouse. Bill grew tired of fixing cut pipes and replacing the things that went missing. 'Look, will you leave her alone for Christ's sake,' Bill would beg. 'I've gotta live with her, she's coming to me all the time, just lay off a bit.'

Bill also had his own troubles. By that stage, he'd been with Fran for almost forty years. They'd had their fair share of fights, but as Bill got closer to retirement something shifted.

'So you're going to be home every day?' Fran had asked.

'Yeah.' Bill had expected some excitement. But that's not what he got.

'I couldn't put up with you every day,' Fran said.

That's when the shit really hit the fan. Fran took him to court for his superannuation and bought him out of the house. Bill moved into his caravan.

Fran might've got the house, but, in a way, Bill got the town. Almost everyone sided with him, including Paddy.

We move to the other side of Bill's caravan, the scorching side, and stare across the highway to Paddy's empty house. It's a clear view. Whatever happened to him and Kellie that night, someone should have seen something. Bill or Fran or someone at the pub. Sound travels here, too. Someone should have heard something.

'I don't think it's anyone in the town that's done it,' Bill tells us. 'Everyone's sort of older, I just can't see it.'

He brings up other out-of-town rivalries. He tells us Paddy pissed off a lot of people in his previous town, Daly Waters. That he had a long-running feud with the woman who owned the pub across the road from his place there, and that he'd been banned from it and the town's other nearby pub, the Hi-Way Inn. 'They hated him,' Bill tells us. 'They really hated him, the whole town.'

It's not the first time this has come up. 'Paddy didn't have many friends around,' Cookie had told us, 'he had a few enemies. So it could have been someone else who sent someone to come fix him.' Cookie had been vague, and he obviously didn't count Paddy as a friend, so it was difficult to know if there was any truth in it. Now, we wonder. Could there have been a person tucked away somewhere with a simmering hatred for Paddy? Someone who had just been biding their time.

On our second-last day in Larrimah, Barry finally admits his potential buyer is full of shit. The bloke's failed to show. Again. We've found him up the back of the pub at the wildlife park, standing beside a tub heaving with millions of wood roaches, dumping rotten chicken into a small red bucket. 'I think he's let us down,' he says. We're struck by the wording: *us*. It's Barry's pub, but in a way it belongs to the whole town.

If the pub doesn't sell soon, Barry will have to close the doors and walk away. It's an awful prospect. Not only would that mean no money for his retirement, but it might also spell the end of Larrimah. A town with no pub is as useless as a pub with no beer.

Then there's the matter of the zoo. Lots of people want to own a pub, but not everyone needs a 3.5-metre croc and five hundred birds to look after on the side.

'I might have to think about selling off the animals,' Barry tells us quietly. He knows a guy in Darwin who might want some of the birds, and Des, the search and rescue captain up at Mataranka, would probably take Sam and some of the snakes for his tourist park. Karen might want some squirrel gliders.

Barry picks up a bucket of raw meat and we follow him through a maze of aviaries to the pond where Sam lives. We've come up here to try to get a glimpse of the prehistoric animal almost every day, but he's only ever eyeballs on the water. Today, as Barry lets himself into a small, terrifyingly low-fenced enclosure attached to the croc pen, Sam appears, drawn out by the irresistible smells of human sweat and rotten chicken.

There really is only one word for Sam: magnificent. Fat and golden with a smooth, blond underbelly, the croc hurls himself towards the pole Barry is dangling meat from. Barry's holding it high, so we can witness Sam in full flight as he lunges for his lunch. But as the reptile moves, the pole suddenly seems too short and Barry's arm too far over the fence. There is an awful moment where we freeze on the small viewing platform, sure Barry is about to lose a limb to this pet he's had since not long after it hatched from the egg. At the last minute, Barry whips the meat out further, spraying us with chicken juice as Sam snaps and gobbles. We can't even complain. Our clothes splattered with fetid liquid seems a small price to pay for Barry keeping his arm.

As Sam stretches out on the bank of his pond to digest his weekly meal, Barry leans up against the now very low-looking fence and sighs. 'This place, it drains your energy. I'm seventy-six this year. I've been doing this for more than fourteen years now.'

You should have retired a while ago, we say.

'Mate, I should never have started.'

While Barry is trying to untangle himself from the Larrimah Hotel, Richard seems to be doing the opposite. He's been wanting to buy property in town for years but says the government won't release any new land because there's a native title claim in progress. Richard's annoyed at the inconvenience, particularly because, he says, Aboriginal people refuse to live here anyway.

What do you mean? we ask.

'They're scared of the place,' he says. 'It's Kadaitja land.'

12

A long-awaited homecoming, kangaroo for dinner and 65,000 years of history

Chasing history is overwhelming; it's like digging through sand but examining every grain as you go. And in Larrimah, we know we haven't gone nearly deep enough. We are intruders on this land in more ways than one, and it isn't sufficient to unearth old war and rail stories. There is a history here that goes back at least sixty-five thousand years.

Trouble is, Richard could be right. There is a conspicuous lack of First Nations people living here in Larrimah, which is completely out of step with the rest of the Northern Territory, where a quarter of the population identifies as Aboriginal or Torres Strait Islander.

In the absence of anyone on the ground to ask, we allow a middle-aged white bloke with a few beers under his belt to give us a cultural history lesson. Richard tells us that Kadaitja is a type of shaman, and that for Indigenous people this is spirit country. 'Best I can work out, probably four or five thousand years ago, a big mob come through here going to a ceremony and they disappeared,' he says. 'And this is all sinkhole country round here. It's not like little sinkholes that the dog would fall into, this is like five kilometres of land dropping away at once 'cos it's limestone country. They reckon the Kadaitja man got 'em and that's why they don't want to live here.'

But like most things around here, that's not entirely true.

Because up the road at a place called Wubalawun, lives a man called Allen Maroney.

Allen is fifty-five years old, a proud Wubalawun man who can trace his direct connection to the land around Larrimah as far back as his great-grandfather. The tract of land that belongs to his people extends north towards Elsey Station and south past Birdum, and Allen's great-grandfather was responsible for protecting the community's borders by walking from boundary to boundary and granting permission for other people to travel through the region for marriage, family visits or to attend sorry business. It would have been a hard job—the distance he had to cover each time was around 100 kilometres and it would take him about a week. Even Allen, who knows the pattern of his country and all its hidden creeks and billabongs better than anyone else alive, doesn't know if he could do it. 'I'm always amazed at the distance he had to travel,' he says. 'My grandfather mastered the art of travel in a very hostile, dry environment. I know where all the waterholes are, my dear, but it would take me a bloody month.'

Allen's father was from near Alice; his connection to the Larrimah region comes from his mother's side. His parents met while working on stations in the Territory, fell in love and then, as Allen puts it: 'all us kids popped out'. Allen is the youngest of four children, and in his early years the family moved around, following the mustering work. But from almost the very beginning, his life was intercepted by two historical forces.

The first was the Gurindji (Wave Hill) walk-off, a turning point for Indigenous rights. In the 1960s, it was well known that conditions for Aboriginal workers on cattle stations were terrible. Pay was sub-standard or non-existent—Allen's own maternal grandfather had spent his life working for little more than sugar, tea and flour. By 1965, there were calls to introduce equal pay for (male)

Aboriginal cattle workers, and in August 1966 Vincent Lingiari, a Gurindji man, led a walk-off of two hundred stockmen, domestic workers and their families from Wave Hill Station at Kalkarindji, 480 kilometres south-west of Larrimah. The protest spread to other stations across the Northern Territory, and eventually a portion of their homelands was returned to the Gurindji people in 1974.

'He's my hero,' Allen says of Lingiari. 'He got land rights and equal pay for Aboriginal people.'

When he was three or four years old Allen's parents moved to Katherine, and not long after he encountered the second force that irrevocably shaped his life. He was taken away.

Allen is part of the Stolen Generations. Officially, the policies that resulted in Aboriginal and Torres Strait Islander children being forcibly removed from their families were in place until 1969, but there are many stories of forced removals in the years after. In Allen's case, he and his siblings were taken to a mission in Darwin in the early 1970s, then lived in foster care in Katherine. His parents were rarely able to visit, and only by securing an appointment via the welfare system, so as well as losing his childhood with them, Allen grew up without access to his country. But he always heard stories about Wubalawun.

'Mum kept telling us, whenever she had a chance to sit down with us, she always reminded us,' Allen says. 'She said to me, "You promise me if I pass away, you need to chase country up and get country back for your big brothers and sisters." So I was virtually chucked into the deep end to sort out Larrimah.'

It took time, but that's exactly what Allen did. He was part of a Land Rights Claim lodged in 1979 (separate from the ongoing current native title claim Richard mentioned). More than a decade later, the Wubalawun Aboriginal Land Trust was awarded 80,000 hectares of land, just north of Larrimah. Allen was able to set foot on his own country for the first time.

125

His heartbeat knew, almost before he did. It thudded, quickly. He looked around at the stringybarks and coolabah trees, the bloodwoods and bauhinia. It felt like opening the door after returning from a long trip. He could sense his ancestors, his mum's presence on the country. He was home and it sent shivers down his spine.

A little while before he'd gone to Wubalawun, a doctor had warned Allen to quit his job as executive director for a community housing organisation in Katherine. 'If you keep on like this, you'll be dead in the next five or ten years,' the doctor had said. Allen had already seen so many of his people dying too young and he didn't want to be another statistic. So when the land claim was granted, it was both a celebration and a relief. He'd been worried he might be an old man before it got through the courts. Maybe he'd never see it.

Wubalawun, which is about 20 kilometres north of Larrimah, was isolated but already had some established houses. Allen moved into a high-set home near the highway, and his sister lived next door until, eventually, she needed to be closer to Katherine. But no one else in his family followed. His brothers had children and jobs and other reasons to stay in Katherine, and Allen's seven children weren't in a position to relocate. So for the most part, Allen was alone.

He wasn't lonely, though, or bored. He had two dogs and enough time to get reacquainted with his county and its seasons. He learned where to find water and where the limestone caves were. Got to understand the way the storm bird sang, predicting a good wet season, or the way its silence warned him when it was going to be dry. He knew, then, he should take it easy with the water from the billabongs.

When Allen was a kid, an Aboriginal family in Katherine had taught him how to hunt using traditional methods and now he adapted them for his country. He caught bush turkey and goannas, turtles and bream from the billabongs, the occasional magpie goose. He cooked pandanus nuts and harvested water lilies. Sometimes, the dogs would hunt a large kangaroo and he'd be eating that for a few weeks. He hated guns—wouldn't let anyone use them on his land—and he only took what he needed. The rest he protected, even king browns and pythons as big as his legs. If a snake came inside, he'd just shoo it on. It was the animals' country, too. They had a right to be here, to roam freely without the expectation that someone might come along and blast them for the hell of it.

Once in a while, Allen would ride his pushbike the 20 kilometres to Larrimah for a case of beer. The people in Larrimah were never friendly, but there was one resident who'd always be up for a chat.

'How you going, mate?' Paddy would say and then he'd start asking questions. What was Allen's life like, out there? How far had he ridden? 'Long way, hey,' he'd say.

'That's why I'm having a beer,' Allen would reply.

It was pub talk. Nothing important. But Allen liked Paddy—he was good at spinning a yarn and he always took an interest. Plus, he was an old bushman, Allen could tell straight away. Paddy had spent time out on the land.

Allen was home in Wubalawun when police were searching for Paddy, but from his quiet patch of country he was unaware of the commotion in Larrimah. No one came to ask him any questions—it was a shame, because his knowledge of country meant he might have had some answers. Instead, it wasn't until a few days later, when he was back in Katherine, that Allen picked up a newspaper and learned what had happened. 'There's my drinking buddy gone,' he said to himself, sadly. And he thought, right away, that whatever had happened wasn't an accident.

We ask Allen if there is any truth in those stories Richard had told us, and he laughs at the simplistic white version of his ancient culture. People aren't afraid to live here, he says. But he can see why some people might say that, because the Kadaitja do come through sometimes.

'Where we're situated is what we call bush-traveller country, my dear,' he says. 'It's like a border crossing and they're more like hitmen.' He tells us that the Kadaitja step in to settle an injustice. If someone kills or marries into the wrong circle, the Kadaitja can harm the wrong-doer, who will get sick or even die, without injury or marking. Even with an autopsy, there will be no sign of what happened.

'A lot of those Kadaitja are from the desert area and they have to walk through our country,' Allen says. He describes how the Kadaitja travel in strange ways—they never drive, never get a lift, but sometimes you might see a man in Larrimah who'd mysteriously appear in Darwin a few hours later.

'You can actually tell when there's trouble in the community by the clouds,' Allen says. 'You'll see a long thin cloud, like the one a plane makes but long, like a snake. That's when you know someone's in trouble. Someone did trouble and there's a hitman after them. And when you see them, you know. You don't come out of your house, you lock your house up. That still happens today, my dear.'

There's some credence to the stories about missing people, too, Allen tells us. He always warns his family when they come to stay. 'Don't go walkabout, you won't come back. You'll follow somebody. If you're male, it will be a nice Aboriginal lady who'll sing out to you. You follow, you don't come back. You'll just keep walking and walking and before you know it, you can't turn around to see where you are.'

It's happened to two people he knows, Allen says. It nearly happened to his brother.

Can it happen to white people? we ask. Could it have happened to Paddy and Kellie?

'No,' says Allen quickly. 'He's an old bushman. He was established. He won't go walkabout just because of that. And they couldn't find his dog. If he went walkabout, they'd find his dog waiting.'

Whatever happened, Allen is certain there's no way Paddy is above ground. His country would have given up that secret quickly; the circling birds would be a tell-tale sign. He is convinced the cause of Paddy's disappearance is another person—which, as Allen knows better than most, isn't a new story out here either.

Like the rest of the nation, Wubalawun country is marred by a shameful history that began with white settlement. Colonial violence and foreign illnesses took the lives of thousands of Aboriginal people and we are still only learning the full extent of the massacres that took place during the Frontier Wars. And out here, you only have to go back a few generations to when land was being claimed and cleared for cattle to find traditional owners being killed or forced off the land.

'Back in my great-grandfather's day, Mum was telling me, they used to hunt men on horses and actually shoot at my family members,' Allen says. He stops short of calling it a massacre, and says his mother found it difficult to talk about, so he never pushed her for details.

'There's history but it's not well documented and I don't like bringing it up because it makes me very upset. My people were getting shot at. Just for being the owner of that country.'

Allen's family story is one erasure within another. On top of being driven from their land all those years ago, now Indigenous people are being edited out of Larrimah's narrative altogether. On one hand, we can understand how the Kadaitja tales might give the impression Larrimah is a place for people to fear. But you only have to look up the road to Allen, living off the land in Wubalawun, to see that this can't be true. And when we start digging deeper, we find many more stories of Indigenous people from all over the Territory who, at various times, have called Larrimah home.

When Darwin was evacuated after the bombing in 1942, Aboriginal people were sent south and forced into camps—one compound was set up near Birdum. Known as the Larrimah Native Settlement, the little information we find on it suggests it was basically a prison that incarcerated Aboriginal people for the duration of the war and beyond. Once they were free, many of them stuck around permanently.

In 1943, a man named George Holtze—the son of a Russian-German man known as Wallaby and a Jingili-Warramunga woman called Litirngali—was granted a grazing licence to run horses and cattle at Birdum. It was a right not often afforded to people like George, who was considered 'half-caste'—especially because his wife Alice was a so-called 'full-blood' Aboriginal woman and therefore a ward of the state. Like so many others, the Holtze family was subject to racist laws of the day—they had their children taken away from them and had to apply for a licence to employ their own family members. Even though they lived next door to the Birdum Hotel, they weren't allowed to buy liquor, and in 1956 George was sentenced to six months' jail with hard labour for supplying his wife alcohol.

There was also a group of residents at Wubalawun community during the 1980s and we hear of several other Aboriginal people who lived in town for extended periods. Cookie tells us he has Aboriginal heritage.

Even Richard concedes that despite the widely circulated stories that Aboriginal people won't live in Larrimah, he's friends with an Aboriginal woman who used to live in town. He gives us a number for a woman named Kirsten Jimmy, who lived in Larrimah for three and a half years with her two young sons.

Kirsten is a Gurindji woman from Kalkarindji, but she now lives in Katherine. She tells us she came to live in Larrimah because of her grandfather, whose mob was from the area. Her father, Jimmy Wavehill—one of the original protesters from the Gurindji walk-off—was a second cousin to Allen Maroney's mother. Allen and Jimmy are both named as claimants in the ongoing Larrimah native title claim.

'I felt like I was home, you know,' she says. 'Because of the spirits, and my grandfather. Poppy knew that I was back there. I just wanted to show myself that I'm his granddaughter and I'm coming back to the land.'

Jimmy had lived around Wubalawun with his father during the war years and he'd shown Kirsten some of the sacred sites in the area, places with spiritual significance that she describes as beautiful. Allen had told us about them, too—small billabongs, secret rockholes and a special tree. The most significant is at Birdum. The storm bird dreaming threads right through that area.

There are only a handful of people alive who know those stories. Like the war and rail years, these are Birdum's endangered narratives.

13

A faceful of grasshoppers, some Russian peanut farmers and the loneliness of a ghost town

It's hard to imagine a time when the people-watching around Larrimah was better than it currently is, but those who travelled on the train known as Leaping Lena talk of buffalo hunters, anthropologists, miners, men seeking medical attention for spear wounds, stockmen, Russian peanut farmers, Chinese people in national dress, Aboriginal people going to corroboree and murderers under police escort, all travelling alongside one another in the same train carriage. We can't make the trip as they did, on board what was widely thought of as one of the Territory's most uncomfortable modes of transport, but we still want to go to the old rail terminus at Birdum.

Having refused to ride Lenny's death-train, the only other way to Birdum is to limp through kilometres of blacksoil country in a ute, hoping like hell you don't sink without trace. That sounds like an exaggeration, but it isn't. No one can tell us exactly what blacksoil is, but everyone agrees it eats cars, and it's one of the reasons this whole region has been a transport nightmare. Whether it was the Overland Telegraph line, the original Stuart Highway, the rail or the upgraded Stuart, they've all fallen apart somewhere around Birdum, in part because of blacksoil. In the 1950s, a 10-mile stretch of bitumen highway literally sank into a pit of the stuff near Larrimah, claiming six trucks but no drivers.

But blacksoil or not, Barry has offered us a ride—except, he tells us, the ute only has two seats, so one of us is going to have to climb into the tray.

'I can throw in a chair,' Barry says, by way of compensation. He's the picture of outback chivalry as he installs a camp chair in the ute-tray. It's the kind that has a beer pocket in it, but it's so decrepit even the weight of a tinnie could send it sprawling. As if he can sense us silently questioning the safety of this set-up, he ferrets around the glove box and produces an ockie strap. 'Here you go! A seatbelt.'

Once we're on the road, Barry launches into a characteristically brief explanation of what we're likely to find in Birdum.

'A ghost town,' he says, like it's obvious. 'And probably some ghosts.'

Of course, there's no way to hear him from the tray of the ute, fending off facefuls of grasshoppers. As we drive into a patch of head-high grass, Barry knocks on the back window.

'Can you stand up?' he shouts. 'I need you to look out for blacksoil.'

The brutality of time is everywhere in Birdum. We crunch through brittle grass but there's almost no sign of the three hundred thousand soldiers who passed through here during the war.

'Here's a toilet if you want to use the bathroom,' Barry laughs, pointing at a hunk of metal that was once something called a flaming fury, an old latrine systern that was burnt off for hygeine. There's also a floor of bottles stuck neck down in the unforgiving earth, which might have been a bathroom, or part of the general store.

In the middle of it all is the replica pub Barry and the LPA built. In the quiet of the late afternoon, it feels like a skeleton, the only real structure in this ghost of a ghost town. Barry points out a rusting beer fridge and the cobwebbed festoon lights are still hanging, but it's been a long time since anyone brought a generator out here.

'We'd get sixty or seventy people out for a party,' Barry tells us. But then he asks, 'That's pretty good, right?' And there's something in the way he asks it that feels sad, like he's looking for evidence of something he's lost sight of, too.

Barry's long pauses grow even longer, until they're almost indistinguishable from the silence. Insects buzz, as if to remind us that this is a place of stillness, somewhere nature has taken back.

He leans against the rusting corrugated iron half-wall that marks the edge of the skeleton-pub. Barry's wearing a gorgeous beat-up hat with an orange feather and he's accessorised his cut-off khaki shirt with a notebook in one pocket and a pen in the other. For the first time since we arrived in Larrimah he talks, directly, about his cancer.

'It's two years, now, since I was diagnosed,' he says. There is another long pause. 'I don't think it will ever come better, or that's what I'm told.' He has prostate cancer. They can treat it, but it's only a matter of time.

As the sun sinks, the tree shadows lengthen and the night animals begin to trill. The birds call to each other, filling the expansive nothingness. The yellow grass glows golden, but there's a menace behind it. You wouldn't want to be here on your own after dark. It would be easy to get turned around.

The soldiers and medics who were based here during the war wrote about how strange it was to lie in their rough, hand-built huts, with no walls to muffle the noises outside. It was like the darkness amplified the sounds. They would wake in the night to footsteps, thinking something as large as a dingo had turned up to scavenge. But the torch would reveal only a harmless little bandicoot.

A curlew wails. As we look out over the vastness of it all, we think of Paddy and the possibility of his body and Kellie's in a shallow, unmarked bush grave, the kind of lost that may never be recovered. But then again, Bill Jacobsen, the rail worker Lenny and Barry told us about, was shot about 100 metres from where we're standing—in line of sight of his own house. Even finding a body virtually on your doorstep doesn't guarantee answers.

Early the next morning, we pack up our bags and farewell the shower-ants and toaster-spiders in the room. Saying goodbye to Barry is awkward. It's not clear whether we're friends or journal-ists or something in between, so it's also unclear whether a hug is appropriate. We chance it; his frame is thin and bony.

'Drive safe,' he tells us. 'Let me know when you're safely back in Darwin.'

We promise we will, and that we'll come back soon. Then all of us shuffle awkwardly, wondering what to say next.

'Richard will help you with the bill,' Barry says, finally.

Richard seems to fit more cleanly into the category of people you do not hug when you leave town and he's on the other side of the bar, anyway, behind a statue of a pig's head wearing a cop's hat.

'How was your stay?' he asks, even though he's seen us twenty times every day since we arrived. Still, it's a hard question to answer; we've got none of the things we came for and a lot of things we didn't. Anyway, he's not asking about the book, he's asking about the room, and it's hard not to think back to the first day we arrived and Richard's irritation with blow-ins who complain about the dust.

We can see his point. Places like the Pink Panther are an endan-gered species. Australia might have a collective nostalgia for a remote pub on the edge of nowhere, but the idea of a far-flung beer is often nicer than the long drive through the nothingness to get it. It's the paradox of distance: remoteness is both the appeal and the problem.

So we keep quiet about the toaster-spiders. To enjoy outback

Australia, you have to leave something behind. Tripadvisor is full of people who come to places like the Larrimah Hotel and get fixated on dated decor and dust, and blowflies and the smell of bore water—and somehow miss the bigger thing they've stumbled into.

Before we pull onto the highway, we drop into Karen and Mark's for a final goodbye. They offer us a cup of tea and we get talking about the old progress association minutes.

Karen is unsurprised by the shemozzle—she tells us she and Barry actually started a third progress association, the Larrimah Community Projects Association, not that long ago. Karen was the president and the fledgling organisation had been awarded a $7000 grant for a rail heritage project, to restore the passenger trolley Lenny is so fond of. Except, Paddy was the association's treasurer, and he went missing before the money hit the account. They couldn't withdraw anything without his signature. And, anyway, it didn't seem right to press forward with their shared plan without him.

'Paddy was enthusiastic about the future and that's what we loved about him,' Karen says. 'He was seventy. And he was still enthusiastic about the future and no one else here has been.'

She's put the association aside, for now; maybe she'll come back to it one day, she says. There's a brief but loaded silence as we weigh up what all the not-knowing has cost Paddy's friends like Karen and Mark and the prospect they might never find an answer. Part of us feels guilty; in asking questions and writing about Paddy, we've obliged ourselves to finding an answer. But that's not something we can guarantee.

'Drive safe,' they say when we finally wrench ourselves away, a pleasantry that carries a lot of weight out here. We've already said our goodbyes to Lenny, Cookie, Bill, Karl and Bobbie. The closed sign is hanging on Fran's gate. As we eye the rear-view mirror, the tiny town is drowned by the bush around it, and we're struck by how foolish we've been in thinking that this was ever something small or contained—how can anything be tiny out here in space so vast the horizon collapses in on itself at the edges?

The Stuart Highway is a scar running up the centre of the country, so long and straight you can go hours without moving the steering wheel. As the sun shifts, shadows creep over the red dust and the wildlife play chicken with oncoming traffic. While we drive, stories we've heard creep to the surface. There's a bigger pattern of disappearances, we've been told—and we start to wonder if it could be true.

There are twenty-five active missing persons cases in the Northern Territory, according to the Australian Federal Police Missing Persons website. At least fifteen of them, including Paddy, were reported last seen on or near the Stuart Highway.

'It's like the Bermuda Triangle,' someone had told us one night at the pub, off-hand. 'Some people say there's a serial killer roaming up and down that highway. Or a crazy truckie.' They'd laughed, but we'd run the theory past Detective Sergeant Matt Allen, who assures us that while the disappearances might look like a pattern, they are not. 'What people have to understand is that the Territory is a unique place and the Stuart Highway runs essentially between Adelaide and Darwin. It's our main highway, and major centres— Katherine, Tennant Creek, Darwin and Alice Springs—the Stuart Highway runs through them.'

Paddy's place is right on the highway; the road trains shake the shade cloth he uses for privacy. Even if a serial killer is out of the question, other people passing through might be relevant. Paddy hated truckies pulling up in front of his place and leaving a generator on all night and he was never shy about confronting Fran's customers when they parked on his side of the highway.

Once, Richard told us, Paddy unhitched some bloke's trailer and the truckie had driven four hours before he realised what had happened. The guy was livid. It's an expensive prank, the kind of thing that might make someone angry. A lot of trucks pass through Larrimah. There are a lot of opportunities to piss off the wrong person. Drug runners and grog runners weave up and down this highway, too.

There's no evidence to suggest any of these theories are true. There's no evidence to suggest *anything*. It's possible that whatever—or whoever—happened to Paddy, came from outside the town and left again, taking any evidence with them. And if that's the case, the person, the evidence and the answers could be anywhere.

So we puzzle and rehash and drive, and let the road swallow us until we feel tiny.

A few weeks later, a headline appears on the front page of the *NT News*: 'Paddy Moriarty inquest probe'. The date is set for 7 June 2018 in Katherine. It will be less than six months after Paddy disappeared.

PART TWO

The disappearing town

Six months after the disappearance.

14

The sound of falcons being shot, an octogenarian looking for love and a quest for justice

At the centre of Katherine—a block back from the highway, behind the supermarket and down the road from the rifle shop—is the local courthouse, a modern building with a nice lawn and a view of McDonald's across the street.

Any other day, it's quiet. Those who've been summoned here slip furtively inside the cider-coloured building and disappear just as discreetly, taking their DUI and domestic violence convictions with them, hidden in deep pockets and under wide hats. But today, 7 June 2018, the area is pulsing. Cameramen haul their equipment across the lawns, photographers light-test their cameras, journalists try unsuccessfully to tap into the free wi-fi from Macca's.

And a small bundle of people from the tiny town of Larrimah are grouped on the benches out the front, wearing their good town clothes and breathing in the smell of cigarette smoke and McNuggets, still trying to unknot the series of events that brought them here.

Inside the courthouse, we are corralled into a small room. It doesn't look like your typical courtroom. Rather than a judge's bench at the front, there is just a low desk and the middle of the room is consumed by a comically oversized boardroom table. The public gallery is a single row of chairs shoved up against two walls—there aren't nearly enough of them.

Greg Cavanagh enters, unsurprised by the overflow. He has more than two decades as the Northern Territory's coroner, investigating deaths in a landscape roughly the size of Mongolia that dishes up the occasional croc attack; for him, the unexpected is expected.

Once he's in place at the understated desk at the front of the room, Mr Cavanagh immediately puts everyone at ease. Chalky-haired, lanky and bulb-nosed, he is firm and knowledgeable, but effortlessly relatable. Early on, he confesses he's a little hard of hearing. 'I'm an old man, I need a hearing aid and I haven't been able to afford one yet. Not that I can't afford it. But it's ten thousand dollars. I'm not going to pay that.'

As the coroner, Mr Cavanagh's function is to establish the manner and cause of death, aided by Counsel Assist Kelvin Currie, a well-dressed, amiable man whose job is to examine the evidence, guide the coroner through the case and ask questions of witnesses on his behalf.

An inquest is not a trial. It is not designed to apportion responsibility, but instead to inquire and to establish the how, when and where of a death. But when there's no body to tell the when and where, the how seems impossible—like trying to catch a bus without knowing the time or location it might stop. Mr Cavanagh and Mr Currie have their work cut out for them.

It's unusual for an inquest to be held so soon after a person goes missing, and Mr Currie addresses this right away. Most of the witnesses are older so things have been sped up, he says. With almost everyone hovering around seventy, six months can be a long time.

Mr Currie suggests this is not the sort of case where witnesses should be allowed to listen to proceedings, which explains why everyone from Larrimah has remained outside on the benches. We spoke to them on the way in—the whole town had been notified to appear, with two exceptions. Cookie and Lenny were left off the list. Lenny had turned up anyway, just in case.

Fran and Owen have been called to attend, but we hadn't seen them out front with the rest of the town. We're eager to hear from them, especially Owen. Given his refusal to talk to media, this might be our only chance to get his side of the story. But, first, the rest of the town has some things to say.

The first person whose relationship with Paddy is a focus is Richard Simpson. In Larrimah, Richard positioned himself as a good mate. But the first witness, Mark Rayner, admits he's heard whispers of arguments between Richard and Paddy. 'Then again,' he says, 'Richard has arguments with everyone in town . . . We heard that he told Paddy that he was keeping the tourists away and costing Barry money at the pub. His behaviour was a little bit erratic.'

Barry is called into the room next and when he's asked the same questions about Paddy and Richard's relationship, he says the opposite. 'I've never seen them argue,' he says. 'And they used to sit together and talk. I don't think there was a problem.'

'There's a suggestion in some of the materials that maybe Richard was a little bit jealous that Paddy seemed to have a bit of a run of the hotel,' Mr Currie says. 'He was more 2IC than Richard. What would your response be to that suggestion?'

Barry looks uncomfortable. Finally, he says: 'He seemed to be getting an attitude later, you know. He was getting, like, a bit angry in his character and that. I actually thought he might be on some substance but I'm not sure.' He then reveals he fired Richard a few days ago.

If there was a problem, according to the brief of evidence, chances are it was about the dogs—Richard had three of them. Barry confirms this, says they were American staffies. Looked like pig dogs to him. He never trusted them.

'Where did he walk them, do you know?'

'Not sure. Mainly down the front of the property. He wouldn't walk them far. He's never gone too long.'

'So you wouldn't think he'd be walking them past Paddy's place?'

'No. He never took that much time.'

Barry tells Mr Currie that he never saw Paddy's kelpie, Kellie, interact with Richard's dogs but that he had caught Kellie roaming at night, and when he told Paddy about it he became a bit defensive. 'He sort of went into denial a little bit about that and said, "No, my dog mustn't roam at night," but it did. I seen it.'

The dogs keep coming up.

It's Mr Currie who asks most of the questions, but Mr Cavanagh intervenes every now and again, to add something, pose a question, greet a witness or clarify a point of law. They've obviously worked together extensively—their questions weave in and out of witness statements like a well-rehearsed duet. But it's also apparent that this whole process is not as clear-cut or linear as we'd hoped. It's full of backtracking and repetition and the narrative gets buried in witness diversions, confusion and misunderstandings.

Nevertheless, the spotlight intermittently returns to Kellie. Paddy's kelpie is the main reason police believe her owner has met with foul play—it's unlikely some natural misfortune would befall a man *and* his dog, and if Paddy had a medical episode or accident, they were sure Kellie would have howled or returned to town. So, as well as trying to establish the character and habits of the man who disappeared, Mr Currie tries to get to the heart of Kellie's personality.

Veronica Elliott and her husband manage a cattle station that runs right up to the back of Paddy's property. Veronica tells the inquest she first met Paddy at a rodeo at Daly Waters, fifteen years ago. In recent years, she only saw him occasionally when she popped into the pub to pick up her mail but they'd usually have a chat.

A couple of months before he went missing, Paddy asked Veronica if she might have a dog for him. His old border collie, Rover, had died about a year before, and Paddy missed the company. As it turned out, Veronica did have a twelve-month-old kelpie that wasn't working out well with the other ten dogs on their station but would make a good pet.

Paddy was excited—he'd owned kelpies before. He adopted Kellie about five or six weeks before he disappeared.

'Did [Kellie] get on with other dogs, or was she a bit snappy?' Mr Currie asks Veronica.

'She was all right. She wouldn't get in a fight or anything.'

'Now, your understanding of that dog, perhaps dogs in general, if she were alive but Paddy was not, where do you think she'd go? What are the possibilities?'

'She should have been at the house or at the pub because he went to the pub every day. Or she would have come back to us.'

'She hasn't come back to you?'

'No.'

There's a ten-minute break, and as we file outside for some fresh air, we notice Richard has been exiled. Standing alone outside the courthouse doors, he looks rougher than usual, despite his neat, stone-washed, short-sleeved shirt. His beard is longer and parted in two, and the hair on the side of his head looks haphazardly shaved.

The break is over quickly and Karen Rayner is called next. She's dressed in a knitted white jumper with a blouse underneath, black pants and high-heeled boots, accentuating her stature. In a confident voice she tells the inquest that, although it was the pub, specifically the animals at the pub, that brought her and Mark to Larrimah, she hasn't been back there since a couple of months before Paddy disappeared because of Richard. She'd finished up managing there in June 2017 but stayed on doing the paperwork, to help Barry out, until one night Richard confronted her while she was working. He was hyped up, angry, as if he were on something.

It came out of nowhere. She'd just been talking to him and he'd seemed fine. 'He just kept coming in and out and running, like literally running,' Karen says. 'He was incoherent. You couldn't make out one sentence. Then he turned around and he said, "You upset my mate, your family is in big trouble here." Then he ran off again.'

Karen says Barry saw it happen and she asked him to do something about Richard threatening her. But Barry had just said, 'Well, maybe you better go, I don't want trouble.'

You can tell the incident still wounds Karen. Barry was her friend. She'd done a lot for him and he didn't stick up for her. She refused to go to the pub until two days ago, when she heard Richard had left. During her absence, she and Barry were still speaking, she says, but the relationship was strained. She wanted nothing to do with Richard. From the confrontation onwards, the only thing she ever heard of Richard was at night, when she could hear his dogs carrying on from her place and Richard telling them to shut up. Usually it was Kellie roaming that set them off, she says.

We're still wondering what it all means—the dogs, the dismissal, the jealousy—when Bobbie Roth is called into the room and the focus shifts entirely. Bobbie's role in the inquest is to answer questions about the five years she spent working for Fran, washing dishes at the teahouse. At one point, Bobbie and Fran were so close that the Roths offered to keep Fran's money in their safe.

'How much money was it that you were holding for her?' Mr Currie asks.

'Between twenty-seven and thirty thousand,' Bobbie says. But Bobbie was abruptly let go from the teahouse when Fran hired a new person to replace her. He came and took the money back for Fran.

Bobbie is softly spoken at the best of times, but the courtroom seems to muffle her even more. She looks small beside the board-room table, shrinking into her smart black coat as if to disappear herself.

Mr Currie asks if Fran talked about Paddy.

'She was always accusing Paddy of stealing things from her property and she didn't like him.'

'How much did she talk about that?' Mr Currie presses. 'Was it an ever-present topic or did it just come up occasionally?'

'It was a pretty ongoing thing.'

'So every time you went to wash dishes you'd hear about that?'

'I wouldn't say every day. It depended on what was wrong. If there was magazines missing off the tables, Paddy would get blamed, or some small thing, she'd blame Paddy.'

'Did she ever say what she wanted to do about that or with Paddy?'

Bobbie's voice wavers. The answer catches in her throat for a moment, then comes tumbling out, accompanied by tears.

'She used to say, "I'll kill Paddy." And she also used to say she'd kill her husband, Bill.'

Then, Bobbie reveals she heard a gunshot around the date Paddy disappeared.

The gunshot doesn't linger in the hearing long, though. Bobbie's husband, Karl, is next to be called.

'Now, your wife says that she heard a gunshot around about 15 December,' Mr Currie says.

'No, I've got my doubts about that. I'm fairly attuned to rifle shots, being ex-military. But my hearing is not one hundred per cent, either.' Karl says he doesn't remember hearing a gunshot.

'Do you hear, from time to time, things that sound like rifle shots around Larrimah?'

'Occasionally, yeah.'

Mr Currie asks what the shots are.

'Barry at the pub,' Karl says. 'He keeps exotic birds and that and he has falcons come in every now and then harassing the birds. I think he pops one off every now and then.'

Karl says that sometimes a fire at the dump would cause cans to explode, too—that might be mistaken for a gunshot.

Next, Mr Currie addresses the threats Fran made against Paddy.

Karl says that Fran would often enlist his help; he'd ordered and installed some CCTV cameras for her when she claimed Paddy had been pinching stuff. But the requests went on and on until Karl began to hide when he heard her coming.

One day he spent hours up on her roof after the TV stopped working, only to find the cord had been cut in half. Karl says Fran admitted she'd done it.

'That was the last thing I ever fixed for her.'

'Did you ever hear Fran making any threats towards Paddy?'

'She used to say "I'll kill him" or "I'll bash him" or something or other, but I don't think it was . . . you know, it's just one of those things you say, really. I don't think there was anything . . .'

'No plan behind it?'

'No plan behind it, no.'

Mr Currie also asks Karl about firearms: why does he still own so many, given how long ago he left the army? Karl tells him it's a hangover from his days shooting feral donkeys and stray bulls.

'I used to have probably thirty or forty different firearms, now I'm down to about eight,' he tells the inquest. 'And I haven't fired a rifle in probably fifteen, twenty years. They're just there, locked up.'

'So you really hadn't had the use of them since you got to Larrimah?' Mr Currie asks.

It feels as though Karl looks directly at us. 'I think I shot a buffalo out the back once.'

Bill Hodgetts takes the stand next, but it's all stories we've heard before, mostly about Fran and Paddy's rivalry. When Mr Cavanagh adjourns the inquest for lunch, everyone spills out into the bright heat of the courtyard and we wander over to the Larrimah group, clustered along benches in the shade. We are introduced to two men who've been sitting quietly in the courtroom watching. Phil Garlick and Kevin Horner are friends of Paddy's. Phil used to look after Paddy's place when he went away, and Kevin has done a couple of stints working at the pub. One of the first things Phil asks us is whether either of us happens to have a grandmother who is single; although we appreciate an octogenarian who is bold enough to be his own wingman, the answer is no.

Kevin lives in Darwin's rural area and Phil moves around in his caravan, so they've both travelled a long way.

Why did you come? we ask.

'We want to know what happened to our mate,' they tell us. 'We want justice.'

After the break, we all settle back into the air-con and a man we've never seen before is called into the courtroom. He's bald on top with a large, white moustache that droops down both sides of his mouth and threatens to spill off his chin. His short-sleeved button-down shirt is checked with bright orange, pink and purple, and his rust-coloured shorts look too small for someone appearing in court.

His name is Maurice Darby and for four and a half years he occupied the strange hinterland of being both Paddy's friend and Fran's employee. Maurice was Bobbie's replacement and Owen's predecessor. His duties ranged from preparing pies and pastries to mowing the lawn and doing the teahouse dishes.

He lived in the bungalow next to the kitchen, and every day, around 4 pm, he'd see Paddy drive his quad bike home from the pub. Once Paddy pulled up around the back of his place, Maurice would jump the fence and go in for a beer.

The questions move on so quickly you could easily miss it, but it's there for all to hear: from Fran's teahouse it's impossible to not see, or at least hear, Paddy come and go between his home and the pub.

But there's no time to linger on this because Maurice is straight into Paddy and Fran's relationship. Mr Currie asks if Maurice knew about the 'kangaroo incident'—not the one just before Paddy disappeared, the one that boomeranged between the two properties.

'Yes,' says Maurice.

'There was a telephone box on the corner, which is no-man's land. And at some stage during the evening a large kangaroo was knocked over by a road train or a ute and it's . . . gone to no-man's land.'

According to Maurice, Fran immediately accused Paddy of dumping it there and demanded Maurice throw the carcass over Paddy's fence. He told her to do it herself. And she did. The next night, when Maurice was having beers with Paddy, the subject came up.

'Paddy said, "I've got a kangaroo over my fence." I said, "Yep, Fran threw it there." So he said, "What am I going to do with it?" Now, if you look at the back of the teahouse, your Honour, it's got louvre windows. It's easy to lift a couple of louvre windows up and back the rear end of the kangaroo in. And the first thing that Fran does is turn the lights on and then turn the oven on. So the first thing that she's cooking with the oven backed onto the wall is the kangaroo's bottom that's been dead for a couple of days.' Maurice finishes with a casual: 'Now, that created a little bit of drama.'

This is a version of a version of the kangaroo story we've heard before, but in the one we were told, Fran paid Maurice to chuck the kangaroo over Paddy's fence because she couldn't physically do it. Someone told us Maurice then used the cash to buy him and Paddy some beer, which they drank while plotting to throw the marsupial under Fran's kitchen window. Which version is true, we can't know.

Even though Maurice maintained friendships with both Fran and Paddy throughout his teahouse tenure, he left the job on bad terms. Maurice says he wants to set the record straight.

'In fact, I wasn't sacked,' Maurice tells the inquest. 'I left her in a bit of a quandary . . . Fran was getting a little bit greedy and a little bit money-hungry at that stage towards customers and the way she was preparing food . . . She was starting to rip people off and I said, "Fran, the time's come for me to move on. You can't keep telling people they're homemade pies when you buy them at Coles/Woolies and put the top back on and charge them at thirteen dollars fifty when it's costing you seventy-five cents a pie."'

Despite all his other revelations, this feels like Maurice's defining speech. The reason he came here. With that done, he's dismissed.

We've almost forgotten about Richard until he walks in. He talks about the fight he witnessed between Owen and Paddy right before Paddy disappeared. 'I couldn't hear the exact words, but I could hear the raised voices and whatnot,' Richard says. 'And that's all the incident involved at that stage.' He says that at the pub later that day, when Paddy fronted up for lunch and beers, Richard asked him what happened.

'I said to Paddy, "Hey, mate, you know, what's going on up there?" So he told me about the fact that Owen had come out and told him to shut his fuckin' dog up or he'd shut it up for him, and, as I said in my statement, I've said it a couple of different ways, but essentially he said, "You shut your mouth, you old cunt, or I'll take your knees out from under you."'

Then he denies any conflict with Paddy, says he 'never had cross words with the man'. Never had cross words with anyone in Larrimah, he says.

'How did you get on with Mark and Karen Rayner?' Mr Currie asks.

'Well, I reckon I picked Karen thieving out of the till so I confronted her about that behind the bar and she unfortunately took great umbrage to that and decides that she needs to completely walk out of the pub and have nothing more to do with the pub at all, even though she was morally contracted and bound to continue on.'

'So you wouldn't regard that as cross words?'

'That'd be cross words, cross words with Karen, yes, for sure, yep.'

Anyone else? Mr Currie asks. Then Richard confesses he'd also had a run-in with someone who pulled up out the front of the pub recently. Richard went out and told him to get fucked.

Richard is asked about guns (yes, the pub owns one—they use it to shoot eagles and hawks, which they feed to the snakes and crocodile), drugs (he's smoked a bit of weed over the years and was using OxyContin after his accident, but nothing now, except beer) and his dogs (no, they never interacted with Kellie). On the subject of the disappearance, he says he's sure Paddy didn't get lost. 'I mean, this guy is an experienced bushman, you know. He's not going to go out there and get lost, and even if he had have gone and tripped over a log, broke his leg, whatever, perished, you know, dehydration, bit by a snake, not only would the hawks have found him, the search would have found him. And where's the dog?'

'Now there are some people in Larrimah that think you might have had something to do with it,' Mr Currie suggests.

'Well, they would be goddamn fools, wouldn't they? Paddy was my mate. Why would I?'

'One of the suggestions is that perhaps you were a little bit jealous of the fact that Paddy seemed to be 2IC at the pub, and not yourself?'

'No, not at all.'

'Another suggestion is that sometimes, either under the influence of alcohol or something else, you'd become a little bit erratic?'

'Yeah, I'm hearing a few stories about this. Apparently, I yell out and that sort of thing, and I'd like to know what it is if I've actually done this, apart from going off my head [the other day]. I very, very seldom even drink too much. I have a couple of times . . .' Richard trails off and Mr Currie asks what drinking too much in Larrimah looks like.

'Drinking too much in Larrimah would be when you are losing control, you get drunk and you hit a customer, you know?'

Whether or not he was involved in Paddy's disappearance, Richard was still front line on Paddy's last night at the pub. He was the one serving the booze and hearing the stories. And that is important.

'In the lead-up to Paddy's disappearance, did you notice anything different about him?' Mr Currie asks.

'No, nothing. Just Paddy being Paddy, every day, the same thing, always happy, always telling good stories, and, yeah, just a good bloke to sit down and have a beer with, and he used to be fantastic with the customers, you know, just every customer that came in he'd greet them.'

'Good for the pub?'

'Absolutely, yeah, and good to watch too, you know, he was just a good man to have around.'

15

A rejected gardening book, a lover (not a fighter) and a case of osteoarthritis

Fran arrives the next day looking neat, if a little casual, in white shorts and a white singlet with a pale, striped blouse over the top. But it's obvious she is out of her comfort zone. Plus, she's the first person to bring legal representation: barrister Tamzin Lee.

When she first speaks her voice trembles, but after sharing her fifty-year legacy of Territory pie and scone-baking, Fran warms to the crowd. Mr Currie does his best to wrangle the dialogue into something approaching a chronology, but it's clear he's not the one steering the ship as Fran takes the packed courtroom audience on one sharp left turn after another.

Fran outlines the full history of her fractured relationship with Paddy, including the story almost nobody talks about: how they were not always enemies. She says she kept an eye on Paddy after his triple-bypass operation and would take meals across the road for him, or invite him in for a cuppa. But establishing how long the friendship lasted—or, at least, the *neighbourliness*; Fran won't call it friendship—isn't easy. In part, because Fran only wants to talk about the fallout, and in part because it's hard for her to give the dates and times. Mr Currie establishes that Fran met Paddy at Daly Waters thirty years ago and she and Paddy probably had about five good years at Larrimah. And then, as Mr Currie puts it with characteristic politeness, 'things went . . . sideways'.

To establish how sideways it all went, Mr Currie reads extracts from his pile of papers, which amount to a lowlight reel of civic dispute. Fran, when she can, adds or comments. She's not evasive so much as easily diverted, but the effect is much the same: she doesn't always answer the questions—and the answers she does give are often to questions that are not being asked. Mr Currie attempts, at least half a dozen times, to pinpoint a specific year something happened. 'When was it, to your recollection?' he asks. And then, 'How long . . .?', and 'But when . . .?' and 'I've just been trying to work out when approximately that was . . .?' He is unflappable. 'But the question I want to know the answer to is, when approximately did that start to happen?' His persistence pays off and the details begin to emerge.

Probably, the trouble started with a large red umbrella. It was bought on a Friday to spruce up the front of the teahouse, and sometime the next night, it disappeared. The police report about the incident reads: 'The umbrella was new and cost $200. Taken overnight 22 May 2010. Believes Moriarty has taken it.' Police drove the 75-odd kilometres to Larrimah to speak with Fran, who told them she thought the umbrella was over at Paddy's house. It was a tip-off that turned out to be partly true. There was *a* red umbrella at Paddy's. 'Members attended Moriarty's house,' the report says. 'He denied any involvement in the stealing of the umbrella and produced an umbrella he owned which was small and old . . . He did admit that he had heard [Fran] had been accusing him of stealing it from her, so to stir her up he got one of the red umbrellas from the pub and put it on the table out the front of his house to get back at her for allegations she was making.'

A little over a month later, July 2010, 'Fran attended Katherine [police] front counter to report the theft of a quantity of books and folders containing memorabilia of the Northern Territory and Katherine area from her teahouse. She suspects that Moriarty is the offender. She believes this because he watched her leave her premises when she went out.' But the police report goes on to say that when Fran got home to Larrimah, she called the station again to say she'd changed her mind—maybe tourists had taken the items, after all.

'No, no, no,' Fran says when the file is read out in court. 'That's definitely wrong.' She tells the inquest she followed scraps of evidence over the road to Paddy's place.

It looks like there was a year-long break in the hostility, then, in July 2011, Fran showed up at the Katherine police station with a petition. She'd been complaining about Paddy threatening tourists and badmouthing the teahouse, but the police couldn't do much without evidence. So, she'd asked anyone who'd been threatened to write down their contact details and when she had about twenty names, she took it to the cops. 'She wants something done before something bad happens,' the report says.

Ten days later, Fran told Mataranka police Paddy had put a glass bottle under a customer's tyre. Two months after, she accused Paddy of breaking a plastic fitting for the hose connected to her water pump. 'Members attended,' the file says, 'inspected the water pump and found no issue with the pump. It was in good working order. Inspected the tap fitting and found there to be some damage and the rubber O-ring perished inside.' The complaint was cleared because of insufficient evidence.

Mr Currie moves on with his feud timeline. There was another detente, and this one lasted until March 2013, he says. But then Fran told police Paddy and his dog, Rover, had entered her yard one night. Paddy claimed he was just getting his dog, but police served a trespass notice.

On 13 April 2014, 'Fran reported Moriarty stalking her and deterring her customers away by his behaviour. Fran alleged Moriarty was sitting in his front yard looking at her teahouse with binoculars and telling customers as they called into her business not to eat there as the food was not very good.' She told police she planned to get a protection order against Paddy.

Then, a week later, Fran complained to Mataranka police that someone had cut the hose running from the water tank to her teahouse and flooded it; it actually happened three times in two months, she said, but on this occasion she was sure her ex-husband, Bill, was the culprit. Police attended but couldn't say whether the hose had been cut or just burst with pressure from a kink. And Bill had an alibi—he'd been drinking at the pub all day.

In October 2016, Fran lost the personal violence restraining order hearing against Paddy and was ordered to pay costs.

And then, on 23 September 2017, 'Fran made a complaint to Mataranka police that Bill Hodgetts, her ex-husband, and Patrick Moriarty had tipped oil over her new plants to kill them. Approximately $500 in value. Believes both of them have destroyed her plants together. Believes their motive was because the settlement with Bill had been through court and he was unhappy with the outcome.' Police attended and found insufficient evidence to proceed with an investigation.

The timeline of grudges stops a few days before Paddy's disappearance. The last incident was also the last time Fran saw Paddy: Tuesday, 12 December 2017, the day Paddy threw the second kangaroo into her yard and then looked up and smiled at her. But it's not the roo prank the inquest is concerned with. It's what came after.

Owen got back to the teahouse around 4 pm that day, Fran says, but she didn't tell him about the kangaroo until the next morning, by which time Owen already knew there was roadkill about—he could smell it. Fran was in a hurry to get on the road, so the conversation was short, she tells the inquest. 'I said, "I'm going to Darwin now," and I took off.' But, it turns out, there was a bit more to it than that.

It takes a bit of putting together—Fran doesn't remember all the details, but Mr Currie has transcripts of her initial police interviews. Fran told police then that she'd made it clear to Owen that Paddy was responsible for the carcass. In response, Owen had told her he'd already had words with Paddy.

'Did he seem upset?' Mr Currie asks.

'Pardon?'

'Did he seem upset?'

'No,' Fran says, quickly. 'No. Owen's a very private man. When you talk to him you'd understand what I was saying. No, he didn't— he was angry because he was upset—well, not that upset angry, but you know.'

'So he was angry, you say?'

'Yeah, yeah, yeah, I would say, yeah. Not grr, grr, but angry upset, you know.'

'Did it cause you concern that he was angry?'

'No, no, no. He's a very private man and no. Didn't concern me. If it did I wouldn't have gone away.'

Mr Currie refers to a transcript of Fran's 30 December police interview. He reads Fran's statement back to her—she told police she'd said something to Owen before she left: 'Don't do anything stupid because I'm going to Darwin and I don't want to come back and bail you out of jail.'

Mr Currie asks why Fran was worried Owen might do something stupid, but Fran corrects. She wasn't worried, she says, it was just because he was upset. As far as she knew, that day was the only time Owen and Paddy had spoken to each other. But, as Mr Currie clarifies, Owen did know about the years of trouble with Paddy. She'd told him everything when he came for the interview for the caretaker role.

Was part of Owen's job to protect her? Mr Currie asks.

'[Owen wasn't there to] protect me, [but rather] to help me look after everything and keep everybody off my property, to stop people from doing things to my property . . . That was it. But not for anybody to hurt anybody.'

'Okay, I accept that. But the person you wanted help with . . .' Mr Currie starts.

'The only person that had ever helped me is Mr Owen and he's the only one who's been honest, hasn't taken anything, pinched anything. He's an honest man.'

'Okay.'

'An honest man,' Fran says. It's like she's on repeat. Owen wouldn't accept food, wouldn't even take a gardening book she'd bought him as a Christmas present. He's an honest man. She says it over and over. 'I only wish to God there was more like him around. He's honest and he's trustworthy.'

Having failed to pin Fran to a chronology that wasn't documented via police statements, Mr Currie turns to the matter of her finances. Was it true that she had between $27,000 and $30,000 in someone else's safe, around the time Bill moved out?

Fran admits she'd given the cash to Bobbie to look after—it was mostly from a Ford station wagon she'd sold for $18,000.

'So where did that money go?'

'Into the business and into paying the bills and I bought this car here. I paid it off, you know, monthly.'

Mr Currie clarifies. 'His Honour heard that the twenty-seven to thirty thousand dollars in cash . . .'

'I didn't have thirty. It was twenty-seven or twenty-five.'

By the time Paddy had gone missing, Fran says the $30,000(ish) was gone—spent on replacing plants, a new car and new appliances. She still had a stash of about $7000, which police found hidden in the freezer when they searched the teahouse.

'That's my super,' she says. Fran didn't have a safe, so she stashed it to keep the business afloat during the wet season.

The inquest isn't supposed to be a list of Fran's grievances and gratitude, but it kind of works out that way. As well as Owen, Fran's best friend, who is also named Fran, is lavished with praise.

The Frans met at the Katherine Woolies, a few years back. Katherine-Fran worked in the butchery and Larrimah-Fran would strike up a conversation when she went in to buy meat for her pies. 'We became friends and then I met her husband through her,' Fran says. He helps her out a bit, trying to keep the old police station from falling into disrepair, inspecting the roof to see if it can be fixed, things like that.

'They're the people that visited your place on 12 December, aren't they?' Mr Currie clarifies.

'Yes, that's right. Yes.'

Katherine-Fran and her husband, Lloyd, were there the last day Fran saw Paddy alive. In fact, one of the reasons Paddy might have chosen that moment to dump the kangaroo is that Katherine-Fran and Lloyd had borrowed Fran's car and Owen was out of town, so it would have looked like nobody was home.

As Fran relates it, Katherine-Fran and Lloyd were heading to Queensland for a few months and needed to drop Lloyd's work vehicle to Mataranka. But all their gear was packed in their own car, so they borrowed Fran's. After the drop-off, they returned Fran's car and headed off to Brisbane. They were in a rush so they didn't stop, just beeped the horn to say thanks.

'And then they went to Queensland?' Mr Currie asks.

'Yes, that's right.' Fran didn't see them for a couple of months after that.

Mr Currie has one more question about Fran's friends, Fran and Lloyd. He approaches it delicately. 'They're also the people who . . . Did I see in the brief of evidence that you are leaving your estate to?'

'Yes, that's right because they—'

'So you've made out a will to them?' he clarifies.

'That's right because they've been doing a lot of work with looking after me and at the moment, through all this that's happened, I've got breast cancer.' Fran's voice breaks. 'I found out a couple of days ago.'

⌣⌣

It's probably lucky for Maurice that he got in quick with his denial that Fran fired him, because she brings it up. He was definitely fired, she says, because she caught him pinching money off her.

It's not the only inconsistency in their recollection of events. Fran also told police that it was Maurice who'd claimed Paddy was dealing drugs.

Mr Currie puts it to Fran that Maurice has already told the coroner he never said that.

'He did. I can swear on my life, on my kids, he did, he did say that.' Fran took the claim so seriously that the day of the haircut she planned to give police a voluntary statement about it. 'I just thought I was doing the right thing, but—because he'd done a lot of things to me and I've never done anything to him, never ever. And Maurice Darby did tell me that.'

'When you say you've never done anything to him, are you saying that he's the bad guy and that you don't retaliate?'

'No, I never abused him and I never would—I've never done anything towards him to do what he done to me.'

Mr Currie takes a while to clarify she's talking about Paddy before continuing.

'Never screamed across the road at him?'

'Yeah, I screamed at him once—years ago, you know, I went crook at him for, you know, for doing things, yes.'

'Okay. Didn't throw a kangaroo over his fence?'

'No. I can't even walk up the stairs,' Fran says. There is another long kangaroo-carcass anecdote, but at this point of the inquest they're starting to blur together. The subtext is clear, though. Fran says she wasn't strong enough to lift a kangaroo.

Thirty-five minutes into her evidence, the coroner offers Fran a break.

'No, I don't want to—I want the fucking thing to be over and done with,' she says. The coroner suggests that even if she doesn't want a break, she might like a glass of water. But it's like the offer unravels something.

'Your Honour. I don't lie, I don't bullshit. And I've been through hell.'

Fran's counsel intervenes—will there be many more questions? She's been on the stand for a long time, and perhaps a few minutes' break would be helpful.

Fran ignores her and ploughs on. 'I wouldn't hurt a flea. Everything's been happening to me. I've been to the police that many times . . .' In her distress, Fran starts rattling off expenses. 'That's where my money goes. My money goes into the property. And I do my tax every year and Centrelink get a copy of my tax return and my—all my income and the outcome every year. I've been doing it for thirty-five years . . .'

Fran has opened a vault that can't be closed again. It's difficult to watch. 'I work hard,' she pleads, as the coroner offers to speak to her directly.

'May I call you Fran?' he asks.

'Yes, darling, you can call me whatever you like.'

'Well, how about Fran?'

'Fran, everybody knows Fran.'

'Okay. Do you want to keep on going until it's finished or do you want a break?'

'I don't want—I want to keep going because I don't . . .'

'That's what I thought, you want to keep going?'

'Yeah, I want to go. I just . . . what I'm telling you today, even if a couple of things said in there is a bit different. I've been threatened and I've been abused and I've been blackmailed. And this is not the last of it—that they're going to hear of this, either, and somebody knows what I'm talking about.'

It's a loose accusation pointed at no one in particular and Mr Cavanagh breezes past it. 'Okay. Next question, Mr Currie.'

The coroner and Mr Currie are careful when they proceed. They reassure Fran that once the questions are done, it will be over. But there's nothing easy about what happens next.

Fran begins by recapping how hard the last six months have been. Then there's the ten years of harassment and damage at the hands of an ex and a neighbour, she says. Tens of thousands of dollars' worth of damage. It always happened when she was out of town—at least until she had Owen there to look after the place, of course. And then there was Paddy's disappearance and the police investigation and now the breast cancer. Her dog died, too. The coroner expresses sympathy. So does Fran. 'I know, everything fucking happens to me and I don't hurt anybody,' she says.

The suspicion and the investigation are killing her, Fran tells the inquest, killing her and Owen. He's been getting pains in his chest—he's got a bad heart, he's had a bypass before. The stress is bad for him, she says.

'You can only go through so much before you start to say—I was going to take it—do myself in,' she says, suddenly looking every bit her age. 'It was that bad. I told the—my doctor. I went to see my doctor. I woke up one morning at four o'clock in the morning numb from the bottom up . . . I wanted to just go—go to sleep and I didn't want to wake up anymore. Then I thought no. I thought about my dogs, I thought about my business, I thought about . . . Owen. I thought about everything and I was like, "No, I'll get up and I'll have two Panadeine Forte, a cup of hot chocolate," which I did and I went back to bed and I woke up and I felt a bit better, so I was right.'

The whole mess has also affected her business. It was hard to bake and serve customers when there were police all through her property and teahouse, searching the incinerators and pumping out the septic system, rifling through her freezers.

Mr Currie nods, but he's puzzling his way through Fran's police statements. One detail stands out, he says. She refers to herself and Owen together—she uses words like 'we', 'us', 'our' over and over again. Like everything that's happened has happened to both of them.

'Well, when it happened to me it happened to him because he's there,' Fran says. 'He's my caretaker, you know. He's there. He—I can't say I pay him, you know, because he won't take any money. He's there to look after my property and he looks after me as well because he respects me for who I am.'

'So what you're saying is that if you're distressed, it distresses him?'

'Of course he—not distresses him, but he would get upset, yeah.'

Mr Currie suggests Fran has been quite protective of Owen.

'Well, he looks after me, I look after him. I treat people how they treat me,' Fran says. She wasn't worried about Owen because, once again, he's an honest person.

Mr Currie asks what Fran means by 'honest', but she never quite gives an answer. The night Paddy disappeared, Owen's car didn't leave the property and neither did hers, she says. So Mr Currie pushes on, trying to establish Owen's character and the nature of the relationship between them. Mr Currie finds page four of Fran's statement from the end of December. She'd told police that when she saw the officers across the road at Paddy's place and discussed it with Owen, Owen said: 'Oh, I thought they came for me.' In her statement, Fran said she got goosebumps 'and straightaway it clicked'.

Mr Currie asks Fran to clarify what she meant by 'it clicked'.

'Just about the drugs. I thought that was a drug bust across the road.'

Then Mr Currie takes Fran back to the conversation she and Owen had before she left for Darwin. The one where she'd told Owen not to do something stupid. When Fran had told Owen about the kangaroo, had he also said: 'Oh, there'll be trouble here today.'?

Fran tells the court that's correct. She thought, at worst, that Owen might go over and punch Paddy.

When she got back from Darwin on 15 December everything seemed fine, but then she tried to give Owen some gardening books and things got tense.

'He looked at them, and then he said to me, "You know I fucking don't want any presents. I won't take anything."' Fran and Owen didn't speak for two days; she was offended, she says.

Mr Currie asks if Owen's demeanour shifted. 'In those days following, the way you described it to police, he was a bit grumpy, Owen, wasn't he?'

'He's always grumpy. He's always grumpy.'

'He loses his temper a bit, doesn't he?'

'No, he's straight down the line.'

'Doesn't lose his temper?'

'He can easily if you upset him, yeah.'

The coroner intervenes: 'Haven't you called him a cranky old prick?'

'Yeah,' says Fran, 'I call him a cranky old prick. I still do.'

Mr Currie looks back at the pile of paper in front of him and continues to quote Fran's statement. '"He's very highly strung. He's very bad tempered", yes?'

'Bad tempered if you upset him, yeah, of course,' Fran says. 'He's a bushie. He has lived in the bush for years and years and years.

And he's—I can't explain it. You will see. All I know is I love him to pieces as a person, that's all.'

'Okay.'

'I get cranky too.'

There's a long back and forth as Mr Currie tries to establish Fran's disposition. In one of her police statements she'd said, 'I guess I'm as bad as Paddy', but when she's presented with the quote she gets defensive.

'You've got to be fucking kidding,' she tells Mr Currie. 'I haven't got a mean bone in my body.'

Mr Currie reminds Fran that she said it the first time she was pulled up by police, when she found out Paddy had gone missing.

'Yeah, yeah, yeah, when you say it like that, that rings a bell.' Then Fran tells the whole story—the funny thing, she says, was she thought the cop was investigating a drug bust and the officer had to tell her Paddy was missing. 'I said, "Oh"—I said—"I never murdered him." And the officer grinned and he said, "What?" I said, "Yeah, I'm as bad as Paddy." It was a joke, which doesn't turn out to be a very good joke, does it?'

'No,' Mr Currie agrees, it is not a joke that has dated well.

'No,' Fran goes on. 'But now, how many times have you said, "Oh yeah, no, I'm going to murder him," you know, like that?'

'And you used to say that a fair bit, didn't you, about Paddy?'

'No, no, I can't remember saying that a lot, no,' Fran says.

Mr Currie tries for specificity. 'How many times, do you reckon? Less than ten?'

'Fucking million, million, millions of times,' she says. 'Oh, I don't know . . . what I've been through, do you think it's going to fucking take me ten years to do it . . .'

'So you're telling me that if you were going to kill Paddy, you would have done it a long time ago?' Mr Currie asks.

'And I wouldn't do it anyway. I'm riddled with arthritis. Imagine me carrying a dog and a bloody body. Oh, come on.'

'So that's the issue, really, isn't it? It's you're not strong enough anymore?'

Fran takes offence. 'What do you mean, anymore? I'm strong, yeah, strong in here.'

'Okay.'

'But I've got arthritis, yes, osteoarthritis.'

'Okay. And that's what stopped you from killing Paddy?'

'No, no, no, no. That's not my nature,' Fran says. 'That's not my nature. I'm a lover, not a fighter. That's why I never retaliate against Paddy.' Then she corrects herself. 'Retaliated.' We are, briefly, relieved that the other town residents aren't here to hear it—the shifting of Paddy from present to past tense.

There's a bit more. Apparently, Fran had also told police about a black sedan and a station wagon with a spotlight on top of it that were hanging around when Paddy disappeared. It's potentially an important detail, but it doesn't get the weight it deserves because we're all still wondering what kind of person cheerfully admits at an inquest that they threatened to kill a probably murdered man 'fucking million, million, millions of times'?

16

A bushie who finally talks, a gentle red nose pit bull and a case of osteoporosis

Ten minutes is all Mr Cavanagh allows for everyone to digest the smorgasbord of strangeness, then we're collectively thrust into a different kind of unexpectedness: Owen Laurie.

His tall figure enters the courtroom, stooped like a person accustomed to ducking through low door frames. He's dressed in a blue polo shirt tucked into grey-beige pants with a black belt and sneakers. A thick brown jacket adds bulk. As he moves to sit down, he removes a brown Akubra-style hat—not dissimilar to Paddy's good hat, and probably worn just as regularly. Underneath, what's left of his greying hair matches a goatee, which forms an inverted egg shape around his mouth.

Like Fran, Owen has legal representation. His barrister, Matthew Littlejohn, has been present for all the proceedings. Owen rests the hat on the table but leaves his gold-rimmed tinted glasses on, so we still feel like we're not seeing all of him; he's somehow found privacy, even in this open courtroom.

Fran always refers to Owen as a 'bushie', and while he certainly looks like he's lived off the land, he's no Crocodile Dundee type. He's tough but not unkempt; looks capable but not gung-ho. On a cattle station, he'd be the guy who'd disappear into the background—he wouldn't attract the word 'character' or 'larrikin' like so many other bushies.

'I've read the interviews you've had with police,' Mr Currie says.

'There are just a couple of things I want to touch on in relation to those. The first one, if I can ask you about your history. When the police asked you about that you generally gave the answer that it would take too long. Is there a short version we can have for the court?'

'Not short, seventy-two-year-old history, I guess,' Owen begins, even though he's seventy-one. His dad was a timber worker and Owen started school on the NSW south coast, then attended high school in Wagga Wagga until he was fourteen. Since then he's had several occupations: he was in the army for eleven months, was a railway worker for about twenty years, worked in the timber industry, in mine maintenance, as a bore runner on cattle stations. He's lived in New South Wales, Queensland, Western Australia and the Northern Territory. He was once a proficient boxer, did the tent shows around Wagga Wagga in his late teens.

His voice is confident and he's not evasive. We get the impression there is a sense of humour there, somewhere deep under all the layers of this Larrimah mess. Though, perhaps, it's been a humour not everyone has understood.

Owen tells the inquest he was married for ten years, has four children. After his divorce there was a relationship with another woman, who moved to the Northern Territory with him, but she's not mentioned again, so we assume she's no longer on the scene.

When he was sixty-five, Owen says he broke his back and had to retire from his bore-running gig, which involved fuelling up, servicing and running bores to make sure the cattle weren't short of water. He lived in a caravan on Manbulloo Station, near Katherine, for five years, but last year the station was being sold and he was told he'd need to find somewhere else.

Then one day someone showed him an ad in the paper: a woman in Larrimah wanted a caretaker in exchange for somewhere to live. He phoned Fran up and she told him to come down and have a chat.

'At that chat she told you all of the trouble she had been having, didn't she?' Mr Currie asks.

'At that point, the garden and things, yeah.'

'And the way she described it, there was effectively something close to a ten-year history of someone across the road not being very nice to her?'

'I don't know how long it was, but yeah, she said that, yeah, that they had been poisoning her—him or her ex-husband—had been poisoning the garden. I don't know which one, I hadn't been there, so I don't know who did it.'

'But she told you a lot more than just about poisoning the garden, didn't she? She told you about people creeping across the road and stealing things, all that sort of thing?'

'Yeah, she did say he stole something, yeah.'

'An umbrella. Did she tell you about stealing an umbrella?'

'She told me a lot of things that happened there.'

Owen says when he arrived at Fran's there wasn't much of a garden. He could still smell the glyphosate poisoning in the ferns. But he agreed he could build one and construct some fences and do whatever maintenance work was required in exchange for a place for him and his dog to live.

'Did you also regard part of your role as to keep the property safe?' Mr Currie asks.

'No. She may have had that idea, but I didn't. I'm not putting her down, I'm seventy-one years of age. I'm not a security officer or anything like that. My job was to build a garden for her.'

Whatever the exact arrangements were, Owen needed accommodation and he didn't mind the sound of the work. But, in hindsight, he admits there were a few red flags in that first meeting with Fran.

'If I had known there was trouble in the town, like I found out since, the disputes that are going on all over the town, I wouldn't have come there. I wouldn't have taken the job.'

He's not just talking about the relationship between Fran and Paddy, he says. Even though he didn't go to the pub and didn't know anyone else, the tentacles of town-wide tumult seemed to reach Owen via Fran.

'A lot was happening in Larrimah, it has been going on from years ago,' he says. 'All that stuff had been going on, I didn't want to get involved in anything like that.'

'Are you involved in any of that, though?' Mr Currie asks.

'No. I've never been anywhere in Larrimah but the place where I live.'

'Are you still there in the job?' Cavanagh asks.

'Yes, I am, yeah.'

'Knowing all the trouble?'

'Yeah. Now, yes.'

To own a pit bull says something about a person, even though there are mixed opinions on what that statement is. Owen Laurie owns a red nose pit bull called Ruby.

'A red nose pit bull?' Mr Cavanagh raises his eyebrows.

'Yeah. But I can get veterinary evidence as to her nature, because she's a very gentle-natured dog, as they are if you treat them properly.'

This is a well-worn argument by pit bull owners, one that can single-handedly fire up talkback radio or letters to the editor. But there's no denying the breed has a bad reputation. Children aren't mauled by labradors. Rappers trying to look tough don't name themselves Poodle.

Did Owen ever set Ruby on Richard Simpson? Mr Currie asks.

'No. Never happened, nothing like it happened.'

Then the questioning lurches in another direction: to a dinner party at Fran's around 11 or 12 December, the week Paddy disappeared. Fran's friends Fran and Lloyd came over and Owen was invited to eat with them all. Owen wasn't a social creature and he agrees that accepting the invite was out of character for him.

'What persuaded you to have dinner with them?' Mr Currie asks.

'She asked me to go and meet her friends and have dinner there, so I did. She's the boss of the place.'

'During that dinner was there much conversation about Paddy Moriarty?'

'Not that I can recall.'

The questions circle back to the garden, which Owen admits he was proud of but continues to deny he was responsible for protecting. He does say Fran instructed him not to plant in certain spots that would give the troublemakers easy access to her plants again.

'And a few weeks after you got there, when you were planting plants around the fence, she said, "Don't put them there, Owen." Remember that?' Mr Currie asks.

'Yeah.'

'Tell us the rest of the conversation after she said, "Don't put them there, Owen."'

'I can't remember the whole conversation, but I was joking with her at the time and I said, "Well, if anyone touches my plants, it will be the first murder in Larrimah."' Owen insists he wasn't serious. That people say things like that all the time. 'I had no intention to murder anybody over a garden,' he says.

With the voice of someone who's seen it all because he *is* someone who's seen it all, Mr Cavanagh interjects: 'People have been murdered for less, sir.'

Owen continues his own character assassination.

'Would you regard yourself as a person that loses their temper?' Mr Currie asks.

'Yes.'

'A lot?'

'Yes.'

'Do you regard yourself as highly strung?'

'No.'

'Do you regard yourself as very bad tempered?'

'Yeah.'

'Did you say to Fran, "I would say something if I'd done it. I'm seventy-one, not well. I would get a free air-conditioned room and three meals a day, but I don't want to go to jail for something I didn't do"?'

'Yeah. And I stand by that, too. If I would have done it, I would have said so. I would have told people.'

Mr Cavanagh corrects him on a point of fact about Darwin's jail: 'It's not air-conditioned,' he says dryly.

After a day and a half of questions, we've realised the inquest isn't going to lay out all the answers. The whole thing is so full of contradictions and repetitions it can't possibly be assembled into a coherent narrative. But Owen's questioning is particularly discordant.

It's almost like someone is drawing an asterisk—Mr Currie keeps penning lines that go in every direction, but they always meet at the same point in the middle. Mr Currie returns over and over to that one encounter Owen had with Paddy across the highway, the one Richard witnessed. There is surely a tactic at play here. When Mr Currie pivots to something else, he always comes back to much the same questions, as if trying to catch Owen in a contradiction.

During one of the returns to the dog incident, Mr Currie asks where Kellie was on Fran's property and what Owen did about it.

'It came to the northern end of our property . . . It didn't come inside the fence. I told it to get going—dog running across the road like that. That's the main highway and the dog may get killed or something, you know.'

'And so you're saying, "Get out of here," or something like that?'

'Yep.'

Mr Currie asks what happened when the dog went back over the road, what Paddy did and how Owen reacted.

'I just said to him, "Keep your dog at home, Moriarty." And he said, "Shut up." And I just said, "Come here," and that was it. He disappeared.'

'So when you said, "Come here," what were you attempting to suggest?'

'Ask him what he meant by, you know, telling me to shut up. All I wanted was him to keep his dog at home sort of thing, you know.'

At this point Mr Cavanagh intervenes to ask if that was all that was said. He pushes: is Owen telling the truth?

'Yes,' Owen asserts, and Mr Currie steps back in.

'Was it an aggressive conversation?'

'No, no, it wasn't an aggressive conversation. I just wanted him to keep his dog at home. Our voices weren't raised. My voice was raised only enough to carry across the highway, which is not very far. And I wasn't angry or aggressive about it, I was just asking him to keep his dog at home.'

'Didn't swear at him?'

'No, not at that point, no. I've never sworn at him because I've never spoke to him again or since.'

'You said, "Not at that point," and then corrected yourself. Was there a point where you did?'

'No.'

'So no swear words used by you?'

'No, not—no. Well, I don't know.' Owen has backed himself into a corner. He might not remember his exact words, but we all know how we speak. We all know what we probably would have said in the face of confrontation—if we're the type of person to insert expletives and which ones we favour. Owen concedes. 'Well, I said, "Keep your fucking dog at home," or something. The gist of this is really I told him to keep his dog at home. Whether I used a swear word or not.'

The admission leads to a string of questions about aggression: if there was anger behind Owen's words, whether he and Paddy had shouted at one another, like Richard said. Owen says Richard's version of the conversation never occurred, but he does admit that he spoke to Fran about the encounter with Paddy. She'd been complaining about the roadkill she believed Paddy had thrown over her fence and Owen told her he'd 'had words' with him.

Did Fran seem upset about the dead roo under her window? Mr Currie asks.

'No. Just the normal way she is with Paddy, you know,' Owen replies.

'What is that normal way with Paddy?'

'Well, you know what she's like with Paddy, you heard her talking about him. She spoke about him the same way she normally does.'

'She seems to be emotional when she was speaking about him, too?'

'She gets emotional about it, yes.'

'Was she emotional on this day when she was talking about it?'

'Not particularly.'

Then Mr Currie puts Fran's account of the fight to him. In her version, both Paddy and Owen were swearing at one another. She says Owen called it a 'barney'. Owen denies ever having used that word, again denies swearing.

'Fran must have had a poor memory or something. Because nothing like that was said at all.'

'Well, see, Fran told me under oath that that's what you said,' Mr Cavanagh says.

'I'm telling you under oath that I didn't say that,' Owen insists.

The questions divert and return all over again. Each time he comes back to the incident, Mr Currie pushes Owen a little further, poking more of Fran's claims at him.

Fran's statement indicated Owen told her he'd gone to jump the fence to confront Paddy and that Paddy ran away, frightened.

Didn't happen, Owen says.

Fran told police Owen was angry over the incident.

Not at all, he says.

The questioning about the confrontation goes on and on. Did Fran warn Owen not to do something stupid, because she didn't want to bail him out of jail? Not that day, he says. Maybe another day. But possibly that day. There was some conversation like that. And what was Owen's intention when he called for Paddy to 'come here'? Was he trying to start an argument? What would he have done if Paddy had come over the road?

'I'm seventy-one years of age, I'd hardly be throwing fist fights with anybody at my age,' Owen tells the inquest. 'Something violent like that I'd break all me bloody bones, you know. I have osteoporosis. I wouldn't be able to engage in an altercation, for my own health.'

Owen is asked if he feels protective of Fran, and he says he doesn't, but that he didn't think what Paddy had been doing to his landlady was right. His police statement is read back to him: 'Well, he's been over there harassing that woman for ages. Can't be a real nice sort of bloke. He's got to be terrorising old women.' In the statement, Owen talks about wanting to give Paddy a hiding.

'At the time you were talking to the police you weren't talking about osteoporosis and breaking all your bones,' Mr Currie says. 'At the time you were talking to the police you had it in mind that if he had have come over you could have given him a bloody good hiding?'

'I could have done.'

'Which is different from the version you just gave His Honour where you said you couldn't?'

'I probably couldn't either, as I said I've got osteoporosis. What are you trying to say, that I would have belted him? I may have tried to but it didn't happen.'

The next time Mr Currie comes back to the argument, he puts more of Fran's claims to him.

'She says you said, "The fucking bastard," and you said, "Oh, there'll be trouble here today,"' Mr Currie says.

'That didn't happen. Nothing like that was said at all.'

Mr Currie says Fran told police that's when she told Owen not to 'do anything stupid'. Owen still disputes the conversation, but agrees that then Fran left for Darwin to pick up a couple of water features. When she arrived home, Fran had said the first thing Owen said to her was: 'I didn't do anything.'

Owen agrees it sounds like something he might have said, but it was in relation to the garden—he hadn't done any work while Fran had been away. He'd just been in his bungalow reading and mucking around on the computer.

But Fran also claims Owen said he didn't go in the garden because he 'didn't want any conflict with Paddy across the road'.

'I can't remember saying that,' Owen says, and denies he would do such a thing anyway; he'd forgotten about 'having words' with Paddy almost as soon as it happened.

Mr Currie says Fran believed he was quite worried about that conversation, and that Owen and Fran spoke about it on several occasions.

'No, not that I recall. We may have spoken about it. As I said, Fran talks a lot.'

'You don't, though?'

'No. I don't contribute much to conversations anywhere,' Owen admits. This is probably the longest conversation he's ever had.

Just outside Fran's place, in what Maurice Darby called no-man's land, is a phone box. For anyone who's travelling through and needs it, the phone box is a saviour. For Owen, it is the opposite.

'On the Saturday evening, sixteen December, at or about six thirty, six thirty-one, did you go down to the phone box?' Mr Currie asks.

'I can't remember going in the phone box, but I may have done, because I have used the phone box. I'm not saying I didn't go there; I'm saying I can't remember going there.'

'Can you remember getting a virus-type message on the computer?'

'Yeah.'

'What did you do in response to that?'

Owen says he tried to use the computer management system to sort out the problem, but when he was unable to resolve it himself, he jotted down the telephone number it listed for tech support. Skype wasn't working, so he'd gone to the phone box.

'Whilst you were there, either near the front of your property or the phone box, did you see Paddy coming home from the pub on his red quad with Kellie the dog on the back?'

'No.'

'Didn't see them come home that evening?'

'No.'

'See, the evidence is that Paddy left the pub on Saturday the sixteenth at about six thirty pm, a bit later than normal. The evidence is that from the phone box out the front of your premises at six thirty and six thirty-one two phone calls were made to the number of the virus company that you had on your computer. The calls didn't get through, no answer. And it seems like it may have been a coincidence that those two things happened at that time, or it may have been the time when you saw Paddy?'

'I didn't see Paddy. I would have heard him if I had been making a phone call. I didn't hear the quad bike. Didn't hear anything.'

'See, the suggestion is that you went to sort it out with Paddy, didn't you?'

'Didn't happen. I just go straight back inside from that phone box, been on my computer and resolved the issue.'

Mr Currie asks if Owen usually logs off his computer when he's done.

Yes, Owen replies, usually.

'Would there be a reason to leave it on?' Mr Currie asks.

'Not necessarily. Sometimes I have left it on.'

'Why would you do that?'

'Forget about it. I might be doing something else and leave it on.'

'So something more pressing?'

'I don't know about more pressing . . . There's not much pressing goes on out there.'

'Okay. See, your computer remained logged on from sixteenth December through to eighteenth December.'

'Could be.'

'The only time it wasn't logged off.'

'Could be.'

'Had nothing particularly pressing to do?'

'Nothing.'

Finally, Mr Cavanagh calls it a day. 'Thank you, sir, for your cooperation,' he says to Owen. 'Thank you for coming along. You may go now. Cheerio.' It's a line he's used after every witness, a light-hearted farewell so at odds with everything that has preceded it, it takes us by surprise every time.

'The inquest will not be finalised today,' Mr Cavanagh announces formally. 'The inquest will be adjourned *sine die* to a date to be fixed, and investigations will continue. And when it recommences it will finish, and submissions may be made before it finishes. Thank you.'

With that he opens a door and disappears into an invisible room at the back. Everyone else shuffles into the foyer. Journalists whisper among themselves, wondering what to lead their stories with after that fatberg of information, all the while keeping a look out for Fran and Owen.

Outside, we all stand around squinting in the sun, standing a little straighter each time the door opens. Finally, Fran emerges holding the hand of a woman with long, black, shaggy hair pressed under an Akubra. The media moves in, following her down the street, as a man, perhaps a police officer or maybe just a friend, stands between her and the journos and cameras. Uncharacteristically, Fran has nothing to say. She points her head at the ground. She puts her hands over her face. She grips the collar of her striped blouse and pulls it up to her forehead.

She only just makes it to the edge of the lawn when someone spots Owen coming out a side door, his barrister by his side. The press is divided; they don't know who to approach. Eventually, Owen strides forward, head up, hands in pockets, silent, and catches up with Fran. They walk side by side, ignoring the cameras and each other, until they're ushered into a legal office and the crowd disperses, rushing off to file stories, or record pieces-to-camera in front of the courthouse, none of which could truly capture what has gone on here today.

Later in the evening, we bump into the photographer from the *NT News*. He'd just popped into Woolworths to grab a few things and saw Fran in the freezer section.

What was she doing? we ask.

'She was buying pies.'

One year after the disappearance.

17

A soon-to-be-homeless crocodile, a plate full of rissoles and a lack of closure

The twang of an old cowboy instrumental leaks out across the Never Never, the kind of tune that resurrects the memory of Paddy, with his lush moustache and wild stories. On the verandah of the Pink Panther, someone rehashes one of Paddy's old yarns—the one about the time out at Heartbreak Hotel when he got involved in a shootout with some drunks who came into the pub. Paddy didn't pull the trigger but he did load the guns—had a great time doing it, everyone reckons. He used to tell the story all the time.

It's late November 2018, just shy of the one-year anniversary of Paddy's disappearance; the wet season has begun and everything has come to life in vivid shades of green. This afternoon, the improbably pink pub has come to life, too. The car park is more full than it has been in years.

It's a strange thing, to have a send-off for someone who's missing. No one knows what to call it, until Karen Rayner mentions Last Hurrah and the name sticks. The event is a triple wake, really: partly for Paddy; partly to farewell Barry, whose cancer is getting worse and who has finally sold the pub; and partly for the pub, which won't be the same without the two of them.

That we've been invited is an honour but also feels like an intrusion. We've turned up with an honest sense of sadness, plus forty plastic knives and forks that Karen requested we bring. There's a level of closeness—a loss of objectivity—that we suspect makes us bad journalists. But we've brought our notebooks, too, which we suspect makes us bad people.

Barry's looking a little gaunt, but also like someone has lifted a huge, pub-shaped weight off his shoulders. He's matched a pair of Hawaiian shorts with his khaki shirt to usher in his retirement and celebrate the sale of the pub. We joke that he looks like Tropical Barry and he says he likes that. There's talk of drinking the pub dry before the handover although, frankly, the group doesn't quite look up to the task. But, just in case, Barry has dumped a giant esky on the deck so nobody has to man the bar.

We're surrounded by familiar faces but there are a few conspicuous absences: Fran wasn't invited, nor were Karl and Bobbie, and Cookie is still banned from the pub for Mars bar–related crimes. Nobody's seen Richard since the inquest.

But the others have turned out and it's good to see them. Karen takes a break from rolling rissoles to give us a warm hug, and Mark waves while he sets up the barbecue. Lenny is tossing one-liners at anyone who'll listen, while Bill sits quietly nursing his beer.

People have come from Darwin, Mataranka, Katherine and Tennant Creek—even Hervey Bay in Queensland—to pay tribute to Paddy and farewell Barry's reign over the pub. Sprinkled between the regulars are former pub staffers, people who work on surrounding stations, travellers who stopped in years ago. But, even though the crowd's larger and more diverse than usual, pretty much everyone's north of sixty and wilting in the 42-degree heat. When the musician calls out 'Get your dancing thongs on!' a guy called Wingnut is the only one who complies. Everyone is roasting, subdued, a little sad.

And then something magic happens.

There are a few drops of rain on the tin roof, which quickly climax to a deluge, drowning out the music, sweeping in under the verandah, forming puddles around the entrance.

It's Wingnut who notices the time. 'Four thirty,' he says, pointing at the clock. 'Exactly when Paddy would've been going home for the day.'

'He wouldn't have left in this,' says Barry, looking out at the torrent. 'He would've been stuck here.'

In the wake of the short-lived downpour it gets a bit easier to breathe.

As the sun sinks and the flies pass their mantle on to the mosquitoes, the music picks up and Wingnut manages to get a few people—the two of us, mostly, we don't have the heart to turn him down—onto the dance floor. Bernie Flynn, the muso who played all the Back to Birdum festivals, alternates between instrumental Irish jigs or ballads, things Paddy liked, and pub rock favourites: INXS, Cold Chisel, Creedence Clearwater Revival.

'"Ghost Riders" was Paddy's favourite song,' Bernie tells us—he loved the cowboy instrumental. Bernie's wearing a Pink Panther Hotel singlet, accessorised with double pluggers and an Akubra. He says he's been playing gigs around the region for fifteen years—Paddy turned up often and would always put in a few requests. 'One night he made me play "Guitar Boogie" three times.'

The music is great, but what's even better is that it drowns out the eerie silence that's settled over the Pink Panther. Just beyond the reach of the festoon lights, the cages of Barry's zoo sit empty. He's sold or given away the birds and snakes and squirrel gliders and now pretty much all that's left are the three crocs, two emus and a cockatoo named Shirley. Des Barritt, the search and rescue captain from Mataranka, has been trying to adopt Sneaky Sam for his Mataranka stock camp tourist venture but the whole thing has generated so much more paperwork than he could have imagined. For months, he's been corresponding with bureaucrats in Darwin about crocodile cages and transport methods and whether he lives too close to the Roper River—in the event of a dramatic flood, they worry, no one could guarantee the huge beast wouldn't escape into the wild. It's enough to tempt a bloke to stage an illegal adoption, Des tells us.

The barbecue is fired up and Karen lays out salad and cheese and beetroot, cling-wrapped twice as protection from the insects. Someone points out a clean-cut man engaged in quiet conversation with some people on the other side of the room.

'That's Steve, the new owner. Seems nice enough but he's a businessman. It's hard to know what to make of him.'

We can't help but stare. Up until now, the pub's new owner has remained anonymous. Mysteriously so. It's not just his identity— there's also the substantial mystery of why someone would buy this place. We've watched as the media courted him, rebuffed by 'no comments'; most outlets couldn't even confirm his name. And now, here he is, next to a plate of uncooked rissoles.

We had assumed the person who'd take over from Barry would be another Barry: an old bushie, scruffy, not very good at accounting, the kind of person who's okay with a cutlery divider under a tea towel as the till. But Steve is actually an accountant. He's wearing a black polo shirt bearing the logo of the Tennant Creek caravan park he owns with his wife. His greying hair and beard look recently trimmed. We're about to wander over and ask him why he's signed up for this folly, but the speeches begin.

One by one, between Bernie's songs, people sidle up to the microphone. The tributes are fragile and earnest—in a town this size, nobody is used to public speaking and everyone's nervous, so the words bubble up when people can't contain them anymore.

'We're glad we knew Paddy,' Mark says. 'Paddy was as much Larrimah as Larrimah itself. [Knowing him] was a valuable piece of life for us.'

Wingnut—who nobody calls by his real name, Garry White—
takes a bit longer to get there. He's desperate to honour Barry
and Paddy, 'two of the best blokes you'd ever meet', but he's
worried he might cry. After a few false starts, he finally takes
the microphone.

'If it wasn't for Barry, this place would've been closed down
years ago,' he says. 'It was Barry who kept it going. I remember
at the beginning, I helped paint the pub pink. Forty litres of pink
paint—I got to hate pink by the end. I love this place. I love Barry.
Barry Sharpe, one of the Northern Territory legends. And you can
say that. Best bloke I've ever met. He's like a big brother to me.
Paddy was also like a brother.'

Everyone nods. It's a sweeping tribute, but with so much
changing and leaving, it's hard to know what to mourn.

From across the verandah, dozens of versions of Paddy gaze back
from a photo board Karen has made and put on display. Paddy's
always smiling, always wearing a hat—his expression is at odds
with the Irish wreath laid under the pictures. His friends had hoped
to place his signature hat here too, but it's still police evidence.

Bernie strikes up some Santana and a man who tells us he might
have some photos of Paddy—and who other people tell us might
be a drug dealer—gets sentimental, too. 'I got a night off to come
down here,' he says. 'Some things you can do and some things you
must. I'll miss the pub. The place will still be here, but it will be
different. It's the way of the world, I suppose.'

The night hovers between madcap and melancholy, and in the lulls
between songs, memories and tall tales spill out.

'Remember that time the baby crocodile they used to keep in
a fish tank on the bar bit a Chinese tourist?' someone says.

'And that bloke who came in saying he was God—he wouldn't
leave.'

There was the time another blow-in demanded to be airlifted out after a tiny spider bit his neck—Spiderman, they called him. And a ghost in a Model T in the car park, and the parrot out the back that someone taught to swear at the tourists.

The esky is filled again, and sausages and rissoles are barbecued. Over a plate piled with assorted meats, we finally corner Steve (it turns out his last name is Baldwin) for a chat about his plans for the pub. He's friendly and we speak for a while, but it's all small talk and pleasantries. He evades the big questions like: why have you done this, what are your plans for Larrimah, do you know how to feed a crocodile and what's the financial logic behind buying a rundown pub in a dying town whose population are half-banned and all elderly?

Around us, the crowd moves around the kitchen and bar—sweeping, clearing plates, opening drinks—like they own it. They kind of do. Most worked here at some point, usually more than once, and not always on purpose. Suzi Geddes and her husband George McLean, a musician who died earlier this year, first came to Larrimah to play a single gig and ended up staying five months. Wingnut worked here five times, and Syd Bowden and his partner Alex Martin worked, drank and lived here.

'It's nice to see the place full again,' Suzi says. 'It's special. Unique. Full of history. The people who drop in, you get to know them and what they drink and it just feels like home.'

She and her husband had even talked about buying the place, before he got too sick, so the evening is especially bittersweet for her.

'It's a changing of the guard,' she says. 'The end of an era.'

Barry's about the only one who's not sentimental about it.

'I don't feel emotional,' he says. 'I feel relieved.'

We've already spent almost a year trying to resurrect Larrimah's past—as if reanimating some lost era might answer the question:

what the hell happened here? Probably, we'd hoped that if we could understand the town's history, we might be able to predict the future, but that feels like a fool's errand now. So much is changing.

Last month, the nearby Wubalawun community won an almost two-decade battle for native title rights over one square kilometre in Larrimah. Allen Maroney and Jimmy Wavehill are claimants. Allen hopes that younger generations might move into town and contribute to the economy—he says there are about 150 people from three families (the Maroneys, the Daniels and the Birdums) directly connected to Wubalawun. He is interested in setting up farms for young people and investigating the possibility of a cultural centre with a barramundi pond attached, maybe even farming yabbies. He doesn't want to take over anything in town, but he'd like young people to feel proud of and connected to their country.

There are other possible futures that could drastically change the shape of the town—some of them are even related to Paddy. ABC journalist Anna Henderson won several awards for her documentary *A Dog Act* and now Hollywood is interested, too. A filmmaker from Los Angeles turned up recently, keen to tell the story.

Also, fracking looks to be going ahead in the region and there's talk the hotel could become a workers' camp. Larrimah's residents seem to have mixed feelings about it all, but they're not too invested in abstract possibilities. Out here, ideas come and go like swarms of stink beetles so you don't gamble on or get upset about something that might never happen.

There is part of us that follows the news stories about Larrimah's prospective futures with a sense of trepidation, even announcements that would be good for the town make our chests tighten. Because there is more than one way for a town to be extinguished. Jeannie Gunn, the writer who brought sentimentality to the idea of the Never Never, might have known how we felt. Her homestead, on Elsey Station, was the beating heart of her flawed but mythic version of Never Never country—it was beloved by soldiers, local elders and station-owners. So when the news arrived that it would be demolished to build a new road, people expected her to be gutted by its erasure. She was relieved.

'I prefer it that way,' she said. 'It can never be a low-down shanty. The last has gone as we left it. All my lovely memories, and which my dear men had before they passed on, cannot be damaged.'

It's getting late, and there's less and less laughter. Someone refills the esky and clouds of cigarette smoke ward off the mosquitoes. When Bernie plays 'Desperado', no one says a word.

We've heard so much about the pub's wild years—the parties that dragged on for days, time passing in a haze of rum and pranks and punch-ups. But tonight, the Pink Panther's chequered history of shootouts and brawls and last-minute weddings seems like a distant echo. At times, what happened to Paddy seems distant, too, like it's another town's story.

'It's bizarre,' Karen admits, in the quiet between songs. 'Like it happened to someone else. I know that's so cliché to say, but it really is. Every time we come into town, it's the same thing. We shake our heads in disbelief. We know he's gone. Know he's not coming back. We can't believe it actually happened here. We can't believe it happened to Paddy. People can have their opinion about Paddy, whatever they like. But we knew him for three years, and he was a great bloke.'

Des reappears from an impromptu nap in his swag in the car park. Wingnut alternates between dancing and sweeping people up in long hugs. Ronald Hill, a beekeeper from Mataranka who everyone calls Rusty or Rusty Bees, speaks up softly.

'I'd always look forward to coming down here,' he says. 'I'd knock off with the bees at four-ish. Paddy would sit on one side of the pub, I'd sit opposite and we'd chat for a couple of hours. Every morning Paddy used to walk his dog around the dump and look for flowers. He'd ring me if he saw any, so I'd know for the bees. And he'd check on my water, in case a donkey knocked it over. I didn't ask him to do that, he just did it. That was the kind of guy he was.'

Around 9.30 pm Bernie puts down his guitar and announces a minute's silence. Barry and Mark turn out the main lights, someone unplugs the clattering fans. Everyone stares out at the empty scrub beyond the red dirt that serves as Larrimah's main street, their faces lit by coloured festoon lights. It isn't exactly silent: the air is thick with the sounds of frogs, and the drinks fridge buzzes in the background. But there is enough quiet to remember the bloke who isn't here, whose bar stool is empty and whose absence haunts the place. The bloke who was the catalyst for all the other changes, all the eras that seem to be coming to an end. The bloke who'd never be quiet for a whole minute, like this, not Paddy.

The morning after, everyone's sitting around in the only patch of breeze eating leftover rissoles. Lenny wanders in, his unkempt toenails scraping over the edge of well-worn thongs.

'How are you feeling, Lenny?'

'I'm fit as a fiddle . . . with two broken strings.'

Everyone laughs, even though we've all heard the joke before. Maybe it's the familiarity that makes it funny. Kiwi, who's temporarily helping Barry at the pub, whistles as he picks up the empties in a wheelbarrow to take them for recycling. When this is all over, he and Barry are planning a holiday. Apparently, when Kiwi asked him where he'd like to go, Barry said: 'Somewhere quiet and remote. Somewhere with not many people.' Larrimah was already taken, so they're going fishing in Far North Queensland.

'Anyone want another cup of tea?' Barry offers and there are a few takers. Someone asks if it's too early to crack a beer. It's not. There are a handful of tinnies floating in a tepid pool of water in the esky; the crew didn't quite drink the pub dry, but they got close.

Paddy's bar stool sits empty, and in the space around it, conversation turns back to the Last Hurrah.

'I sort of expected Paddy to be here,' Barry admits. 'I had to keep reminding myself he's not showing up. He's lost. But he'd have enjoyed last night.'

'It was a good send-off,' Karen agrees. 'Everyone who came knew Paddy, so it was meaningful. It didn't end up being a circus. It meant something to everybody here. Everyone here missed him.'

But whatever closure this gathering of people and memories offered, it's incomplete: while Paddy is still missing and the inquest hangs open, it's hard to draw a line under any of it. 'We live in hope the police will find evidence to take this forward,' Karen says. 'I'd really hate to see that justice was not done, it'd be so unfair. And Paddy was such a fair person.'

There's talk of another memorial, a real one, when this is all over.

'This one's just a practice run,' Barry says. When they can, the town will do something more formal. They've got their eye on a patch of land over the road where they could put a plaque or a statue: a man and his dog, maybe, if they can get permission. Because what they can't do is bring Paddy home. And even if they could, nothing here is the same anymore.

PART THREE

The disappearing outback

Almost two years after the disappearance.

Almost two years after the disappearance

18

An angry ghost woman, a mobile phone black spot and a highway of tears

It's around midday, early November 2019, and we're tearing up the Stuart Highway in a panic, a dying man on the back seat of the car. In the rear-vision mirror, he's a crumple of bones in a sack of clothes, curled up, eyes closed, his breath terrifyingly light. As we drive and cry and check for a pulse, and worry if we're doing the right thing, we know this situation was probably inevitable. After all, we're the ones who set out to document the death of a town.

Still, if we hadn't arrived when we did, it would probably have been a whole lot worse. If we'd shown up later in the day, with this heat, maybe it would have been a dead person we were transporting, not a dying one.

Driving and crying. Driving and crying. It goes on for what feels like forever. But just fifty-two minutes after we leave Larrimah, we pull up at the Mataranka clinic. It takes five people to extract our fragile passenger from the back seat. The staff already know, we'd called them hours ago asking for help, but still they ask: 'What happened?'

What happened was this: we'd gone to Larrimah to visit Barry because we heard he wasn't doing so well. We just wanted to see him, have a cuppa, take his mind off the dying for a bit, then catch up with whoever

else was around. Maybe even meet Brent, Fran's grandson, who was running the teahouse.

Barry had moved into the old railway house Karen and Mark Rayner owned. Karen had been caring for Barry, despairing for him. The house wasn't fit for habitation, she'd told us—it had been destroyed years ago by a drug dealer and subsequent police raid. But after he sold the pub, Barry asked if he could stay there a few weeks until he organised something else. Then he'd just become sicker and sicker, and soon it wasn't possible for him to move. Where would he go, anyway? He was refusing the hospital or any other supported living situation and he didn't want to burden his children. All Karen and Mark could do was take him meals, do his washing, clean up and check in and make him comfortable. And keep trying to convince him it wasn't the best place for him to be.

The day we were visiting, Karen was working out of town for the week and Mark was working on a nearby station, so we'd arranged to go to Lenny's shed and have him take us to Barry.

'I'm waiting on a new knee,' Lenny told us. Him and half of Larrimah, we thought as we followed him the 30-odd metres to Barry's. Lenny was using a walking stick and it still seemed like a tremendous effort to propel himself forward. He'd also been having seizures. 'I had one over at the pub the other week. Kept hitting myself in the head.'

Despite Karen's warning, the house was a shock: incomplete walls exposing their silvery insulation innards, bare wooden floors, no ceiling, no doors. A bird fluttered madly, trapped in the roof cavity. And the heat. It was hideous, even with the old air-conditioner Mark had hooked up. But there wasn't enough time to fully absorb the state of the house because Barry was lying on the floor in the kitchen beside an upturned chair, knee bleeding.

'There were bats in the roof,' Barry said, by way of explanation.

'Did you have a fall, mate?' Lenny asked.

'I dunno,' Barry said.

'How long you been lying there?'

Barry mumbled something about last night, that he'd been standing on the chair because of the bats. But it didn't seem possible he'd have been able to climb onto a chair. He was arrestingly thin, his skin an alarming shade of grey. And there were no bats.

We managed to shift him from the floor to a chair. Mid-move he'd asked: 'Who are you?' We told him our names and he smiled. 'Oh!' Recognition flickered briefly, then faded. He told us about the party that kept him up last night. It would have been all right if he could sleep but some revellers came in and made a racket, playing music and dancing. Some of them were naked, he said, it was revolting. A man lay down on Barry's kitchen table and wouldn't move. They dressed Barry up like an emu. They wouldn't leave him alone. He thought they might come back, he said.

Lenny pulled us aside. 'I think you need to call the ambulance.'

We agreed, but it wasn't that simple. Barry hated hospitals—he'd always said he wanted to die in Larrimah.

The next couple of hours were chaos. With no mobile reception and Barry's landline misbehaving, one of us went to the pub to phone for help, the other stayed with Barry, cleaned his wounds, made him tea and listened to a series of escalating imaginings. He had filled the empty house with people who weren't there. A little girl had been hanging around on the verandah, Barry said—she's the nice one, he reckoned, but the woman in the half-built bedroom down the hall was terrifying. He kept calling to the ghost woman: 'Sorry! We'll keep it down!' Then he started talking about a horse in the other room.

At the pub, we phoned the clinic in Mataranka and asked them to send the ambulance. They said it was coming, then called back to say it was not. We called triple zero, who patched us back through to Mataranka—with the emergency operator on the line, they agreed to send the ambulance. But moments after we hung up, a surly nurse called back and said they weren't coming: 'Just bring him here yourselves.'

Barry's daughter had been calling the pub all morning, worried. She was flying to Darwin that night to come and see him. Get the ambulance, she insisted. We called again and this time a doctor in Darwin, sounding annoyed, told us we'd need to drive Barry to the clinic in Mataranka. An ambulance wasn't coming.

Mataranka was 75 kilometres away, with no mobile reception most of the way. What would we do if he got worse in the car? What if he died? Just getting him into the high-set four-wheel drive was going to be a problem.

Back at the house, Barry had at least decided he wanted to go to hospital. It was too hot, he told us, and the ghost woman in the other room was angry. He was really frightened last night, he said. So we grabbed his medication, along with a book of phone numbers and his Hawaiian shorts, which he insisted on packing.

Getting Barry into the car was an awful trial-and-error operation that took far longer than it should have. And then, as we turned onto the highway and drove past Fran's house, Barry sighed. 'It's funny, isn't it?' He sounded tired but his voice was clear. 'Even after all this time, how you don't trust someone.'

Then he'd laid down and closed his eyes. We'd looked at one another, unable to speak but thinking the same thing: had we just heard Barry's last words?

We'd hit the accelerator and silently begged him to keep breathing. We must have made our own lungs take in air, but it didn't feel like there was ever enough oxygen in the car.

As we watch the staff at the clinic put Barry in a wheelchair and push him up the path into the building, one of the nurses says: 'If we'd known he was like this we would have come.'

The panic begins to drain and, in its place, the anger rises. We've been thinking and writing about isolation and remoteness for years, but for the first time we really understand what it is like to be so far away from anything, especially help. In the end, out here, the only thing you can rely on is yourself.

In a way, it's also the first time we've really understood Barry—or, for that matter, everyone in Larrimah. It's easy to romanticise an unconventional outback life—weird and sprawling, a series of adventures and misadventures. A life with rough edges is charming, but when the person you've always relied on—yourself—can't take care of you anymore, the rough edges close in.

We follow Barry's wheelchair into the treatment room and are relieved to hear the locum nurse who'd refused to send an ambulance has left for the day.

The staff buzz around Barry, checking his blood pressure, taking his temperature, asking questions. They all know him—he's been coming to the clinic for years—and they're cheerful and concerned. Barry perks up. He's still beyond pale and making no sense—at one point he comments that this wait at the motor vehicle registry is very long—but at least he's sitting up and talking.

We start to wonder if our concerns are misplaced but then the nurse tells us she's phoning Katherine Hospital to find him a bed in their palliative care unit. The clinic manager says their driver will take him there. Moments later, when the manager has disappeared for her lunch break, the driver approaches us and asks if we're going to Katherine. Yes, we say, we'll meet him at the hospital. 'If you're going there anyway, you can take him. It's a waste of time us both going,' he says and walks away.

Our stomachs sink, and before long we're doing it all again, driving through 110 kilometres of out-of-contact territory with a dying man on the back seat. We cry, again, but not as much because this time Barry is sitting up, staring out the window. He talks occasionally, but it never makes any sense. At one point he fiddles with the door and we put the child lock on, worried he will tumble out onto the highway. Looking at him there on the back seat, shrunken against the door, we're shocked anew at how tiny he is. We'd never realised how short he was; somehow, he always seemed bigger when he was at the pub, in the middle of it all.

By the time we pull up at Katherine Hospital Emergency Department, we're all exhausted: Barry with sickness, us with fear. Inside, they don't have a bed yet. 'And you are . . .?' the triage nurse asks us. It's an uneasy question. What are we, to Barry? His friends? His writers? His journalists? We settle on friends and take seats beside him in the freezing waiting room.

They say someone's true nature presents itself at the end, that when all the context and agenda and artifice are stripped back, you're left with base character. We sit there for more than two hours and the whole time Barry is mild-mannered and good-humoured. Other patients come and go, doctors check on him occasionally. One asks Barry what year it is. He snickers, as if they are fools. 'It's 1942!' he says. Barry was born in 1942.

He dozes, on and off, while we take turns to step outside and make phone calls. His daughter and sister are about to board a plane in Brisbane, they'll meet us at the hospital tomorrow morning. Karen and Mark call, assure us we've done the right thing.

Barry remains oblivious. 'This is a long time to wait for a battery, isn't it?' he says. He isn't angry or frustrated. It's that same wry observation. Look at the world, isn't it strange, that's the way it is.

Next morning we work our way through the hospital corridors to Barry's room, where we find him on his side, sleeping. We don't want to disturb him, so we continue down the hall to a little tearoom where his daughter Karen and sister Netty sit, talking to a nurse. Both women greet us with warm hugs and tears; they are generous in their sadness, and happy to share stories.

'When we were children Barry would always give me animals for presents,' laughs Netty. 'For my birthday I'd get a lizard or something else he'd picked up out in the bush.'

Karen tells us her childhood was a little unusual, too, because of Barry's love of wildlife. 'We lived in a reptile park for a while,' she says.

Netty is anxious to be with her brother and we don't want to intrude but they insist we come and say goodbye. It's an awful farewell, we're marooned between grief and false optimism. We hold Barry's hand and chatter, say goodbye like we'll see him again soon. He's unresponsive, a curl of exhausted bones in a too-big green hospital gown, paler than ever under the fluorescent lights. Eyes overflowing, we walk out into the cement sauna of the hospital car park, get into the car, and silently start the drive back to Darwin. Crying and driving, again.

Barry's rapid decline in health is a shock in more ways than one. It heightens our awareness of the world, and makes things seem more urgent. It's not just the old publican and his stories that are slipping away, it's a whole era.

We'd set out to capture something of Larrimah, the people who lived there, and what happened to Paddy. Now we realise how precarious it all is. Most of the people we want to speak to are in Barry's age bracket. They're slowing down, waiting on surgeries, battling illnesses. Without history-keepers like Barry, towns like Larrimah take another leap towards extinction.

On the way back to Darwin, we cue up the audio of our old interviews with Barry and the car fills with his husky laugh and funny stories. As we listen, we jot down all the names he mentions, the pieces of history he suggests we follow up.

Later, when we are home, we take stock of the contact list we've been accumulating over the past two years. It's awful. Scraps of paper, names scribbled in notebooks, business cards. There's a rodeo clown, a clairvoyant, four people called Tony/Toni, a convicted drug dealer, a couple of politicians, some cattle barons, the family of a murdered man, a few cops and a lot of ageing alcoholics, most of whom are hard of hearing. A lot of our leads are spectacularly vague. 'There is a guy who worked at Katherine pool who knew Paddy. Dunno his name. Not sure how he knew him. Just ring Katherine pool,' someone tells us. And a few people point us to a guy who used to own the Torrens Creek pub over in Queensland. Paddy would go over there for long stints, they say. But he doesn't own the pub anymore so he could be anywhere. His name's Terry, someone tells us, but no one knows his last name. Could be Bowen. Or he might live in Bowen.

There is also a bunch of people it's almost impossible to get in touch with—people who don't have phones, or who spend the wet season hibernating in far-flung pubs and the dry season out mustering. People who live in communities with no phone reception and English as a second, third or fourth language.

'You just have to get out there and go to the pubs and walk up the main streets and ask people, that's how you'll find what you're looking for,' a friend who's spent almost her whole life in the outback advises. So we start formulating a plan, mapping out an itinerary, phoning whoever we can and inviting ourselves to their places. In four months' time, in March, we'll pack up the car and drive to see what—and who—we can find.

19

A publican who went troppo, a million bats and a town set on repeat

The March road trip doesn't happen. COVID-19 happens. As the world is held hostage by the death flu, the Northern Territory shuts up shop. Borders are closed, biosecurity zones are set up, people are told to stay at home. It's a weird time to be writing about a town that's tiny, isolated, precarious and fractured because suddenly we're all trapped in our own tiny, isolated worlds. It turns out intimate proximity, a lack of alternative company and nowhere else to go is a recipe for disagreement. Spouses contemplate divorce over the way their partners stack the dishwasher and parents tire of their own children's singing. Now, feuds over murdered buffalo or homemade pies don't seem so trivial.

For the people of Larrimah, life continues in quiet seclusion but there are adjustments: the pub and teahouse are temporarily closed, tourists disappear, scheduled surgeries like Lenny's knee are postponed, and driving to Katherine now requires paperwork due to restrictions on movements in and out of Indigenous communities. Places like Mataranka, with high rates of chronic disease, overcrowded homes and limited access to healthcare, are particularly vulnerable to COVID-19. Whole communities could be wiped out if the disease made its way there.

Newsreaders use the word 'unprecedented' over and over, but that's not entirely true, and First Nations people in the Northern Territory are acutely aware of it. Pre-1950s, police in these parts would head out in the 'leper van' on 'leper duty', rounding up any 'suspects' and transporting them to the leprosarium in Darwin. Those people were isolated away from home, never to return to country. We should be thankful to be self-isolating in four walls that are, at least, our own.

And, in a way, our COVID limitations help us uncover something extraordinary.

We shudder when we find it: the bones of a man and his dog in the scrub near Larrimah, covered in a loose scattering of leaves and branches, each with a single bullet through their skulls. Their story is buried in the archives, in a folder tucked at the back of the box of police diaries, and it's such a weird coincidence to be looking at *another* missing man with *another* missing dog that it sends goosebumps down our arms.

On 10 January 1959, Larrimah's sole police officer Constable Alan Lake and Aboriginal tracker Ginger received information that two Aboriginal stockmen had stumbled across the remains of the man and his dog 3 kilometres from Larrimah, just off the highway. Frightened, they took off and told their boss what they'd found. He reported it to police.

Police arrived at a strange scene. Clothes and blankets and tins of food were strewn around, as if the man had been camping, and the bones were laid out on a swag, a pile of folded clothes under the skull as if they'd been used as a pillow. There was a makeshift structure—some sort of windbreak made of branches—on top of the bodies. Constable Lake patrolled the area for evidence, and Ginger was left to guard the site overnight while they waited for back-up. Two days later, it was declared a case of homicide and police began inquiries.

The next bit really gives us chills: the man who met his death beside his dog in the lonely patch of Larrimah scrub was Irish.

When police started asking questions, they learned that a man named Thomas Lahn, about fifty years old, had stayed at the Larrimah Hotel about a year before with his small fox terrier. One witness said the man was German, another claimed he was Austrian, but the two men who saw him last at the Larrimah Hotel said Lahn 'appeared to be Irish'. Also, despite an extensive search of the area around the bodies, no weapon was found.

That's all the diaries reveal and we need to know more, so we apply for access to the inquest documents.

While we wait for approval, we trawl the libraries, the internet and the NT Archives for other things. We read every book we can find about the outback, watch grainy documentaries, dig through microfilm newspapers and magazines. We spend months squinting through the slanted curls of twenty-six years of handwritten, white ant-eaten Larrimah police journals. We find someone who has been compiling a history of the Brunette Downs races, an iconic race meeting that has been running since 1910. Paddy must have attended in his years working on the station there. The woman lets us thumb through hundreds of photos from the 1960s to the 1990s. We stare at every cowboy. None of them is Paddy.

We listen to hours of mini-disc tapes of interviews conducted by the late journalist and author Andrew McMillan, who often went to Larrimah to write. Fran Hodgetts, Barry Sharpe and Barry's former partner Ann Kanters are all in there, their voices finding us over a distance of some fifteen years. The tapes are an enticing mess of repeats and contradictions. A lot of it is the same people fighting about the same things.

In Andrew's research, there is also a map that uses little triangles to mark sinkholes and craters around Larrimah. They are every-where, pockmarking the landscape like clusters of terrifying pimples. We go back to wondering if Paddy's disappearance was accidental. Perhaps the ground beneath him simply crumpled, consuming him and Kellie.

We confirm that Bill is Lasseter's grandson; his mother was one of only two legitimate children the prospector had (though there were many children born of his extra-marital dalliances). It's a shock—not because we thought Bill was a liar, but it's an impossible thing and it is also true. The old guy in a caravan behind the pub probably has the answer to one of Australia's biggest mysteries: the lie that was a billion-dollar reef of gold. And if Bill, a descendant of Australia's greatest liar, is telling the truth—well, what does that say about who can be trusted?

Eventually, we receive approval to view Thomas Lahn's inquest file. It's a slim folder; a sad, brief ending to a person's life, topped with black-and-white photographs of a human skull half buried under the natural debris of the bush. Reading through the statements, it looks likely Lahn's death was suicide. People staying at the Larrimah Hotel reported that he'd been depressed, down on his luck. He had even said he would shoot himself, and he did own a gun. It's just the gun wasn't *there* with the bones in the bush.

There are other strange things about the case. The dog's collar was buried beside Lahn's body, the body was lying down, and, most notably, another man's pants were found nearby. No one admitted to taking the gun. The men who made the initial grisly discovery say it wasn't them—they were scared of the dead man. But by the time they'd found Lahn, his remains had been there about seven months, so anyone might have stumbled upon the scene.

The conclusion police appear to be pushing is that someone who happened across the body took the rifle Lahn had used on himself. The coroner isn't so convinced. His report says: 'I am quite satisfied on the evidence that at least one other person unknown, and who has not come forward, was at the camp where Lahn's body was found, either at the time of his death or afterwards. The rifle Lahn is known to have owned has not been found and was probably removed by this person and what appeared at first to be a windbreak of boughs was erected after death probably to conceal the body.'

After all this, it's a frustrating conclusion: an expert coming in and saying 'what we know is that we don't know'. Inquests are, sometimes, terrible things—the promise of an answer that goes unfulfilled. Given the way it's going, it's possible, even likely, that Paddy's inquest will also have ambiguous findings. Although he's probably met with foul play, there's no evidence to pinpoint a murder and no way to rule out the dozens of other strange possibilities. The elements hide things, out in the Never Never. Sometimes forever.

Between all the archival work, we'd also been looking for relatives of Bill Jacobsen, the man who was murdered at Birdum in 1936. We'd doubted his daughters could still be alive—Ethel and Rose were born in 1930 and 1934—so we try to find anyone who'd come to that strange family reunion in 2006. Then we discover that of the eleven people who made the trip to Birdum in matching T-shirts, only five are still alive—and one of them is Ethel.

She's living in a nursing home in New South Wales and is a little forgetful, but Ethel has spent a lifetime wondering what happened to her father and that's a trauma even a failing memory can't erase.

'I don't really know anything about my father's death because I wasn't told anything. I wasn't very old myself,' she tells us. 'I think I was about six years old. I don't even remember seeing my father off that day. But I do remember I said to him, "Oh, will you bring me home some lollies." Which seemed quite silly because the shop we ran was full of them.'

Her mother wouldn't talk about the murder, Ethel says. It was too painful. But when they were older, Ethel and Rose spent years going through documents, writing letters to archives and bureaucrats, and visiting clairvoyants, trying to uncover the truth.

The sisters came up with a few theories. Someone who'd known their father had told them Bill, who worked as a fettler on the rail, was a stickler, wouldn't allow anything on the train that wasn't supposed to be on it, and there was a lot of gold being smuggled up and down the tracks at the time. Perhaps someone needing to transport something illegal had gotten rid of the person stopping them from doing it? Their mother, Dolly, was reasonably well off—she owned the house and businesses—and they figured that might have been an incentive for someone to want Bill out of the picture. One psychic said that although she sensed that Bill's murderer was definitely a man, she kept coming to a woman's name. Ethel remembers her skin crawling with the realisation: she'd met a man who'd known them in Birdum when she was still young. He'd worked on the trains with her father and was friends with her mother. His name was Bill Alice or Bill Alison. Could it have been him, they wondered? The not knowing gnawed. A creaking sense of injustice.

It wasn't just the lack of answers, it was the lack of a resting place, too. Even though they knew where their father died, for a long time the family didn't know where he was buried. In 1957, they put ads in newspapers and went on to visit Darwin several times, searching for his grave. It took almost forty years, but they finally found him: in an unmarked grave in Pine Creek. Sheer luck had it the man who had buried Bill was still around and able to identify the plot for them.

Being able to place a plaque on their father's resting place meant a lot to the sisters, but it did little to ease the pain of not knowing how he'd gotten there. 'Rose and I always thought of our dad. Always,' Ethel says. 'We always wanted to know who killed him.' Rose died without answers in 2013. Ethel is almost ninety. Time isn't on her side.

With the pandemic keeping us at home, we make phone calls. We try to tee up a time to speak to Fran again, but she's not well; we write letters to Owen and send them to places we've heard he might be living, but he's either not there or doesn't want to talk.

Then we start in on strangers. A lot of the people we contact turn out not to have met Paddy, but they all know of him and, without exception, everyone is exceedingly helpful and full of yarns.

The stories we hear about Larrimah are something else. There's one about an old publican who'd go troppo every year in the wet season, ban everyone, close the Larrimah Hotel and drink the whole top shelf. Sometimes he'd sneak out, drunk, and let people's car tyres down or turn all the taps in their gardens on.

One man tells us he once fixed a power point in one of the old sheds in Larrimah and found a huge blob of black goo. It turned out to be gelignite. 'I phoned an army demolition guy about it and he reckoned it could have blown up half the town,' the man tells us. Someone else claims that back in the 1980s when there was no speed limit, they made the almost 200 kilometre drive from Larrimah to Katherine in fifty-eight minutes.

A couple of people say it wasn't unusual to wake up to freshwater crocs walking up the highway or soaking in the pool at Green Park caravan park during the wet season.

We sift through hundreds of other incredible stories about Larrimah, and just when we think we've heard it all, we come across a man named Albert Wilson.

'I spent twenty years off and on in that shithole,' he tells us. 'The place has always been trouble with a capital T.'

For whatever reason, Albert's family made a move to Larrimah in 1978, and even as a seventeen-year-old Albert could see there was something strange about the place. There were about eight residents, dope was growing in the gutters of the pub and fighting seemed to be

a favourite pastime. Even the local cop was an alcoholic. One night, Albert ran into him, drunk outside a Katherine pub, about to drive two hours home. The cop was so pissed he could barely stand, so, despite not having a licence, Albert took the keys and drove them home. The next morning the officer fronted up at the Larrimah Hotel, where Albert was working.

'Did you drive me home from here last night?' he asked.

'No, you dickhead,' said Albert. 'I drove you home from Katherine.'

'But you don't have a licence,' the cop had stammered. 'You'd better come up to the station.' Albert thought he was in trouble but the cop just issued him a licence and back-dated learner's permit.

Albert's family moved to Alice Springs for a while, and when they returned to Larrimah in the 1980s, things were no better. The pub, Green Park and the Top of the Town were all still fighting and there was bad blood between a bunch of local station workers who came into town to drink. People checked who was in the pub before they went in; often it was safer to drink on the verandah. At one point, someone stole the pub's mascot Pink Panther and blew its head off with a shotgun.

Then, there were the petrol wars. All three establishments sold fuel and at the time the average price was around 75 cents per litre, but to draw customers in, each servo kept lowering the price. It got so out of control, petrol was down to 45 cents per litre—probably the cheapest in the country. People from Elliott and Daly Waters would drive up to fill 44-gallon drums. Albert, then working at Green Park, was repeatedly sent to rub out the pub's petrol prices on the chalk sign on the highway. Since it was a short-lived inconvenience (they'd just rewrite them), one night he decided to take it to the next level. Under the cover of darkness, Albert slipped over the highway and painted the pub's sign with furniture polish so they couldn't write on it at all. He did that twice, and on the third occasion he got a belting.

It sparked another fierce battle with one of the blokes at the pub, who started sabotaging Green Park. One night he came over to the caravan park and threw an olive python into one of the guest's tents—while she was inside. That time Albert was the one dishing out the flogging.

Despite his active involvement in the town's troubles, in 1989 Albert found himself president of the Larrimah Progress Association. The previous president had quit in a huff and stormed out, and with only two people left at the meeting, and the other refusing to take over presidential duties, Albert stepped up. But when the rest of the town heard about his self-appointment, there was a confrontation involving firearms.

By 1996, Albert had had enough of the bloody place. He moved to Katherine, sold his mum's house to Cookie and vowed never to return. But after the Katherine floods in 1998, he was struggling to get back on his feet. He phoned a mate who owned the Dunmarra Roadhouse, south of Daly Waters, and asked him if he had any work.

'I got some work in Larrimah, if you want it?' the bloke replied.

Albert didn't. But he was in a tight spot, so begrudgingly returned to Green Park. By then Fran had opened her teahouse and Albert had only been back a short time when someone painted over her signs. His antics during the petrol wars had become the stuff of legend and he had some paint in a suspiciously similar shade out the back because he'd been doing up the toilet block. Fran told everyone he'd done it. In Larrimah, Katherine, Mataranka, everywhere Albert went, friends and strangers approached him, telling him off for picking on the nice lady with the teahouse. It got so bad, Albert ended up sending a letter warning her to stop slandering him. One day Fran fronted up to collect her mail and fired more accusations at him. Both she and Bill wound up being banned from Green Park.

Fran never let up. She seemed to thrive on trouble. And so, years later, when her neighbour went missing, Albert did wonder if it was possible the woman who had tormented him for so long would take things that far.

'I don't think [Fran] did it,' he tells us. 'Paddy was a larrikin, a bit of a bragger. He could have upset someone with his antics.'

Albert admits he only knew Paddy in passing—they weren't great mates—but when the Irishman went missing, the rumours found their way to him because people knew of his long-time connection with Larrimah. 'I heard the body got chucked in with Barry's crocodile,' he said. 'Or that he could be sitting down south somewhere laughing his head off and just did all this to stick it to Fran.'

But we look beyond what Albert says about Paddy because his perspective on the town aligns with so much of what we've dug up: no matter the era, it's always pranks and bar fights and warring neighbours. It's not the people who are the problem. The people have changed over the years, many times over. The problem, it seems, is the place.

'In the end I moved to Katherine driving taxis to get away from the mongrel town, it was driving me around the bend,' Albert says. 'You didn't know if you put your keys in the car if you were going to have brakes.'

The Larrimah rumours get wilder. We hear about treasure hunters who go scavenging around Gorrie Airfield, certain there are old army vehicles buried out there that are now worth a mint; about a man everyone called the Grey Ghost who used to chase people around town on a ride-on mower; and about a bat plague that closed down Green Park for a while. No one could go outside without an umbrella, and when the wildlife rangers came to check it out they estimated more than a million bats were roosting there every night. Also, apparently half the town *did* eat that pet buffalo.

Charmaine Roth tells us that not long after she moved to Larrimah in 1998 she caught some Russian spies gathering intel. The army was holding a series of war games around Larrimah, a practice for the real thing, she tells us. There were tanks crashing through the bush, planes flying overhead, men with guns traipsing around people's backyards. Charmaine was working at the pub and says the staff were in on the games too, encouraged to report any 'baddies' they encountered to the team playing the good guys.

'These tourists came and stayed for a few days,' she remembers. 'There was just something about them. They had these massive cameras and they reckoned they were bird watchers, but it was dry season, there were fuck-all birds around.'

Charmaine phoned to report the bad guys, thinking it was all part of the games. 'Next thing we've got military police here and everyone got taken in and interviewed separately. They wanted to know a description of these people, the type of cameras they had, the type of car they were driving. It turned out they were actual spies—Russian, or maybe German—and they were there gathering information. They were legit baddies.'

Of course, the pie wars rate a mention. Andrew McMillan interviewed Fran in 2006. Interview isn't quite the right word—it's more of a wild monologue outlining Fran's bitter feud with Charmaine's sister, Di Rogers, who ran the pub and then bought Green Park. 'Then she started making pies exactly like mine, painted over my signs on the road out of town twice. First time cost twelve hundred dollars to get done. I couldn't prove it, but I know they done it. So people coming in asking for Fran's pies, she'd just say "These are Fran's pies." They'd say, "No, they're not Fran's pies, they're burnt. Fran's pies aren't burnt." So I got on the phone and blasted her from one end of Larrimah to the other.

'Then I heard she was delivering pies out to Borroloola on the mail bus, no refrigeration for hours. She had a big sign up at the chicken shop in Borroloola: Larrimah pies. I'm Larrimah pies. I've been here twenty-two years, everybody knows if you go to Larrimah, you have a Larrimah pie, which is Fran's. Why not put her name? Say, "Di's pies, Larrimah", not Larrimah pies.'

Fran told Andrew she was worried that if someone ate an unre-frigerated pie and got sick 'they'd say Fran's no good, she's gone down the gurgler, her pies are off'. So she went to the health depart-ment and made an official complaint, which led Di to confront her. 'I told her, "I'm Larrimah pies, you're just a Johnny-come-lately." I said, "I don't mind you doing it, but you do it wrong, you put your name on it."'

Fran was also bitter about the Larrimah Progress Association falling apart and, like Barry, she blamed members of the Roth family for it. Even though Fran told us she was never friends with Barry, she revealed to Andrew that she and Barry teamed up to fight Di when she tried to get a takeaway liquor licence at Green Park. And they won. 'She undercut me, now she wants to undercut the pub,' she said, back then. 'Who needs another takeaway? It's fifty metres between here and there.'

We track down Di in North Queensland, where she runs a pizza bar, and she scoffs at the suggestion she stole Fran's business. 'Silly old bag,' she says. 'I only started making pies because everyone was complaining about Fran's pies.' Di tells us she called her pastry business 'Di's Pies' so that they didn't cross over with Fran's, and that the transport of them to the supermarket in Borroloola was cleared by the health department, but Fran continued to make complaints. 'So I just thought, stuff it, we're not doing it anymore. If you're going to be this petty about this shit then don't worry about it.'

Di gave up on the takeaway liquor licence, too, in the wake of a tsunami of complaints led by Ann and Barry, who she says had been making life difficult for her since she ran the pub. 'They'd do everything to make our lives shitty,' she says. 'What they did to our family was just not normal.' In the end it all got too much for her, and in 2008 she moved to Queensland and made a rent-to-buy deal with someone from Katherine to take over Green Park.

But a short time later, the place burnt down. It happened on the only night of the year Karl and Bobbie—the fire-and-rescue crew—were out of town. A lot of people believe the fire was deliberately lit, so we track down the police record, which says the fire began at 2 am but wasn't reported until morning. By then, the extent of the damage meant investigators couldn't prove anything. No one received a pay-out and Di went bankrupt. 'Everything I had put into Larrimah, I lost. For five years I was on the bones of my arse and I had to start again. All that hard work . . .' The sentence trails off as Di thinks of what could have been.

Our file of peripheral information on Paddy grows, too. Once, the Irishman had been eating dinner at a pub with a bunch of mates and a bat landed in his meal: 'He just picked it up and threw it out and kept eating!' his friend Ray Aylett tells us. Megan Ashley, who lived two doors up from Paddy in Daly Waters, says he taught all her kids to crack whips. But some stories are dark. One man tells us he's heard Paddy was twisted up in a $20 million drug bust at Hidden Valley Station, about 100 kilometres south of Larrimah, back in the 1990s.

We look it up and it's a sensational case involving an ex-footy star, the Calabrian mafia and, allegedly, the mail-bomb killing of a police officer investigating the case. 'Call this bloke, he knows something about it,' our contact says. We dial the number and the phone call lasts one hour and forty-nine minutes and is hugely entertaining, but the guy denies knowing anything about Paddy being involved in the drug bust. Later, a woman tells us that she thinks some drug dealers Paddy dobbed in during his Heartbreak days had been biding their time and finally came for him. More than one person suggests Paddy was tangled up in the IRA.

These are, in some ways, far-fetched theories—but a certain kind of lawlessness attaches itself to the remote communities

Paddy spent his life in. Outside the reach of phone reception and a consistent police presence, a person could easily get wrapped up in someone else's wrongdoing.

Another woman tells us she heard a guy was paid to 'knock Paddy off'. She was sceptical at first, she says, but around the time she heard the rumour, the man suddenly came into a heap of money. 'He was telling everyone he won forty thousand dollars on Keno up in Darwin,' she says. We add it to our list of things to run by police.

Of course, these are theories—rabbit holes that begin with the words 'what if' and end with murky frustration. We find ourselves obsessing, going over and over the possibilities, asking questions we cannot answer. Questions no one can answer.

20

A family full of Patricks, a horny border collie and a man without a past

For police, Kellie has always been the key to the case. It's partly because if Paddy had met with misfortune, they were sure she'd have barked or come back to the house or the pub. 'If we find Kellie, we'll find Paddy and vice versa,' Detective Sergeant Matt Allen had told us, early on. 'They must be together somewhere.'

It's a comforting idea—that whatever happened, the two of them were together. But as the case progressed, the police started to consider the possibility that Paddy and Kellie had been separated. They'd even had a few tip-offs about Kellie being alive. So they put call-outs in the media for anyone who might have picked up a young kelpie on the highway, thinking she was a stray. Kellie was distinctive: reddish brown, tan socks, two tan spots in place of eyebrows, light patches on her chest, a pale tip on her tail. Police hoped she might turn up at a shelter or at someone's house—even someone adopting her from the side of the road would give police a point of reference. The place where the dog was picked up might be a place they could search for Paddy.

'To cause harm to an animal, let alone a human, is obviously very untoward,' Detective Sergeant Matt Allen had told us. 'There's a possibility that somebody who was involved may have dropped Kellie at an animal shelter, not just in the Territory, I'm talking anywhere in Australia.'

It's something we'd considered, too, right back at the beginning of all this. Four months after the disappearance, we'd taken out a map and marked all the towns on the Stuart Highway. Then we'd looked at other likely routes across to Queensland and Western Australia. We pinpointed the animal shelters in those towns and enlisted some young journalists to make inquiries. Between them they called, emailed and messaged more than fifty shelters. They found a dog that looked a lot like Kellie in a shelter in Tennant Creek, 500 kilometres south of Larrimah, who'd been dropped in around the time Paddy went missing. But she wasn't Kellie.

Even now, more than two years on, we search for Kellie—at every dog park, on every shelter website, at every beach we visit. We can't help it. She's everywhere and nowhere. Just like Paddy.

More than a few people have told us Paddy warded off questions about Ireland with the throwaway quip 'Potatoes, potatoes, potatoes', or a phrase like 'I was poor and it was cold'. So when it comes to Paddy's youth, there's very little to go on.

Police must have had the same challenge. Anything before Paddy's arrival in Australia is a black hole.

We have a few clues, though. The first is a copy of *Every Man and His Dog*, which features Paddy and his previous dog, Rover, on the cover. There's something strange about seeing the image, immortalised in hardcover: the pair of them sitting on the steps of the Pink Panther Hotel. Paddy's clutching a XXXX Gold and wearing a straw hat, staring straight at the camera with the faintest of smiles. Rover, a handsome black-and-white border collie, is grinning beside him. And together, with the chaos of the highest bar in the Territory behind them, it's like they've captured the essence of the Australian outback. It's not surprising that, of all the pairings, it's Paddy and Rover who made the book's cover.

But the real goldmine is what's inside. A one-page story about

Paddy's life, written in first person. Mostly, Paddy uses the opportunity to talk about Larrimah, the Pink Panther, his womanising, Rover, and Rover's womanising. 'Oh yeah, I've had plenty of women in my life, no dramas,' Paddy told the writer, David Darcy. 'But, I've never settled down. I just done the rounds a few times. I've had a lot of different kinds of women . . . don't worry about that. Yeah, there was a lot going on in the sixties. Some pretty wild stuff. No, I've never had a missus, just me dog, no dramas.'

Paddy also details the lengths Rover would go to for love (or lust), including a story about the randy dog who, over the course of a week, walked more than 100 kilometres back and forth to a nearby cattle station to mate with two dogs, resulting in twenty puppies. 'So he sowed his seeds, all right, no dramas,' Paddy reckoned.

The glossy photograph of the grinning bachelor and his bachelor dog is at odds with Paddy's unsavory words. But we set our feelings aside in favour of the discovery of something we can rely on. Dates. Times. The name of a ship. Paddy's account in the book pins down his arrival in Australia to a 1966 voyage to Darwin on the *Fairstar* as a ten-pound Pom. He would have been nineteen years old.

At this point, the idea of a clear-cut, verifiable fact makes us euphoric—shipping records are something that can be checked. But we search the archives for Moriartys and Paddys and Patricks and Patrick Josephs (his middle name), and even people with birthdates that match Paddy's, on the *Fairstar*, which did the voyage to Australia in 1964 and 1965, but not 1966. And then we download the *Fairstar* manifests and go through them, line by line. He is not there.

We check other ships that arrived in 1966, and then just other ships that arrived in the 1960s. We consider any boat docked in Darwin, then Perth or Adelaide, too. We search Moriarty passengers for two decades, on any ship, docking in any Australian port.

Finally, we find a 1972 arrival card matching Paddy's birthdate (30 March 1947)—the handwriting even looks like the samples of Paddy's writing we have from the progress association documents. It's a re-entry card, meaning he was 'returning to live in Australia' not 'settling in Australia'. He listed his occupation as 'forklift driver', his country of birth as 'Limerick Eire' (Ireland) and the most recent address as Harlesden, London.

It's hard to know what to make of the absence of an initial entry card, though. It's possible that Paddy really did arrive in 1966 and there's just no record of it—a mistake on the manifest, perhaps, or maybe he jumped ship. Possibly he travelled at some earlier date. It's even possible he didn't move until 1972 and was mistaken about the arrival date. But it's a weird mistake to make. Back then, migrants spent a minimum of five weeks (sometimes months) on cruise liners to Australia; many describe it as the most exciting, albeit nauseating, time of their life. The name of the boat that gave you safe passage to your new country and the year you came are the sort of thing you remember.

If Paddy had lied about the date he arrived in Australia and the ship he came on, it's hard to imagine why. Presumably, a person might fudge the year or means of arrival to cover shame or wrongdoing, or to make it an easier story to tell. It's also possible to lie to create an alibi, of sorts.

Over the years, a few people have raised the possibility that Paddy was somehow connected with The Troubles, a period of unrest in Northern Ireland that lasted from the late 1960s into the 1990s. It's a time synonymous with bombings and violence. Is it possible, people have asked us, that a young man with a past marred by poverty and injustice might somehow have been involved with the IRA, or the violence more broadly?

There's no way to chase this up, though police have tried. There's no evidence Paddy was linked to the IRA—he was from the south of Ireland, for a start. For a moment, we think we're on to something when we discover that Harlesden, the London address on the re-entry card, had a strong Irish community and a bridge there was blown up by the IRA. But that happened in 1939, well before Paddy was born.

So we keep asking Paddy's friends, over and over—surely Paddy said something about his time in Ireland? Nobody remembers. There are people who spent years chatting to Paddy on the verandah of that struggling pink pub and never asked any personal questions. The people who did ask are vague on details. One woman tells us she thinks Paddy talked about coming out to the Territory from Ireland on some teenage work program, only to be stationed in a place so grim and difficult that he escaped, without even shoes on his feet. It was, perhaps, a version of the 'oranges and sunshine' promises made to UK orphans and children taken by social workers, who were instead subjected to abuse in workhouses and outback postings in terrible conditions, right up until the 1970s. But on second thought, the woman tells us, she's not sure that story was Paddy's—she knows a lot of outback blokes with Irish pasts. Maybe Paddy's story was about how he worked on a ship to get here, because he couldn't afford the ticket. 'It's one of the two stories, I think,' the woman tells us. 'But I couldn't say which.'

So we go back further. We have a birth certificate, partly in Gaelic, with some details: Patrick Joseph Moriarty, born in Limerick, Ireland on 30 March 1947 to Mary Moriarty, of Abbeyfeale. He was born at Croom Hospital, the nearest maternity hospital to Abbeyfeale. No listed father. It's not a lot, but it's enough to get us to some relatives. And what we find is that Paddy has disappeared before, within a small village and a large, close-knit family.

For Francis Foley, it was a curious shock to see a relative he'd never heard of in the pages of the national paper. The story was everywhere—on the radio, in the streets, there was talk of it in all Abbeyfeale's shops and pubs. 'It's strange, really, for a man who left Ireland with no one knowing anything about him, he ends up kind of famous.'

We catch Francis on a Zoom call, early in the morning before his day as a local councillor gets too busy. He's a kind, soft-spoken man in glasses and a blue polo shirt, with short grey hair—we can't see any sign of Paddy in his face.

Francis is happy to talk but doesn't know how much he'll have to tell us. Although he's sure he's related to Paddy—Paddy's grandfather Patrick Moriarty would have been his grandmother Josie Moriarty's brother—until Paddy went missing from Larrimah, Francis didn't know he existed.

Francis lives in Abbeyfeale, in County Limerick. It's a quiet village right on the border near County Kerry and a lot of his family live nearby—Francis is the eldest of seven children. The size of the family, and the tendency to use family names (for example, at least three Patricks), makes the genealogy hard to navigate.

Abbeyfeale is almost certainly where Paddy's mother, Mary, grew up and lived but, although he knew of her, Francis never met Mary. He did meet Paddy's grandfather (also named Paddy), a quiet man who cycled everywhere and liked his food and the odd pint of Guinness. He was a simple farming person; back in the 1950s and 1960s, the region was poor and life in the village was simple. People lived off the land and got around by horse or donkey cart. Even though Francis's grandfather helped build the electrification tower, he died in 1974 at the age of seventy-four, never having experienced the wonder of walking into his house and turning on the light switch.

'That makes us sound very backward here but we weren't,'

Francis says. 'It was just taking time for things to come through in certain parts.'

He speaks about the era with fondness but the story has all the gaps you'd expect for someone who was a child, more interested in games than his grandmother's stories. He can pinpoint where Paddy should have been in the family, but it's a picture that won't shift into focus. Part of the problem, he thinks, was that Francis's parents lived in Birmingham for a while, so they'd lost touch with some of the family in Abbeyfeale for a few years.

'My grandmother, she was telling me stories. But you didn't know the people so you wouldn't retain it,' he says, apologetic.

Over in Royston, England, Mae Screeney—a good-humoured young grandmother to four children under seven—was having a similar experience when the news of Paddy's disappearance broke. She contacted police because she recognised Paddy's mother's name—Mary Theresa Moriarty—as her first cousin, the daughter of her oldest uncle, Patrick Moriarty (born 1897), who was one of fourteen children. Mary, one of three children, was born in 1921 and later in life went to live in the Channel Islands, where she remained until she died in 1995.

Mae's family lived four miles away from Mary. Growing up, Mae's uncle Patrick—Paddy's grandfather—visited every Sunday evening. Mae's late brother was also called Patrick. It's a close community, where people notice things about each other; Mae is sure if there had been another Paddy Moriarty in the area she'd have known about it. So, although Paddy was certainly born to Mary, it's unlikely he grew up with his mother.

In the years since Paddy's disappearance, Mae has tried to unpick how one of her relatives might have been born without the family knowing. The conclusion she's come to is that Paddy was probably born out of wedlock—the birth certificate supports this, with no father listed—and then fostered out or sent to a care home; adoption wasn't legal in Ireland until the 1950s.

'I feel sad that my cousin Mary might never have seen her son after his birth,' Mae tells us, over email. And, as if to make up for it, between school plays and Santa visits with her grandchildren, Mae's been hounding adoption agencies for records. The whole, huge family is invested—Paddy has ten aunts and uncles living in America, plus fifty-two first cousins and 152 second cousins and umpteen third cousins. Mae can't bring Paddy home or make up for the way the past seems to have disappeared him, twice over. But she hopes to resurrect something from his lost past and she also hopes he'll get justice.

Francis agrees it's possible, if not likely, that Paddy was fostered out. Back then, plenty of things were talked about only in whispers, or not at all. Certainly, the idea of a child born out of wedlock would have been taboo in Ireland. Young women were sent away to have babies, and what became of those children in various institutions is a national scandal the extent of which is only just coming to light. 'A lot of women suffered a lot of their lives wondering what happened to their babies, what happened to their children,' Francis tells us. 'It was unbelievable.'

But if that's the case, it's a lead that's almost impossible to chase. According to a genealogist we contact, orphanage records from the 1940s and 1950s are not available and so much of the process was unofficial in those days, anyway. Paddy could have been boarded out to live with a farming family and might have had little or no contact with his mother.

'I suppose it's tragic, really, it's sad that he just disappeared off the face of the earth,' Francis says. 'But then when you look at the other side, tragedy brings something else out of it as well. He'd have been lost completely. We'd have known nothing about him. Unfortunately, there are the circumstances of him going missing, but I know of him now and I never would have known about Paddy Moriarty. So I suppose the quirky thing about it, because of the tragedy of the whole situation, we know about him.'

However poetic Francis's take is on family 'finding' Paddy, Paddy, unknown early years eat at us. How can a whole person be a secret? Someone must have lived with Paddy, gone to school with him, worked with him. So we get in touch with Irish journalists and radio stations, hoping that someone will come out of the woodwork. A few Irish people get in touch to say they did meet him—not in Ireland but in Larrimah or out at Heartbreak Hotel. It's always the same story: great bloke, good storyteller. Had an excellent night. He was a totally memorable character. But when it comes to details, there's nothing.

It seems impossible, but it's not. It's just impossibly sad. What Mae suspects happened is this: Paddy lived in another area entirely, or under the shadow of another family's name—at least until he needed a passport.

In the end, it's not Paddy's family who fills in some of the blanks in his Irish past. We hear it from Paddy himself.

21

Some legless trousers, the world's loudest burper and a shameful history

The home video camera shifts into focus. Paddy is sitting on his stool at the Larrimah Hotel, beer in hand. He shouts to his friend and interviewer Barbara Flynn over the noise of the pub. It's 2010, INXS is blaring and a drunk keeps doing 'the stairs' in the background. Barbara politely tells a woman who keeps interrupting to piss off. Over it all, Paddy keeps talking.

'I came out here in '67 on the *Fairstar*, from Ireland,' he says. There it is, from his own mouth. Casual. Specific. Definite. It's the same ship he mentioned in *Every Man and His Dog* but a different year. The book said 1966.

'You would not believe it,' Paddy says. 'It was a rough ride. Shit yeah. And it took us six weeks. There was no stabiliser [in] those days and I said to the captain, I says, "What's happening here?" I says, "Where's Australia?" He said, "We're not far off, we're about another two weeks to go," and I said, "You're joking."'

We'd discovered Barbara through another one of those lengthy outback phone-chains. Years ago, she'd wanted to make a documentary about women in the Northern Territory. But one night at the Larrimah Hotel when her husband, Bernie, the musician from Paddy's wake, was performing, Paddy had insisted she interview him.

Years later, when she heard about our book, she was kind enough to put a USB in the mail for us. And suddenly we had Paddy, in his own words, in motion.

In the footage, he's wearing his good hat and a short-sleeved blue check shirt, his bushy eyebrows and moustache dancing as Barbara asks questions. Everyone around him is erratic, drunk, but his voice is clear and even, with a hint of an Irish lilt behind the northern Australian accent. A woman next to him screeches something about the lap dancers of Larrimah and Paddy laughs, hard enough to shake his whole body.

Barbara asks if Paddy had experience with cattle before he came to Australia.

'In Ireland, we had our own cattle and they were looking for a stockman over in Australia. They were looking for a horseman, I was a horseman. Me grandfather, he was a blacksmith, me old man was a horseman, and I learned how to ride horses, right. Everything was easy then, Mum and Dad and Grandpa . . .'

Paddy paints a soft picture of his childhood—riding horses to church and the local pub, that sort of thing. But there are precious few details. No names, ambiguous places. 'I used to ride into school about ten kilometres. Me sister, the three of us, used to ride into school and back. That's how I used to learn how to ride horses. And loved it.'

We're only just beginning to generate questions—who is the grandfather, the sister, the mum and dad? Where? How? But the interview moves in another direction and then cuts off altogether. We have nine precious minutes of footage, but every sentence seems to open as many gaps as it closes.

The only thing we're sure of is that there's no sense of shame or secrecy in the telling—if anything, Paddy is fighting the chaos of the pub to make sure there's a record of his past and he strong-armed Barbara into the interview. So we lay the idea that his Irish past had somehow caught up with Paddy to rest. Instead, we salvage a list of names, stations and jobs from the video and return our attention to piecing together his early years in Australia.

Establishing a timeline for Paddy's life is almost as hard as pinning down a chronology in Larrimah; whole decades are murky black holes. But we know this: sometime soon after he arrived in Australia, probably the late 1960s, he worked at one of the country's biggest cattle stations: Brunette Downs. He spent about seven years at Heartbreak Hotel in the Territory's north-east in the 1990s, and bought a house in Daly Waters, south of Larrimah, in 2000.

There are a lot of gaps, but we assume there must be people— close friends, girlfriends, publicans—who Paddy had drip-fed details of his early days in Australia to. So we go looking for Terry, who was both friend *and* publican.

It takes about half a dozen calls to pubs, a local councillor, and even a real estate agent, but eventually we track down Paddy's mate who owned the pub over in Queensland. His name is Terry Taylor and he's living in Bowen, on the north-east Queensland coast.

Terry tells us he was close to Paddy for almost thirty years. Right up until Paddy's disappearance, the pair would catch up over the phone every fortnight. For the decade that Terry owned the Exchange Hotel in Torrens Creek, a town dented with 6-metre (20-foot) craters after an out-of-control fire at a World War II ammunition dump caused an explosion that almost wiped out the place, Paddy stayed with Terry every second Christmas, for a couple of months at a time.

They'd met around 1994. Terry was building houses out at Borroloola, about an hour from Heartbreak Hotel, and would come into the pub on his weekends off. 'Paddy and I first met in the bar—funny that,' says Terry. 'We hit it off good. He was a great bloke. Always laughing and carrying on. Nothing worried Paddy.'

In the years of drinking and yarning and friendship, Terry heard a lot of Paddy's stories. Information about his family was thin but adds to what we learned from Barbara's video. Paddy had told Terry he'd been born out of wedlock and never knew his father but Terry remembers seeing a photo of a couple who Paddy called his mother and father. 'I think it was a stepfather,' Terry tells us, with the benefit of hindsight. 'He never really spoke about anything like that. He just told me that they got killed in a car crash.'

Terry says those photos and a bunch of Paddy's other gear were all burnt in a fire on his property years ago. Paddy reckoned a rough-nut working at Green Park at the time had something to do with the blaze. He'd been having trouble with that bloke for a while by then. It must be the fire that police told us about—the one that essentially erased Paddy's past, leaving him document-less, photo-less, past-less.

Terry does remember talking to Paddy about his early years in Australia. 'When he arrived in the Territory, it was pretty wild, you know,' says Terry. 'There was no bullshit out there. They picked him up at Darwin and Paddy turned up in long pants and the man that he worked for got the knife out and cut the legs off his strides. They took him to Brunette—it took them three or four days' driving to get there. The roads were about as wide as your driveway, and dirt. Paddy wondered where the hell he'd arrived at.'

It must be the experience of so many migrants that their imagining of a place is so much paler than what they're confronted with. Coming from Ireland to the Northern Territory in the 1960s would have been a dramatic shock. And if Paddy had come to Australia on the promise of warmer weather and adventure, like so many others, he probably got more than he bargained for.

Terry thinks Paddy was at Brunette Downs from when he arrived until he took on a yardman gig at Heartbreak Hotel in Cape Crawford. By our calculations, that would have been about twenty-seven years on the station, which, in an industry where people come and go every season, would have to make him one of their longest-serving employees.

Years after they both moved on from Heartbreak and Borroloola, Paddy bought his place in Daly Waters in 2000. Terry had scored a contract renovating the Hi-Way Inn nearby and he moved in with Paddy for about five months. But he wasn't the only one living there.

Paddy had a girlfriend, Terry tells us—he met her at Heartbreak, then she lived with him at Katherine and in Daly Waters for a while. Nice girl. A lot younger than Paddy, though. Maybe thirty years between them.

'He always had young girlfriends,' Terry says. 'In the end, he did push her off, told her to go and get on to her own age people. He was starting to get on a bit and that. But they were together about two or three years. At least.'

The phone line crackles between us. Two or three years? How is it that no one has ever mentioned this woman before? Were they protecting him because of her age? Protecting her? Or did he somehow keep her a secret from almost everyone?

Kevin Horner lives in Darwin's rural area—he's one of the two men who sat through the inquest hoping to find out what happened to his mate. We meet him at midday on a Friday at his local, the Humpty Doo Tavern, the lesser-known neighbour of the Humpty Doo Hotel, whose biggest claim to fame was that in the 1980s it owned a 600-kilogram Brahman bull called Norman who won drinking competitions knocking back a two-litre Darwin Stubby in forty-seven seconds. Located in a small shopping complex, the Humpty Doo Tavern looks less likely to invite a bull into the bar, but it's still a typical rural pub featuring a crowd of pokies, a near-constant traffic jam in the drive-through and a rough edge. A bloke who unofficially holds the title of world's loudest burper (at 110.6

decibels, louder than a motorcycle and on par with a power saw 1 metre away) acknowledges the tavern as his training ground.

Kevin arrives just after we do and we recognise one another, despite the interceding twenty-odd months. He's sixty-eight years old, thin, gangly almost, with a thick head of receding brown hair— and he's keen to talk. So we order beers and fish and chips and pull up a table in the quiet bistro.

Most people know Kevin Horner as Kev the Builder. That's what brought him to the Northern Territory. He came for a two-week holiday but there was so much work he thought he'd stick around for a bit. That was forty-six years ago. His profession is also what brought him to Larrimah; he did some of the renovations on Cookie's house.

Kev doesn't really know what happened to fray relations in Larrimah, but by the end he had to alternate his meals between the pub and Green Park to keep everyone on side. It wasn't always possible to be neutral, though, because it was all so petty and public. And yet, despite the squabbling, there was something about Larrimah that crept under his skin, too. After Kev's wife died in 2014, Barry rang and asked if there was anything he could do to help.

'I wasn't doing so well, so I said, "Let me come and run the pub for a while. There's just one condition: don't pay me. I just need a bed, a beer and a feed."' Kev had filled in for Barry once before, so he knew the ropes. Plus, the place was busy with fracking drillers at the time and Barry needed the help. Kev stayed for eighteen months, working 6 am to midnight, keeping his mind off things.

It was during this time he and Paddy really became mates. 'He was part of the furniture at the pub,' he says. 'He'd bring out all the blarney with the tourists—he should have been on a wage.'

Kev reckons Paddy drank a lot more than police and the others in town let on. He scoffs when we say that Paddy's bank records show he only withdrew forty dollars a night and spent it on eight XXXX Golds.

'Paddy had an enormous capacity for grog,' he tells us. 'He'd drink a thirty-pack a day.' When Kev was behind the bar, Paddy would put most of what he drank on a tab and pay it off at the end of the month. 'He was never any trouble, though,' he says. 'Never hungover.'

Behind the bar, Kev also had a front-row seat to the drama between Paddy and Fran.

'Fran bought a brand-new ride-on mower which broke and she blamed Paddy for it,' Kev says. 'But her grandson or nephew or someone had been there and she was making him do the lawns and he hated it so he poured dirt in the gas tank. When he was at the pub waiting to catch the bus out of there, he bragged about it to everyone, but Fran always blamed Paddy for it.'

Kev concedes Fran had good reason to be suspicious of her over-the-road neighbour. 'Paddy would go over to Fran's and let the gas out of the gas bottles and water out of her tank,' he says. 'And he did stick a hose in her window and wet all her books and flooded the place.' He also says Paddy graffitied some of Fran's signs. 'Barry told him to stop or she'd do it back, to the pub signs, then they'd finish up with no signs in town.'

But Kev had plenty to preoccupy him behind the bar. He'd been trying out a new pie recipe that required three days of cooking and he was also dealing with a shoplifting issue. Someone reckoned they'd seen Cookie stealing Mars bars. Kev was sceptical. 'I said, "Why would he pinch Mars bars, he's a four-needle-a-day diabetic,"' Kev tells us. But Mars bars did seem to be going missing, so Kev installed a fake CCTV camera and waited until Cookie came up to the pub. Kev had counted the Mars bars beforehand, and when Cookie was about to leave, he realised six were missing. Apparently, Cookie initially denied it, but Kev pointed to the little black 'camera' and he broke down and confessed.

We're shocked—Cookie had put up a compelling denial to us.

'He also once knocked off a four-litre tin of tiny taters which had been there for years and long expired,' Kev tells us. 'Someone saw him disposing of the evidence down at the dump.'

We can't help laughing, and Kev does too. He never minded the drama—the daily capers kept his mind off his grief. 'It was better than watching TV, all the antics going on.'

That is, until Paddy. The inquest, the police case, the news reports—it was a different kind of drama. After digesting all of it, Kev has some ideas about what might have happened to his mate. He can't prove any of them. But the question we really want to ask him is about Paddy's relationships and the young women he lived with. He doesn't know about that, but he does give us something.

'I think he had a lot of children,' he says, and our ears prick up because we think he had them, too. The person who told us—one of us, anyway, Kylie—was Paddy, about a year before he disappeared.

✦

Standing beneath the sprawling branches of the African mahogany in the courtyard of the Larrimah Hotel in 2016, Kylie was talking to Karen. They sweated in the heat, swiped the flies and chatted about nothing particularly remarkable: how Karen had ended up here in Larrimah and how long she planned to stay; what Kylie was writing about and why she'd driven all the way from Darwin to Larrimah to do it.

It's difficult to recall how it could possibly have come up—maybe they'd been talking about Karen's son or Barry's children, who'd recently been to visit—but Karen was telling Kylie about Paddy's past. Specifically, that he had children. A lot of children.

'I think the woman was Afghan–Aboriginal,' Karen had said. 'He's got a heap of Aboriginal kids running around.'

Kylie had only met Paddy briefly in the pub the day before, when she'd first arrived. He hadn't spun any of the yarns he was so well known for, they'd mostly just talked about Rover, the old border collie

who was constantly by his side. A lovely dog, friendly. Appreciated a
pat, and Kylie was happy to oblige.

She had barely recalled Paddy's name, yet here she was, hearing
the personal details of the man's life from Karen. And then, suddenly,
there was Paddy, hauling a garbage bin full of empty beer cans right
past them. Karen seamlessly smoothed over what could have been an
awkward encounter. She wasn't gossiping behind Paddy's back—this
was just a fact she was relaying. A detail you pass on in the context of
a conversation about family.

'I was just telling Kylie about all your kids, Paddy,' she'd said.

Paddy paused beside them and smiled. 'Oh, yeah, there's about
seven or eight of them, I think,' he replied cheerfully.

It was a shock—someone not knowing the exact number of children
they had. Kylie simply asked if he saw much of them. No, Paddy said,
he used to take them all to the rodeo though, and buy them cowboy
hats. He smiled at the memory, and continued on his way, the sound
of aluminium on aluminium retreating with him.

It was a passing conversation. It didn't seem like a secret. Nor did
it seem like a lie—why would anyone invent such a large number
of kids and excursions to a rodeo? That night, in the diary she was
keeping, Kylie had jotted it down. Not for any reason. Just the bower
bird behaviour of a writer who accumulates odd titbits that might
one day come in handy. That was fourteen months before Paddy went
missing.

The story of the kids, the Afghan–Aboriginal woman and the
rodeo hats is one a few people who knew Paddy had heard but
it was so light on detail it felt like a whisper. Although Afghan–
Aboriginal heritage might sound distinctive, it is not uncommon
in the Territory, particularly around central Australia, which had a
population of thousands of Afghani and Pakistani cameleers from
the 1860s to the 1930s.

Karen and Mark Rayner had obviously heard about the children from Paddy. So had Barry Sharpe and Richard Simpson. Another woman had told us she'd met one of Paddy's kids; she remembered well because the boy was trouble. It felt like a tangible lead, but after some digging it turned out she was thinking of another man's son.

For every person who'd sworn it was true, there was someone else who denied it vehemently. Denis Watson, Paddy's first boss at Heartbreak Hotel, was sure he didn't have children, and Frank Shadforth, who lives in Gulf Country and had known Paddy since 1983, literally laughed at the suggestion. In fact, he couldn't stop laughing. 'That bastard would say anything,' he said.

Paddy's Queensland friend Terry Taylor gave us a firm 'no' when we asked, too. But then he'd backtracked and said Paddy sometimes joked about kids and that he *might* have one here or there, the results of flings he'd had over the years.

So when Kev tells us he's spoken to the kids, it's like watching an illusion shift into focus. We've been pursuing this hopeless lead for months, perplexed that so many people had versions of the same story—six or seven children, to an Aboriginal woman—but not one of them had ever asked Paddy's partner's name, where she was or where the kids—now adults—were. If it hadn't come straight from the horse's mouth, we'd have cast it aside as another tall tale. Even the police had given up—they'd heard the stories too, but Paddy didn't appear as the father on any birth certificate, in Australia or in Ireland.

We order another round of beers and Kev offers up some details.

'A woman rang the pub asking for Paddy, and when I asked if I could tell him who was calling, she said she was his daughter,' Kev says. 'That happened a couple of times. They sounded like Aboriginal people and they seemed to be calling from a sat phone. Paddy never would talk to them. He'd tell me to tell them he wasn't there.'

Kev says Paddy wouldn't elaborate on the kids but he certainly didn't deny their existence. 'He never really seemed to know how many kids, just a lot. He didn't tell me if they were with the same woman.'

Kev takes a sip of his drink and scratches around in his mind for any other slices of information about the phantom children, but he comes up empty.

Before we leave the Humpty Doo Tavern, he hands over a number for Phil Garlick, the other man who attended the inquest. He warns us Phil is pretty deaf and a bit hopeless on the phone. And he doesn't have email and he doesn't read real well, anyway, so texting won't work. 'Also, he's a millionaire,' he adds.

Phil is usually in the Northern Territory in his caravan around this time of year, but COVID has trapped him at home in Griffith in the NSW Riverina region. We arrange a time to call, phone him up, hit record, and he hangs up on us. We call back and he doesn't know what happened. Can't work out this bloody phone, he says.

'How did you meet Paddy?' we ask.

'Pardon? WHAT?'

It's not going well.

Eventually, we get into a rhythm, and that rhythm is mostly a series of booze-filled anecdotes. Phil's Larrimah connection is through Billy Lightcan—they've been mates for sixty years and used to work for the same trucking company in Katherine. 'But they didn't put us together because we used to drink too much bloody grog,' Phil confesses. Somewhere along the line, he doesn't remember where, Phil met Paddy, and the pair bonded over booze. 'I tell you what, love, we've had some heavy nights on the grog, him and I. He was a top bloke. Whatever he said, you could put your life on it. He was honest with me.'

Paddy was there for some big moments in Phil's life. The pair of them were drinking at the Larrimah Hotel one Christmas morning when Phil received a call that one of his sisters, who'd lived most of her life in the United States, had died and left him a bit of money. Almost a million dollars. How she had so much and why she left it to him, Phil doesn't know.

Instead, he launches into an unprovoked account of what he thinks happened to Paddy, based on what he heard at the inquest. Richard knows something. Fran knows something. Owen definitely knows something. Maybe even his old friend Bill knows something. He sounds frustrated by it all and wants to know why the coroner hasn't come back and charged the lot of them.

When we'd met Phil at the inquest, he was pale, overweight, a heavy smoker. He tells us he's eighty-one now and he's had some bad news from his doctor—we feel it again, the creeping sadness for Barry, the sense that we're running out of time.

But Phil has that bush way of narrating tragedy and hilarity in the same voice, and without letting a beat pass, he hints that he's a ladies' man. It's an easy leap from there to ask if he knew if Paddy had any children.

'He always told me he had seven girls,' Phil says. 'Seven daughters from blackfellas at Brunette Downs.'

It's not much of a lead, but we take it. And then we get another. Megan Ashley, who lived near Paddy in Daly Waters, vividly remembers taking Paddy his mail one day and meeting a beautiful woman, who might have been Afghan–Aboriginal, and a girl who was about eight or nine. Paddy introduced the girl as his daughter.

We trawl through documents, searching for anything on the Aboriginal community at Brunette Downs around the time Paddy first arrived in Australia. Back then, in the mid-1960s, the so-called 'native camp' sat about 300 metres from the main station homestead, with anywhere from sixty to one hundred and twenty people living there at a time, mostly local Wambaya people. The land's traditional owners had always hunted in the grasses and lagoons around the area for their food, but when the cattle edged out the wildlife, many took up work on the station.

As 'wards', the Aboriginal population was the responsibility of a station's management, which received an allowance for 'maintenance' of the people on the property. It happened all over the Territory, just as it did to Wubalawun man Allen Maroney's grandfather. Even though communities were fed and accommodated, Aboriginal people were given no autonomy and very little control over their own lives, and living conditions were often poor and segregated from broader station life. As Allen said, there was a vast gulf between the pay rates and rights of Aboriginal and white workers.

We find years of Department of Aboriginal Affairs audits of the Brunette Downs camp—through the 1960s, 1970s and into the 1980s, the hundred or so people living in the community were housed in a dozen corrugated iron sheds with ant-bed floors and no beds. There are photos of the camp's three pit toilets: hot tin sheds with crude holes in the floor, covered in faeces and ripped-up magazine pages that had been used for toilet paper. Health department reports are scathing: Aboriginal children suffered ear and eye infections as a result of the water supply being cut off intermittently and there were widespread gastrointestinal outbreaks.

It's hard to read, and there's worse to come.

In 1976, a prisoner in New South Wales, held for an unknown crime, writes to the commissioner about his time working as a cook on Brunette Downs. He claims Aboriginal workers there are being exploited, that Aboriginal children are denied fresh fruit, vegetables and milk, and 'the toilet block is not fit for pigs to use let alone human beings'. His letter is passed on to a senate inquiry and the claims are all addressed, but by 1977 another inspection reveals the camp to be in 'an extremely filthy and disease prone condition' and the toilets 'heavily infested with flies, maggots and cockroaches'. For eighteen months, the camp's only three taps are not connected to water, which instead comes via an old trailer-mounted tank that frequently runs dry.

Then came the grog. Brunette was a dry community but illegal grog runners made it out there from time to time, and by 1978, Aboriginal people from all over the Territory were going there to live or passing through, bringing alcohol with them. 'Even children have been reported to me presenting themselves at school rotten drunk,' one official writes.

The more we read, the worse we feel—if Paddy *had* pursued a relationship with an Indigenous woman at Brunette, there's almost no way it can have been on equal terms. We find claims that when the Aboriginal stockmen were working, white stockmen would go down to the camp and have sex with women. We know this sort of thing isn't exclusive to Brunette. It happened all over the country.

We start sifting through old census records, looking for children with the last name Moriarty, or families with seven children. No one has seven daughters, and very few have more than four children living there with them. We come across a fellow who bears the last name Limerick, the Irish county Paddy was from, and wonder if he could have given a son that as a last name. But the dates don't match.

Indigenous naming traditions also mean people can go by kinship names, traditional names and nicknames. An Aboriginal man tells us that, back then, surnames didn't reflect a family lineage: people just chose something they liked and attached it to a child, or employers inflicted their surname on a baby. There's a whole generation of children who were named after racehorses and footballers and pastoral stations.

We need to talk to someone who was there at the time. Paddy wasn't a blow-in who took off after one season of droving—everyone says he lived at Brunette for many years, long enough to accumulate a handful of kids, apparently. So we start jotting down names then trying to find those people. Finally, we come across a story and a name that might clear things up.

On a mid-November day in 1976, just as the season turned from hot to impossible, Tony Willy heard the buzz of a small plane in the airspace overhead. Brunette Downs was a busy station, even back then—at 12,212 square kilometres, it was more than one and a half times the size of New York City and was running about fifty thousand head of cattle. All sorts of people dropped in: politicians, journalists, government officials, pilots mid-race. Today, skidding across the dust in a small aircraft, was the Health Department's flying doctor service.

Although such visits were routine, Tony paid attention because the nurse jumped in her car and drove the 300 metres to the Aboriginal camp, picked up two women and took them back to the clinic. It was the driving that was odd; perhaps they were seriously ill, he thought. So when he returned home to the camp, he started asking questions. And he discovered both women had been fitted with contraceptive devices, possibly against their will and certainly without truly understanding what was occurring.

Tony was furious but unsurprised. About six weeks earlier he had approached the Department of Aboriginal Affairs (DAA) with a similar complaint. In the lead-up to the 1976 Mt Isa Rodeo (which was almost 700 kilometres away but in bush terms was considered right around the corner), Tony claimed several women, both married and single, were fitted with devices—either without understanding, or under the impression it was a mandatory procedure. When some refused to go to the clinic, the nurse drove over and picked them up.

'They can't just go and do that to white ladies, can they?' Tony said to the DAA officer when he reported his concerns, resulting in a flurry of correspondence between the DAA, the Health Department and the then-management at Brunette Downs, which questioned if forced contraception was government policy.

So when Tony started investigating this second incident, it was like history repeating—his earlier outrage hadn't resulted in any real change. There was one small difference between the two events. This second time, the two women fitted with inter-uterine devices were asked to sign consent forms agreeing that they understood the purpose of the device and it had been inserted voluntarily. One of them marked the space with a simple X.

The worst of it—the worst in a series of terrible injustices—is that it was the whitefellas who were the reason for so many unplanned pregnancies on stations. Although they had no proof, the DAA area officer claims non-Aboriginal stockmen were having relationships with the Aboriginal women on the property. 'My mention of relations between Brunette Downs stockmen and Aboriginal women is purely general and based on information I have gained over the years, both in an official and private capacity and I daresay we are in no position to upgrade the social inclinations of any stockmen, white or black,' the officer writes.

In a letter raw with polite rage, Brunette management denies any such relationships, saying they are prohibited and would result in dismissal if proved. The manager at Brunette counter-claims that he has received a complaint from male members of the Aboriginal community that three white men from the Department of Aboriginal Affairs who recently repaired the pipeline to the camp had relations with three Aboriginal women and were supplying them with alcohol.

It was common knowledge that white stockmen had sex with Aboriginal women on stations across the Northern Territory, and that while there were love matches many relationships weren't on equal footing. In some places the 'promiscuity' was described as 'rife'. It was generally accepted as a by-product of isolation and gender imbalance on the stations, and even if it was against some stations' policies, management often turned a blind eye. At some stations, it's claimed such relations were encouraged as a strategy to decrease the turnover in white labour. More than likely, there's a whole generation of children born as a result.

This information isn't like the filing cabinet in Larrimah—the Pandora's drawer of things we shouldn't know. These are things that *should* be known, of course they should. But it's hard to know where to put Paddy in all of this. At any rate, his not knowing how many children he had suddenly makes sense. Any relationship between a white man and an Aboriginal woman (or vice versa) was so taboo it would have likely been kept quiet, and if there were children the father might not have been involved in their upbringing. That was not only usual for white station workers in these circumstances, but also the way Paddy had been brought up, in the absence of a father. But as to what that potential relationship was—whether it was an act of love or one of coercion—we cannot say. The relationship might have been very one-sided. It might not have been a relationship at all. We wonder: could another kind of past have caught up with Paddy?

So we start looking for Tony Willy, hoping he might remember the young Irishman fresh off the boat and employed on the station. Maybe Tony can tell us, honestly, what kind of man Paddy was, at least back then. Maybe he can tell us where to find these children.

Station workers are difficult to track. Many drift around and the Aboriginal community at Brunette Downs where Tony lived has moved. Plus, this was forty-four years ago. Would Tony even still be alive? A quick Google search finds him in the *Northern Territory News* back in 2014 as a representative of one of seven groups awarded native title rights in the Barkly Tablelands. The story is from Tennant Creek so we contact Jasmin Afianos, who used to run the *Tennant and District Times*.

'Yes, I know Tony,' she says. 'But he doesn't own a phone. I can get someone to run over there with a phone for you if you like?' she offers helpfully. 'He is pretty deaf, though. You'd be better off just going there.'

Tennant Creek is a ten-hour drive and several COVID biosecurity checkpoints away. To get permission to go we'd need to prove our visit was essential, and we're not sure talking to a bloke who may have known another bloke almost fifty years ago qualifies.

We move on to another contact on our list: someone we can see in person. Detective Senior Constable First Class Wayne Smith meets us outside the closed doors of Darwin City Police Station. 'COVID,' he explains, ushering us inside. Police front counters are more of a risk to the community open than closed now, it seems.

Detective Senior Constable Smith isn't just part of the NT Police Missing Persons Unit, he *is* the unit. It seems outrageous, the idea of one man covering all this open space, all these tucked-away corners and vanished people. But Detective Senior Constable Smith explains that although more than one thousand people go missing in the Northern Territory every year, according to national statistics, 99 per cent are located. 'Probably greater than that. Anecdotally, I'd say it's ninety-nine point eight per cent,' he says.

There are categories of missing: runaway kids, homeless people, people lost in the bush, people who've voluntarily gone missing. Detective Senior Constable Smith spends a lot of his time dealing with 'concerns for welfare' or 'location unknowns'. He's been in the role since 2016, and in that time, he's only had seven long-term missing cases cross his desk, including Paddy's. They're the hardest and worst cases, and they're especially challenging in the Territory, where distance, isolation, technology, weather, culture, feral animals and waterways with crocs—things that wouldn't necessarily arise elsewhere—play a role. Of the seven long-term missing cases he's worked, police have only been able to locate one person, who unfortunately was deceased.

It's a desperate undertaking, looking for someone who is gone, though the nature of the desperation varies. One strategy that is consistent across cases is that police treat the information coming in via missing persons hotlines, letters or emails seriously. Not all such tip-offs are concrete and a lot of them are borderline dubious. It happens a lot, Detective Senior Constable Smith says, people getting in touch saying they've had a dream or a vision or a premonition; psychics and clairvoyants and mediums who claim to have been contacted from the other side. While they don't seek out such tip-offs, police don't laugh them off.

'It would be silly to not consider all options,' he tells us. There can be real information hidden in peculiar tip-offs. 'You've got to be open to the idea someone might have a piece of information that they know first-hand but they are scared and they might have had a dream about it. Or they might not have had a dream, they might have seen this first-hand and they just want it out there. So you can't rule that out. You've got to keep an open mind.'

The idea of taking every wild theory seriously seems at odds with the sensible setting of the police station. But now we know who we have to go to next. Someone who we'd been made aware of a while ago. We hadn't exactly discounted him, but we hadn't rushed to find him: a man who says he has special abilities and claims to know exactly where Paddy is and what happened to him.

22

Some weird energy, a dead-weird PhD and an even weirder offer

If you stick around an outback pub long enough—until the bar mats are dripping with condensation and the stars outside have risen to a level of spectacle that would be breathtaking if everyone weren't too drunk to notice—you'll hear stories. Not the brash tall tales that get told in the heat of the afternoon, yarns about crocodiles guarding bank vaults or self-decapitating emus. These are quieter yarns about the kind of things that can happen on long, lonely roads.

Somewhere through the second bottle of rum, a long-haul truckie might whisper about the time he'd nodded off and woken to the shock of the truck swerving out of the way of a tree, his fillings buzzing in his mouth. 'It's a miracle I'm here to tell the story,' he'll say. And then, softer, he'll admit that it felt for a crucial second like there was someone else's hands on the wheel.

Next, a bushie might confess to seeing and smelling and hearing things late at night. He'll tell the barflies nursing warm beers after last call that there are sometimes shadows in the trees that look more like people than animals—figures you can only snare in the periphery of your vision. 'Makes your skin crawl,' he'll say. 'It's enough to make you shiver, no matter how bloody hot it is.'

There are strange things in the sky and lights on the road, someone will confess. Almost everyone who's been out here a long time will swear by it. Lights, sometimes called Min Mins, that can't be explained or followed but that are, for a second or two, bright enough to blind you.

The line between fact and fiction is precariously thin, out here. So maybe it's no surprise that as soon as you're outside the metropolitan limits, there's at least one person in every room who'll bet their drought-stricken property on the skills of a water diviner.

Apparently, a diviner can trace things and people by the energies they leave behind on the earth but we have no such powers so it takes a little while to track down Paul. When we get him on the phone, he's in Western Australia's Kalbarri, divining pressure, sickness and cancer. He has a low, gravelly voice with a lilt to it—a kind of suspenseful rhythm—and a habit of saying entirely incredible things as if they're normal. Like, for example, how he's in Kalbarri, divining pressure, sickness and cancer.

Paul's not under any illusions that he's particularly special and he speaks about the divining process much like a mechanic would speak about tuning a car.

'They say four in five males and three in five women can divine. It's no different from how dogs sniff energy. Did you know that when a rattlesnake bites you, they can follow you for up to five years? It's not the scent, it's the energy.'

The most common kind of divining (sometimes called dowsing or water witching) is for water; in Australia, plenty of bore drillers work in partnership with diviners, who will use rods, forked sticks or copper coins to work out the location, flow, depth and salinity of underground water sources. Some diviners even guarantee their work against the substantial cost of sinking a bore. But anything can be divined, Paul says. He just follows the earth's energies, tracing underground streams, geopathic stresses, different minerals.

'It's not that different to what black trackers do, or the way old blackfellas won't go into areas they call badlands. They can feel the energy coming out of the earth with their heads, making them feel sick, so they don't go there. Or old bushies will roll out a swag sometimes and you'll see them twitching and turning and they'll hop up and shift it. It's the energy coming out of the earth.'

Where others might track water or gold or minerals, Paul has learned to track two things: sickness and people.

'What you do is you leave a thread of energy on the earth when you move,' he says. 'I can follow you around, whether you're dead or alive. I've followed people who have been missing for forty or fifty years. Stuff like that.' There's another of his lilting pauses. 'It's not easy finding someone that's dead.'

Paul was at home in northern Australia when a mate from Mataranka called. 'Are you still divining?' he asked. 'Because my friend's gone missing and the police seem to be coming up empty. Maybe you can tell us where he is.'

Paul pulled out Google Maps, asked for some details. Then he tracked Paddy's energy. 'He's about seven hundred and fifty kilometres away from Larrimah, give or take.'

His mate was stunned. 'What's he doing there?'

'He's obviously been carted there,' Paul said. Paddy was no longer alive; Paul was sure of it. So he jumped in the car and drove almost a day to Larrimah. He met his mate at the pub, got out his divining rods, and followed the energy back to Paddy's house. But then, Paul's lungs stopped taking in air. He couldn't breathe, he couldn't move; there were tears running down his cheeks. This had never happened before, and he kept thinking: 'Paddy didn't die here, but this is where the beginning of it all happened.'

It took a while before the whole story emerged from the rods but, gradually, a picture formed for Paul of what he thought had happened. Two men in a small van, maybe a bus or truck, were travelling through Larrimah, towards Katherine. They stopped, maybe to use the phone in no-man's land across the road from Paddy's place, on the edge of Fran's teahouse. Then, something happened. Paul didn't know what, but he knew it was violent—Paddy wasn't killed, but he was badly hurt. It wasn't premeditated. Paddy was just in the wrong place at the wrong time.

Probably, Kellie was barking. The men must have panicked, Paul thought. So they loaded the dog and Paddy into the van and got out of town.

Paul followed the trail of energy, which was smooth until a rest stop 35 kilometres north of town. There, it seemed as if the driver pulled off the highway, hopped out, walked into a paddock in a wide, 200 metre circle and then got back to the car and drove off. It made no sense. Paul thought maybe Paddy had died in the van and the dog had started howling or barking. When the perpetrators pulled over to try to silence Kellie, maybe she had taken off into the bush. That 200-metre loop might have been them trying to find her.

Paul divined that the van eventually set off again, without Kellie. The driver avoided Mataranka, skirted around the town via a series of back roads used by grog runners and drug dealers. As they neared Katherine, they pulled into a truck bay off the Victoria Highway, put the body in the bush, and then headed into town. They stopped at the United 24-hour petrol station and refuelled, pulled up across from the McDonald's and crossed the road for a feed, walked back to the car, travelled up the main street, pulled up at the Bendigo Bank ATM, got money out, returned to the spot they'd left the body, retrieved it, then headed out on the Buchanan Highway, past Top Springs.

According to Paul's readings, it was early morning, about 4.30 am, when the van pulled up at Kalkarindji's rubbish dump. The two men left Paddy in a rubble pile and covered him up.

By the time Paul put down the divining rods he was exhausted and shaken. The level of specificity was unsettling.

'What do you want to do?' his mate asked, after Paul had traced and retraced Paddy's energy. 'I know the sergeant in town. Maybe we *should go to the cops.'*

Paul paused. It was one thing wandering around waving sticks, but another talking to cops about who murdered people. Plus, his reception with the police hadn't been warm in the past. But he did call Chalkie—Sergeant Thomas Chalk.

'What is it you do, mate?' Sergeant Chalk asked Paul.

'I follow people and stuff,' he said. 'Look, if you've got someone pegged for Paddy's disappearance, just tell me to fuck off and I'll go back home. The only reason I came over here is because my mate asked me. I believe Paddy's down in Kalkarindji.'

By the time we ask the question, Paul is expecting it: if Paddy were killed or injured, and his body moved elsewhere, what happened to Kellie?

'It's funny when you follow energy because if you die on a place on the ground you will leave a fairly big energy and a strong energy because it's the shock, it's the energy memory,' he tells us. 'But, I thought, it's going to be fairly hard following a dog through that country.'

And yet, that's exactly what he did. He went back to the rest stop where it looked like Paddy's and Kellie's energies separated and tracked the dog's initial journey to somewhere 15 kilometres off the highway. But getting there was going to be a long slog through thick wet-season grass and scrubby trees, so they enlisted the help of a friend with a chopper. From the air, Paul says, the sticks did confusing things—like the dog had gone around in circles. But then, 15 kilometres from the highway, on top of a hill on the fence line, they found a cattle trough. There were dog prints everywhere. Something had been camping in the trees, walking back and forth to the water trough.

Still, there was no sign of Kellie, or any dog—and Paul was getting the sense that she was elsewhere. About 350 kilometres away. So they headed back to the highway. There, Paul tried to retrace Kellie's path along the sandy track next to the Stuart.

'I'm walking, sticks in front of me, middle of the highway, in the footsteps of the dog going up the highway,' Paul says. 'And the dog and Paddy met. Their energies met. My sticks and my hands floated up over my head. [My mate's] going, "What the fuck's going on?" and I'm going, "That's weird." You could feel their energies meeting again, the dog and Paddy. He was dead and the dog was alive looking for him. I went back and did it again, same thing happened again. Two energies meeting. Weird as hell. One weird feeling.'

And then, after we've exhausted the subject of Paddy, Paul proceeds, in his low gravelly voice, to tell us the location of pretty much every body in Australia. He's got detailed geographic readings and theories on the Beaumont children, three-year-old William Tyrrell and a Scottish woman last seen riding the rail in Melbourne. There are others. It must be hard to live with, we venture, all this gruesome detail and useless certainty.

'It's not really.' Paul dismisses the idea. 'I'm not a soft bloke. I grew up in the bush, and you're removed from it a bit. Obviously, you'd like to catch the perpetrator and deal with them but I don't think you can do that. The trouble is, you don't get a lot of help and support from coppas, politicians, etcetera. People think you're level-headed and probably right, but they don't want to get involved—that's the response you get. Unless you dig one up and find one, you're just another wanker with bent sticks.'

There's a pause, and it feels like Paul is weighing something up. Us, maybe.

'I could take you to Larrimah,' Paul continues. It's hard to say whether it's to prove himself right, or something else. 'Nothing ever changes, it's exactly the same, the energy lines on this earth—they say every thought and action is recorded on the earth, that's the spiritual energy side of life. When you follow someone, it's in millimetres, every time. You could do it one hundred times, it's all the same. Never changes.'

Paul means something entirely different but he could also be talking about Larrimah. The town where people rotate in and out but the same things happen, over and over again.

There's another long pause.

'If you're looking for Paddy and you're serious,' he says finally, 'I could probably find him for you and show you exactly where he is and go and get a digger and dig him up. I haven't had time, but I could probably do that. I have a mate with an excavator.'

It's a suggestion Paul delivers with as much fanfare as you might display when you offer someone a lift to the shops or an extra helping of dinner. Silence hangs heavy on the phone line. It's an impossible possibility. We can't do it. We can't just wander into a dump with an excavator and start looking for a body. But, also, how can we not?

Not knowing what to do with all this, we phone Sergeant Thomas Chalk down in Mataranka, and he confirms a diviner did show up one day with a pair of rods and some ideas about where Paddy and Kellie might be. 'He's turned up and said, "I work on the spirit and that type of thing," and I'm like, "Oh, yeah, righto,"' Sergeant Chalk says. 'I'm not the sort of fella to believe in that sort of stuff. Nothing's off the table with Paddy, I understand that, but when you start talking about diviners, you sort of think to yourself: "Really? Have I gone too far with this?"'

But just like Detective Senior Constable Wayne Smith, Sergeant Chalk says he knew the stakes were so high he couldn't discount anything. He reminded himself of a saying he tries to live by: 'The human mind is like a parachute—it works best when it's open.' Plus, Paul seemed coherent and specific, so Sergeant Chalk jumped in the car with him and headed down to Larrimah.

Paul showed him the whole process and, from the get-go, the way the divining rods shifted unsettled Sergeant Chalk.

'I don't know, he can twist them with his palm or his finger or however he twists them but they do swing around and something's going on,' he says. Sergeant Chalk still isn't sure what that something is. And then there was the way Paul found water and dog prints 15 kilometres into the nothingness on the edge of the highway. That didn't prove Kellie was there—the prints might have belonged to a dingo. Still, how did Paul know there was a bore out there?

There are other things, details Sergeant Chalk says it would be hard to stumble upon without insight. The back roads Paul says the car took around Mataranka, for example.

'There's part of a road that he took me on and, I'll be honest, I'd been here four years then and I didn't even know it was there.'

So there was *something* in it. But, in the end, there's only one question Sergeant Chalk has.

'If he can tell you that Paddy's body is in the Kalkarindji rubbish dump, why hasn't he found Paddy? Because if Paddy was there and he was able to say here's a leg bone or here's a skull or here's the bones, here's where somebody's put Paddy, well, that's something real, isn't it?'

In fairness, it's not like Paul didn't try—he scouted the dump himself, looked around as much as he was comfortable. But he says the place felt eerie and he didn't know whether a murderer might be watching him, so he passed everything on to police, even offered to come back and assist with a search, on his own dime.

Police tried, too, to follow up Paul's theory. They sent a team out to do their own inspection. But they didn't excavate, and since then the dump's mounds and trenches have moved and been filled and covered, maybe even burnt to disguise the smell. A dump like that is a kaleidoscope of change.

There's another person who thinks he knows where Paddy's body might be—and his evidence is a bit more tangible. Senior Sergeant Jim Whitehead, the guy Sergeant Meacham King calls the godfather of search and rescue, is researching where murderers hide their victims. He's got decades of experience as a search and rescue coordinator and it's a job he takes very seriously—he once almost died from kidney failure re-enacting the movements of a woman who became lost at Julia Creek when her car broke down, just so he could confirm to the inquest that it was likely she had died within four hours of leaving her vehicle.

But Senior Sergeant Whitehead noticed that, although there were a lot of rules for how to go about finding living people—police call it lost person behaviour—there's very little to tell police how to find a body, especially one that has been deliberately hidden. So when homicide detectives kept coming to him with a crime scene and a suspect, asking him where they might find the body, he started collecting data. And he turned it into a PhD.

'I call it dead person behaviour,' he tells us when we get him on the line. 'Basically, it's around how we can find homicide victims who aren't at the scene of the crime. There are lots of studies where a body is found and they do a profile to find out who killed them, but I started doing it the other way around,' he explains. 'If you tell me who you think the offender is and who they killed, their relationship, the height–weight differentials, availability of transport—I can suggest more likely places to search for a body.'

In the course of his research, Senior Sergeant Whitehead has discovered that the killer's relationship to the victim is often key to finding where they put the body. 'For example, in intimate homicide—the murder of a partner or spouse—very few of those bodies are ever moved,' he explains. 'Acquaintances tend to move bodies. Employee–employer relationships, father–son relationships, son–mother relationships, things like that, bodies tend to get moved a bit.'

On average, Senior Sergeant Whitehead says, a victim is usually within 19 kilometres of where they were killed. 'I've had one at seven hundred and thirty kilometres, but that's an aberration. Most bodies are less than half a kilometre away. If there's a big height–weight difference, there's a greater chance of a body being moved a greater distance.'

There's even a pattern emerging to predict the direction a killer is likely to head in when disposing of a body. 'I've found east seems to be the best direction if you want to bury a body; the greater majority of my victims have been buried east of where they were murdered. I don't know why yet.'

So what about Paddy? we ask. Given he had a few enemies, if one of them was responsible, where is he likely to be?

Senior Sergeant Whitehead thinks for a moment. His research hasn't looked specifically at enemies. That's too subjective, he says. But an enemy would be an acquaintance of sorts—that's the category in which he classes things like drug- and bikie-related murders and other relationships with bad blood. 'I think he wouldn't be far from town, because people don't want to be caught with a body in the boot. It's incriminating.'

It's an outstanding understatement, but he is still caught up thinking about what could have happened. 'Yeah, I reckon he's fairly close,' he repeats. 'And off a track that's well used, because people are going to go somewhere that's familiar.' He stops for a beat, and comes full circle back to the more risky, more incriminating option. 'Then again, he could have been put in a road train and driven all the way to Coober Pedy and put in a mine shaft, too.'

Tracking down people who knew Paddy is like a tree that keeps growing taller and wider. Every person we call gives us more people to call. Even the people who knew nothing of Paddy pass on lists of new leads. We follow them all and the tree branches out uncontrollably.

Then someone gives us a man's name. A grader driver. Once a mercenary in Africa, they say. Worked around the Barkly region for years. He definitely would have known Paddy. This could be a lead to the kids, we think. When we phone the station the man is working on in Queensland, we're told he's out in camp, no mobile reception, but the manager can run a message to him. 'He'll have some stories for you,' she says. It sounds like a warning, rather than a recommendation. 'He's a writer too, you know. Writes bush poetry.'

When he finally phones us back, with one sentence it's as if he has taken an axe to the whole sprawling tree of contacts we've been growing.

'I've been expecting someone to call me about this,' he says.

Why is that? we ask.

'Because Paddy's not dead.'

23

A maybe-mercenary, a man in the scrub and a policeman haunted by Paddy

We nickname the man the Bush Poet. His voice on the other end of the line is deep, no-nonsense. He'd known Paddy for thirty-odd years. They weren't good mates, exactly, he says, but for decades they worked around the same areas and drank at the same watering holes. They'd bump into each other regularly and stop for a chat, maybe a beer, catch up on news. There's more background, we're sure of it, but since he's already dropped a bomb, we cut to the only question we can ask: What makes him think that a man everyone believes is dead is not?

'I don't think it. I know it,' the Bush Poet says. 'Paddy is very much alive. So is the dog. And I think I know where they are.'

We pause. The Bush Poet doesn't sound crazy or drunk.

The reason he knows, he tells us, is that Paddy told him. He says he saw Paddy, not long before he disappeared. 'Paddy was a troubled man,' the Bush Poet says. 'He didn't think he could stay around.' Something had spooked the Irishman—the Bush Poet won't say what—and Paddy had asked a lot of questions about what it would take to disappear.

We have a lot of questions, too, but the Bush Poet won't go into detail. He says he's no good on the phone but we can meet in person. We can't do that right now, so he says to call again when he's back from camp. He usually comes in on Fridays to watch the AFL, he says, just leave a message at the station again in a few weeks and he'll get back to us.

And then he hangs up, leaving us to ponder the scraps he's fed us.

He's not the first to float the theory that Paddy is alive. When Karen Rayner went back to work for a brief stint at the pub about a year after Paddy disappeared, she fielded phone calls all the time from crackpots who said they'd just had a beer with Paddy in Darwin, or had seen him at the shop in Mataranka. The police received their share of calls, too; it happens often in missing persons cases. But this feels different. And every cop we've spoken to says they take *everything* seriously.

So, a couple of weeks later, we phone the station where the Bush Poet works again. We get the same woman on the line, his boss, and use the opportunity to do a discreet reference check. She tells us the Bush Poet is older and probably should have retired by now but he loves life in the camp and has children who live nearby. 'You should definitely come and meet him,' she says. Somehow, we manage to politely question his sanity; she assures us that, apart from his memory not being as good as it used to be, the Bush Poet is very much of sound mind.

When he calls us back, the Bush Poet reveals more. He'd collided with Paddy at Heartbreak Hotel a short time before Paddy disappeared—he can't remember if it was a few weeks or a couple of months. But he's very certain that it wasn't the usual happy-go-lucky Paddy he encountered.

'He was scared,' the Bush Poet confides. 'He told me he'd seen something he shouldn't have. A drug drop. Dangerous people. He asked me what I'd ever do if I wanted to disappear. He talked about what he'd do with his dog. He was rattled.'

We prise some more details out—we're looking for specifics, things we can verify. The Bush Poet says Paddy told him he'd seen a dodgy truck parked up past the pub somewhere one night and went over to investigate. The truckie had spotted Paddy watching them unload drugs to another truck and had threatened him. Then, not long after, the same truck driver was badly beaten.

'It took a lot to worry Paddy, but he was worried all right,' the Bush Poet says. 'He said he wished he hadn't been so curious. He said, "If I ever run, make sure you look after my dog."'

The Bush Poet says it's a major transport company involved—he even gives us the company name. They hide drugs in cattle crates, he says, because police wouldn't use dogs to search a cattle truck. Larrimah is one of their transfer points, he tells us. Then he warns us to be careful. This is dangerous territory.

It sounds suspiciously like an episode of *Mystery Road*. But there is something about the way the Bush Poet talks about Paddy being alive that makes us pause. Little bits of information drip out, like that the Bush Poet has talked to his daughter about this, that he and another of Paddy's mates who has since died both believed this wholeheartedly. It doesn't sound like the rehearsed script of a prankster. And a lot of drugs do make their way up and down the Stuart Highway.

The Bush Poet's given a lot of thought to where he thinks Paddy might be. 'Go to Gulf Country,' he tells us. Gregory. Hell's Gate. Doomadgee. That's where he'll be. 'You sound smart, you'll find him. I am sure of that.'

His voice is even, clear. At one point it feels as though he's about to say more, as if maybe he has even seen Paddy since December 2017. Had a beer with him. Or maybe he adopted Kellie and Paddy's dog is now his dog. But then he goes silent.

'I'm not real good over the phone. Come see me and I can tell you more.'

We have a couple more conversations with the Bush Poet over the next few weeks. He reveals a little more about his life: that he's won some awards for his writing, that he's a bit of a loner, that he spent years living in Africa because he fell under the spell of the place. He hints that not everything that happened to him there falls into the category of happy memories and we wonder if the rumour about him being a mercenary is true.

But his story about Paddy doesn't waver. He protests when asked if he's having us on. He names the same few places to go looking and sometimes adds in some extras: Calvert. Borroloola. But always they are around Gulf Country. Of this he is certain. That is where Paddy is.

In places with war histories like Larrimah's, it's not unusual to find a leftover bomb laying around in the scrub, even now. That's what the Bush Poet feels like: a bomb in the bush. Potentially explosive or maybe nothing to worry about. Something that would be easier to ignore. A notion so unlikely it could be a practical joke.

But COVID still prevents us from taking him up on his invitation to meet and the waiting gives us time to stretch his words inside our minds. Even if what the Bush Poet is saying is true—if Paddy was frightened for his life and planning to disappear—it's a leap to assume he is still alive. Because if Paddy had seen something he shouldn't have and someone was after him, wasn't it equally likely that person had caught up with him?

And if Paddy did disappear of his own accord, how has he survived? It's been years, and Paddy hasn't accessed any of his money, or run into anyone he knows. His face has been all over the news. Surely, if he were holed up somewhere—even somewhere remote—someone would notice.

The other thing that occurs to us is that such a convincing vanishing act would take a lot of planning. If Paddy had staged the whole thing, would he have been so thorough as to leave everything: his medication, his hat, the food on his table? We've heard repeatedly from his friends that Paddy could be naive. His first boss at Heartbreak Hotel, Denis Watson, told us Paddy was a hard man to talk to, in many respects. 'He had a very limited understanding of the world,' he'd said. 'He wasn't an erudite conversationalist. He was just like a typical bushie. Nothing wrong with it, just not a lot of new information.'

Paddy's Queensland friend Terry Taylor had told a similar story. 'A lot of the stuff he used to just go along with what somebody said because he wasn't educated, you know. It was barely enough to sign his name.'

Could such a person so successfully fake their own death? Their own murder?

And yet. Possibility tugs at the edge of every rational thought we have. Sergeant Chalk's words come back to us: the mind is like a parachute, best used open. We know this is probably taking it a stride further than Sergeant Chalk might have intended, but still, we can't ignore the theory altogether. So we try to get to the base of it: not just whether it can be true but whether we trust that the Bush Poet thinks it's true. And while we're weighing it all up, another person reinforces the possibility of the Bush Poet's story with one of their own. And unlike the Bush Poet, who is a complete mystery, this story comes from someone we know—journalist and former editor Mark Wilton.

Mark saw the dog first. It appeared, walking in the long grass on a gentle, sweeping right-hand bend. It was the kind of turn that made you slow down, but only slightly—the car was travelling about 120 kilometres per hour. Mark didn't really take much notice, it was probably just a dog from one of the nearby stations, he thought. But then, as he squinted through his bug-splattered windscreen into the bright day, a figure came into view. A man walking behind the black and tan dog on the edge of the scrub alongside the verge.

'How the hell have they got out here?' he asked his partner, Fiona Wulf. She sat forward in the passenger seat and stared at the man

in the scrub. Mark took his foot off the accelerator, ready to pull over.

It was 19 December 2017, and the couple was between nowhere and nowhere, on day two of a 2500-kilometre drive from Darwin to Townsville to visit Fiona's family for Christmas. The Stuart Highway had been quiet—it was about 11 am and they hadn't passed another car since they'd fuelled up at Dunmarra, half an hour earlier.

'That's a bit weird, you reckon we should stop?' Fiona asked. The pair of them drove The Track often and were no strangers to rescue missions: drivers bogged, broken down or crashed into kangaroos. They always stopped to offer help. But this man wasn't trying to flag them down and there was no sense of panic or a problem. Fiona and Mark both stared out the window, looking for any sign of distress as they passed within 15 metres of the figures. But the man—older, tanned, wearing a hat, a polo shirt, shorts, boots and a thick moustache—barely even raised his head, which they thought was weird in itself.

Fiona twisted in her seat, keeping an eye on him, and just as Mark was about to pull over, he saw the top of a van pulled in behind some trees.

'Ah, he's right, there's a car in there. Must have just pulled over for the night and he's just letting the dog have a run,' Mark said. He hit the accelerator again.

Three days later, after they'd arrived in Townsville, Mark was scrolling through social media when he saw the story about the search for missing Larrimah man Paddy Moriarty. He skimmed the article, then there was a picture and his thumb froze.

'Who does this look like to you, Fi?' he asked, passing the phone over.

'Oh my God, that's the bloke we saw on the side of the highway.'

Mark tried to call the police straight away, but the 131 number put him through to Queensland police, so all he could do was leave a message. About a week later, sitting in a bar on The Strand in Townsville, looking through social media again, Mark saw another story about the missing man and his dog, this one mentioning a Mitsubishi

Delica police were seeking more information on. It had been spotted hanging around Larrimah around the time Paddy disappeared. Mark had only seen the top of a van as they'd passed by, but he knew a bit about cars. The vehicle he'd seen was an older style van, flat-roofed, light in colour, the kind backpackers drive. It could easily have been a Delica. He phoned the police again and, a few weeks later, when they were back in Darwin, both Fiona and Mark were interviewed separately.

'Are you one hundred per cent sure the person you saw was Paddy Moriarty?' the detective had asked.

'Well, no, I'm not going to say that,' Mark replied. 'I'm one hundred per cent certain I saw a person who looked an awful lot like him.'

'Well, what per cent are you sure it was him?'

'I'm ninety-five to one hundred per cent sure, it's in that zone,' he told them. 'I'm very confident that's who it was.'

The story sinks in and we start with questions we cannot answer. If the man Mark and Fiona saw was Paddy, who did the vehicle belong to? It wasn't Paddy's because his car was at his place. And what was he doing out there? If he had been fleeing trouble, faking his own death and starting a new life, like the Bush Poet suggested, he'd surely have gone further than 180 kilometres from home by day three? If he were deliberately disappearing, would he stop to walk his dog out in the open on the side of the highway? And was the dog Mark saw Kellie? Mark described a black and tan dog, but Kellie was red or brown, with tan markings—although it's not a distinction that would be easy to make driving past at speed. What about Paddy's medication and his hat? Would he leave them behind, willingly? Or was there someone else there with him, hiding in the scrub out of the view of passing cars? Someone who'd forced Paddy to leave.

Despite our questions and doubts, we concede it's plausible Paddy might turn up 180 kilometres south of Larrimah, three days after he was last seen at the pub. He had plenty of mates around those parts. He knew the area well. There might not be a clear reason for him to *be* there, but there was also no reason for him *not* to be there.

'I've thought about it a lot since,' Mark tells us. 'The biggest reason I'm annoyed that we didn't stop is he might not have been missing at all from the sixteenth, but something could have happened to him on the nineteenth. He could have just decided, "I'm going to just take off for a day or two," and then something's happened since then. For all I know, he's died in a ditch somewhere the next day. That's the bit that gnaws at me when I think about it.'

Although police took Mark and Fiona's story seriously, the couple say they don't think enough was done to confirm the person they saw wasn't Paddy. There could have been a call-out in the media, for example, trying to find the man and dog they'd seen while people's memories were fresh. 'If it wasn't him, just find out who the bloody hell it was I saw. I don't need to be right,' says Mark.

Mark was a journalist for decades and his instincts tell him that the police inaction on this front might be a clue. 'They must have information that says we know that he died in Larrimah and "we've got a fair idea of who did it",' he says.

Still, both Mark and Fiona are sure of what they saw.

'I'll go to my grave convinced that the man we saw was Paddy.'

By now, the only thing we can do is go back to police. Most of the NT police force was diverted to COVID duties back in March: monitoring borders, enforcing social distancing. Detective Sergeant Matt Allen tells us he's finally been released from instructing people drinking beer in pubs to sit down rather than stand. 'It was one of the hardest jobs I've ever had in my life,' he says when we phone to make a time to interview him. 'Imagine trying to do that.'

We meet him at NT police headquarters in Darwin, located across the road from Crocodylus Park, a working crocodile farm, research centre and zoo. When the traffic dies down, you can hear the low roar of the lions from outside his office.

Is this where you take the bad people? we ask when he leads us into a small interview room with an empty desk and drab, grey walls.

'No, that's next door. Want to see?' He shows us into a similar-sized drab grey room with padded walls.

It's been two and a half years since Detective Sergeant Allen received that phone call about a suspicious disappearance in Larrimah. In that time, the case management file, which logs everything from phone calls from the public to police notes, has accumulated well over one thousand five hundred entries. He's recently begun a detailed review of the case, and although he works on other things, Paddy Moriarty takes up most of his time.

'We don't put matters like this on the shelf, it's constantly going to be looked at,' he says. 'The only thing that will probably change is the operational tempo. Some days you get some information, some days you're reviewing old stuff, but we're not going to stop working on a job like this.'

Detective Sergeant Allen volunteered to do the case review, but it's also connected to his obligations to report back to the coroner: once his body of work is complete, it's up to the coroner to conclude the inquest. Having spent the past few weeks re-reading statements, double-checking alibis and considering out-of-town possibilities, he's still convinced Paddy and Kellie met with foul play.

'Yes, he had heart issues and, yes, he walks the dog, but for him to go walking and something to happen to the dog around the same location, that's a possibility but unlikely,' he says. 'I was up in that chopper and saw for myself how easy it is to see wallabies jumping around. If someone was lying on top of the ground, we're pretty confident we'd have seen them, or their clothes.'

We ask about pigs, if it would have been possible, with the delay in reporting, for the local wildlife to remove all the evidence of a body. Detective Sergeant Allen says he's been briefed on body decomposition experiments interstate but the results are almost useless given the difference in the environment, weather and wildlife in the north. He's even considered leaving a pig's body out in the elements near Larrimah, to get a clearer sense of the decomposition process in that environment, but he's not sure it would progress the case.

We ask about the possibility that Paddy has children; Detective Sergeant Allen is as curious as we are. It would help police, he says, to have family invested in the case. It would keep pushing police further. And there's always an outside chance that an estranged child is relevant, the possibility that someone slighted by Paddy might want to hurt him. But they've followed up a couple of leads and checked records: they don't have anything to go on.

So we put other rumours we've heard to him: we'd had a tip-off that a grader driver somewhere was telling people he'd been paid to kill Paddy, that it was a claim that stood out because the same guy also came into some money around the same time and said he'd had a big Keno win. Detective Sergeant Allen knows what we're talking about; he investigated it, and there's no evidence to suggest that's the case.

We've also heard whispers that a fence was cut on a station not far from Larrimah. Of course, that's something that happens from time to time, but the timing—if it's true—is chilling. We were told a fence was found damaged soon after Paddy went missing. And then it was found cut again the morning after Paddy's memorial. Is it possible someone disposed of a body, we ask, then came back to clear up the evidence on the one night they could guarantee all Paddy's mates would be busy at the pub? Detective Sergeant Allen nods. Someone did cut the fence but there's no evidence the damage is relevant.

We ask about the Larrimah drug dealer who went to jail years ago—the guy Barry told us thought Paddy had dobbed him in. He'd got caught in 2013 and we'd found the judge's statement, which said a 58-year-old man had built a grow room in a house in Larrimah. Police found forty-six plants and a pretty extensive hydroponic set-up. The man's three-and-a-half-year sentence was suspended; he only spent thirty-six days in prison. Detective Sergeant Allen says he investigated that lead too, but found no connection to Paddy's disappearance.

We ask about the possibility of Paddy being tangled up in the huge drug bust years ago at Hidden Valley Station. And whether there was anything in Mark Wilton and Fiona Wulf's sighting of a man they believe was Paddy. Detective Sergeant Allen says there's no evidence to support either of these scenarios.

While police avenues of inquiry continue to pile up, the answers do not, and we can tell that's weighing on Detective Sergeant Allen. He tells us he's never been so consumed by a case but he's also never had so many unique obstacles.

'The priority is still to find Paddy and Kellie and, unfortunately, I can sit here and tell you I don't know where they are. We look into every piece of information because we just don't know.'

It feels like an opening, a chance to ask if police have received any tip-offs that Paddy might be alive without sounding too foolish. 'We do get calls about Paddy being alive,' Detective Sergeant Allen confirms. 'Not too many calls. And they're unsubstantiated. He's a unique-looking character, with a cowboy hat, moustache, old. Even my colleagues, when they see someone walking around similar to Paddy, they'll take a photo and text it to me. But it's not him.'

We venture: hypothetically would it be *possible* to actively disappear? Could someone hide away for this long? Lie to their friends? Survive without money?

'No, that would be really bizarre and unlikely. It takes a lot to change your identity and as a seventy-year-old male who's got heart issues, with Medicare and health treatment, the car being at the house, his money, his bank cards . . . you'd have to be pretty sophisticated and have the motivation to pack up and leave without people that are so central to you. I find it really unlikely.' It's a compelling set of reasons, but he goes on. 'And Paddy's got his house, he's got his castle, his little ranch, his quad bike. Why would you go?'

It's all completely logical, arguments we've already worn thin ourselves. Even if he was scared—terrified for his life—the logistics of disappearing so thoroughly would be all but impossible to pull off. There is simply no way Paddy's still alive, in hiding. But then, Detective Sergeant Allen catches a bout of our 'what ifs'.

'Nonetheless, anything's possible,' he says.

Almost three years after the disappearance.

24

A lost cemetery, cane toad curry and a cockatoo with chlamydia

The trip we have planned is not an itinerary a travel agent would recommend: a loose 4000-kilometre scramble through some of the outback's least-popular towns. It's not that there aren't things to see and do—gorges, rock formations, national parks and waterholes. It's just that we won't have time for sight-seeing. We'll head south to Larrimah, via Batchelor, then continue on the Stuart Highway through Daly Waters and Elliott, as far as Tennant Creek. From there, the plan gets murky: east across the border into Queensland to find the Bush Poet, who still hasn't entirely committed to meeting us, then up through the Gulf of Carpentaria, wherever the Bush Poet directs us, before coming back to the Territory via Paddy's old haunts: Borroloola, Heartbreak Hotel and Brunette Downs.

A week before we leave, we see a news report that sounds more like an outback horror movie. An Aboriginal family—including two young children—were returning from a fishing trip near Borroloola when they stopped at Heartbreak Hotel, grabbed some food and kept going. They weren't far up the road when a four-wheel drive began tailgating them, flashing its high beams and speeding. Then, someone pointed a shotgun at them and fired.

The family escaped unharmed but there's fury at the perception of police inaction, resulting in a protest at the Borroloola Police Station. One local man tells *SBS News*: 'It's a long time since something like this has happened in Borroloola. We have a history of policemen chasing and shooting our people during the massacre times. There's trauma already inside us from that kind of stuff, and now it just got relit.' Eventually, two of the three men in the four-wheel drive are charged.

As these communities seethe with generational anger, we know it's a bad time to be heading into Gulf Country. But we stock the ute with water, two-minute noodles, jerry cans of fuel and short-bread we've baked as a gift to compensate for rolling into Larrimah again to hassle people with a fresh batch of questions. We also have several hundred passengers on board: mealworms Karen has requested we bring down. She's doing fly-in, fly-out work now, so she's given up breeding mealworms and needs some to feed the squirrel gliders she's adopted from the pub. It's a task we aren't sure we—or the elements—are equipped for. Even though we let the creatures have the best seat in the car—the shady side, with the air-conditioning pointed right at them—we're still worried we might have a mealworm mass murder on our hands.

We hit the road with our thorny to-do list: we need to find three Aboriginal men called Tony, Paddy's potentially illegitimate (or even non-existent) children, a murderer, a missing man and—first up—a probably dead dog.

By now, the dressed-up termite mounds on the way to Larrimah are familiar. Even at 130 kilometres per hour we recognise them: our old friends Soggy Jocks and anthill Santa and another mound wearing a hard hat. Every time we hurtle past, their outfits have grown more threadbare; today, they look particularly ragged. One day, we think, they will be naked again.

The Stuart Highway seems to bend in the early-morning heat. Today it takes us to Batchelor, 100 kilometres south of Darwin and the gateway to Litchfield National Park: a weekend playground for tourists and Darwinites who enjoy drinking tinnies under waterfalls and taking life-threatening leaps from rock ledges, usually in that order.

Batchelor's lesser-known claim to fame is as the birthplace of the world's biggest pumpkin. The gourd, produced in 1912, was so big it took four men to roll it. But before they could send it on a victory tour of Australian cities, the pumpkin went missing. Detectives and Aboriginal trackers went after it and a reward was offered for its safe return. Eventually, a tip-off led to the wreckage of the rotting pumpkin in the bush; it was too late to save even the seeds.

Of course, we are not here to solve a century-old pumpkin-crime. We are here to find Kellie. But in hindsight, perhaps we should have asked the diviner about the pumpkin, too.

We turn off the Stuart and drive past a butterfly farm, an exotic tree plantation and a newly built solar farm and turn into a pretty hamlet. We're armed with a printout from Google Maps, which has a red circle around a house on the corner of two unnamed roads. Paul, the diviner, emailed it to us, with the explanation that last time he divined Kellie, the young kelpie-cross was living here, probably with a couple: a teacher and a tradie. Likely, they'd picked up Kellie on the Stuart Highway, assuming she was a stray, and adopted her.

Paul had tried to fact-check his own claim, twice. The first time he'd gone to Batchelor in search of Kellie, there was no dog at the house, but he'd run into a local cop who said he owned the only kelpies in town. When pushed, the cop did remember seeing a woman with a kelpie down at the supermarket one night. He'd assumed she was a traveller but maybe she was local.

A while later, Paul returned to Batchelor with his wife in tow, and pulled up outside the house again. This time there was a dog there. Two, actually. An old brown kelpie lying under a car in the driveway and a young kelpie rolling around in the grass in the backyard.

'Do you think that's really weird that I could divine from home to Batchelor for a kelpie and there's none in town except for one, according to police, and it happens to be in the backyard I divined, rolling around in long grass?' he asked his wife. 'Do you think that's bizarre?'

She agreed—it was odd. But the gate was locked and nobody was home. There was no way to talk to the owners, and even if there was, what would he have said?

As we pull up in front of that house, we face a similar dilemma. We have a speech planned, but it seems ridiculous now that we might have to use it. 'Excuse me,' we will say. 'We're writers and we've come here on the advice of a diviner who thinks you might have adopted a stray dog that, until now, has been presumed dead but who might be the key to solving a very suspicious missing persons case. Could we please come inside?'

As it turns out, we have no occasion to use the speech. The house is dark and the gate is padlocked. A meaty bull Arab–type dog growls as we approach. We call out, but there's no reply, only baring of teeth from the dog that is not Kellie.

There is no one in the shady street to ask. From the roadside we look around the neighbours' yard, just in case Paul was off by a few metres. But there's no kelpie. We'd stay if we could, stake out the house until its owners returned. But it's already starting to get warm, we're scared the mealworms are looking sluggish and we need to be in Larrimah before 10 am to attend a funeral.

'Here's a good line for your book. A whole bunch of people can't even find a cemetery that's fucking full of bodies.'

Des Barritt is standing at our car window, hands on lanky hips, head shaded by an enormous cowboy hat, looking out into the bush.

'This fucking happened last time I was out here,' he mutters, casually pushing over a waist-high termite mound.

The five-car procession has already turned off the dirt track into the scrub twice. Judy MacFarlane is leading the way. She is one of the graveyard's only regular visitors: her parents and grandfather are buried here on what used to be her family's property, known as Larrimah Station and later Western Creek Station. Indigenous people called it Brolga Valley. She knows the area intimately, but even she can't recognise the turn-off into the trees.

'Is it before the bend or after the bend?' Judy asks no one in particular. Karen Rayner disappears into the scrub on foot.

The morning sun glints off the black tombstone in Des's trailer. It's peaceful here, but unforgivingly dry. If an artist were painting it, they'd only need three colours: rusted-red-earth, ready-to-give-up-green, and already-damned-tan. Karen returns and points in one direction. Everyone gets back into their cars and we follow the procession, the fine red sand jolting our steering wheel as the tyres make a desperate snatch for firmer ground. The cavalcade is slow, not because of the sombre circumstances, but for risk of staking a tyre.

The bush round here is full of elusive graveyards. People have told us about a so-called 'Negro Cemetery', a place where several American soldiers stationed in Birdum during the war were buried after being executed, apparently as punishment for a sexual assault. We'd also found evidence of a Larrimah War Cemetery in Canberra's National Archives but no one knows where it is. Barry once took us to another bush cemetery: a single grave surrounded by relentless scrub. And a truckie found a separate burial ground—a wooden sign and a few wooden pegs as grave markers, about five of them, near Birdum. But the bush changed or the white ants got it or a fire swept through. The next time he was back, there was nothing.

Several wrong turns later, a shout comes from up ahead. 'Found it!'

It's been eight months since Barry died in Katherine Hospital, a sleeping bag of bones curled on a slim hospital bed in the palliative care ward. Grey skin against white sheets, his withered body drowning in green hospital-issue pyjamas. His friends came out here to scatter his ashes a while ago and Judy says by the time she was done confetti-ing her mate around the scrub, there was more of Barry on her than anywhere else. Now the headstone is ready, they've come back for another farewell.

The five little graves look lonely in the big landscape, a cluster of souls clinging to the outback. As well as Judy's relatives, the bush cemetery houses John Pearson, a worker on the Overland Telegraph who died in 1899, and the writer Andrew McMillan, who died in 2012.

Des pulls a rectangular iron fence out of his trailer designed to mark Barry's plot. He confesses it's not that flash because he welded it the other night after an annoying meeting and ten beers. He does some quick measurements, then gets out his angle grinder and starts lopping off the iron limbs to ensure they're the right height. Mark Rayner and another bloke start digging holes and mixing cement while the rest of us stand around swatting at flies and positioning ourselves in shifting patches of shade.

Memorial services are usually nostalgic affairs, reflecting on how short life is and how we should make the most of it. Here, no such graces are observed. Lenny rests his battered frame on the fence around Andrew's tombstone. As Larrimah's oldest resident, we might all be guilty of wondering if Lenny will be the next to go but it is Judy who strides over and leans on the cattle guard around her parents' grave.

'Now, Lenny, do you have a will? You're getting on and you really need to get one.'

As well as being Barry's friend, Judy is the mayor of Roper Gulf, the area that takes in Mataranka and outlying communities like Larrimah. It's a title she doesn't like to throw around—it makes her sound like a wanker, she says—but her responsibilities extend to deceased estates.

'We've had a few people in town go recently with no will,' she says. 'Total nightmare.'

Lenny takes his impending death well, saying he does need to sort something out. He had a fall recently and the evidence is fresh. One eye is blackened and his head is held together by a butterfly clip. His limp has become a hobble; he's still on the waiting list for a knee. Standing in the direct sun, he looks fragile. Someone tries to coax him into having a drink of water.

'Water is for fish and under bridges,' he quips. 'Never drink the stuff.' But eventually he takes a few sips. 'This is the most water I've had in thirty years!'

'Oh shit, what have I done?' Des is looking over the upturned fence he's been working on. Its legs are in the air, all different lengths.

'Fuck me, I think you've cut that one twice.'

'And you haven't cut that one at all.'

'It's as crooked as a dog's leg.'

'Fuck.' Des laughs. He is good-natured but there is more hot-sun waiting as he fixes the mistake.

While they work on the fence, we wander 50 metres away to nearby Pigeon Hole, a now dried-up billabong. Karen tells us it's quite pretty in the wet, you can swim and fish. It was one of the places police searched for Paddy, and it serves as a reminder of what's missing in this graveyard. The injustice that Paddy still hasn't got a plot here goes unsaid but not unthought.

We return to the cemetery just as the tombstone is finally in place. Everyone falls, unasked, into a moment of silence.

'Barry used to love it out here,' Karen says, finally.

'Yeah, he used to come here to poach birds,' adds Lenny. 'I used to come here to skinny-dip.'

This is the closest to any kind of reflection on Barry's life the ceremony reaches. But there's a nest in the tree opposite and almost everyone points out, at one time or another, how much Barry would like the view of the birds and a resting place surrounded by silence and their calls. An eternal dawn service. There might not be a lot of sentimentality but the old man has been deeply seen, by his close friends, and maybe even understood.

This is our first visit to Larrimah in nine months and while there's obvious evidence of the pandemic just about everywhere else, Larrimah has been, in some ways, immune. Social distancing has never really been a problem here. Lenny has, however, been tested three times and Cookie was accused of breaking the self-isolation rules on his way back from a trip to Tassie to see his girlfriend; he's also had a surgery put off. But otherwise, nothing much has changed. Except the pub.

It's like the place is haunted by Barry's absence. The wildlife park is padlocked and even more of the cages are empty. The squirrel gliders have been evicted. Ray, the blind croc, is moving in with Karen. Shirley the cockatoo's feathers have fallen out, exposing her scrawny bird-body. She's recently been diagnosed with chlamydia. Des has had no luck with his crocodile adoption; Sneaky Sam is still out the back.

An eerie silence hangs over the pub but the group from the memorial fill it with beer and pies and chatter. They've had more time to adjust to the changes in town than us, we suppose.

It's hard to say what the afternoon is—a wake of sorts, though there's as little ceremony as there was in the bush. Des tells a story about one night on the piss when he and some mates thought it'd be a good idea to cook a few cane toads legs into a curry. 'Really bitter, inedible,' he says, as if that came as a surprise. 'But next morning I got up and one of those half-legless toads was crawling across the kitchen bench. Fucking unkillable.'

Bill turns up—he doesn't say much, though, and he's even thinner this time, his moustache overshadowing his gaunt face.

Again, not everyone is here: Karl and Bobbie aren't attending the memorial, for obvious reasons, and neither is Cookie. Fran's still down south receiving medical treatment for breast cancer, and she asked Owen to leave before she left town.

We wander over to buy drinks; there's a new face behind the bar and it takes us a moment to realise it's actually Brent, Fran's grandson. We've been messaging with him for over a year.

'It's so good to finally meet you,' he says. We feel the same.

Larrimah has had its share of battlers. For example, in World War II, a handsome young man named Clem was appointed as Larrimah's military hospital cook, despite hating cooking, having less than a week of training and being equipped with no kitchen and almost no ingredients. Still, he claimed a patch of dirt under a tree, baked bread in termite mound ovens and set about supplementing the scant army supplies with snake (not good), bush turkey (not great), wallaby (good in stew) and tinned bully beef (excellent in pies, if you lifted the lid and scraped out the flies). But even Clem's efforts pale in comparison to Brent Cilia's, who rocked up in Larrimah as a 24-year-old gay bloke who'd never made a pie, trying to run a Devonshire teahouse in a place where his nan had become a national media story.

But, Brent tackled the teahouse PR problem head on. He erected a 'Get Sconed At Fran's' sign, learned to bake and set about winning the town over. People say he's a nice kid.

We're keen to chat but he's clearly busy—the wake might be informal, but there are plenty of people ordering beers. We'll be back through town at the end of our trip, so we make a plan to catch up with him then.

Judy appears beside us at the bar to order another round.

'Do you get a local discount, Judy?' Brent asks.

'Well, I should, I'm the fucking mayor,' she replies, then turns to us and winks. 'That's the only time you can use the mayor thing.'

As everyone gets ready to leave the pub, it feels like a full stop on an era. It's so unceremonious an ending to it all, you could easily miss the moment. Barry is gone, and this is definitely someone else's pub now.

Since he took over, Steve Baldwin has cleared away a lot of the mess, and although he's kept the memorabilia, it looks less cobwebby. He's even moved an old piano he found under a pile of junk out back into the bar. He's turned down the volume on the TV, has music playing over a sound system and replaced Barry's cutlery-divider till with a computer and scanner. Across the road, by the museum, there's a dead tree he's painted bright pink and there are rumours he's planning to decorate other trees in a range of themes, from World War II history to sports team colours. Sometimes, he has a singer in to entertain the punters. The pub's shop now has a decent offering of tinned goods and Steve has expanded the merchandise range to include hand-painted key hooks featuring Pink Panthers.

Things are being slowly spruced up. Modernised. Maybe even gentrified.

25

More buffalo shooting, some heat-stroked mealworms and all the ways to die in the bush

We meet Steve in the courtyard under the big African mahogany as light begins to drain from the sky. The air is thick with mosquitoes. Lazy ones. They rarely bite but they buzz in our ears and land on our faces.

It's taken almost two years to pin Steve down for an interview and, to date, we only know three things about him:

1. He owns a caravan park in Tennant Creek.

2. His brother was a politician.

3. His wife, Jan, is not that impressed he bought the Larrimah Hotel.

'She won't have anything to do with it,' Steve says in a tone that sympathises with her stance. 'She's only been here once, got out of the car, went for a walk around, and that was it.'

Steve is Territory born and bred. His old man had a hunger for the frontier, working as a shepherd, wool classer, croc shooter and crane operator but it was buffalo that made his money: shooting them, slaughtering them where they lay, then selling their hides, and later their meat.

'We lived off a rifle for thirty years,' Steve says. 'And we caught barramundi until it was made illegal for inland rivers. Then we poached for another ten years.'

While his dad was out bush, the rest of Steve's family lived in Darwin and operated a little shop selling buff meat for pet food and barra under the table. Then they bought land just outside Kakadu National Park, where they shot a thousand buffalo a year for eighteen years. Eventually, they were selling pet food all over the country. The Baldwins also owned the Territory's first croc farm and built the iconic Bark Hut, a roadhouse constructed from bush timber from seven hundred local trees.

Steve studied accounting and there's something clean-cut about him that tallies with industry stereotypes: his grey hair and beard are short and neat, and he wears transition lenses to beat back the sun. He has an easy, calculated way of assessing a situation, looking around and seeing what needs to be done. But for every stereotype he confirms, he defies dozens of others. He's a man who is comfortable with the lawlessness of the outback and who is skilled at bringing order to it. He's spent his whole life making things work in this nefarious landscape.

'Dad was always on the land and hungry for opportunity,' Steve says, and it obviously rubbed off on him. First, he bought some land from his father and built the Mary River Wilderness Retreat, then he worked his way around the Territory, buffalo shooting, running a tax return business in Arnhem Land, and taking on CEO positions and consulting for Aboriginal organisations across the north of Australia. He even did a fifteen-month stint in Afghanistan in the Ministry of Finance, where part of the job description was making sure he wasn't kidnapped.

Eventually, Steve found himself back in Darwin and at a loose end for about half a day until he spotted an ad in the paper for a block of ten flats for sale in Tennant Creek. He thought there must be a typo in the rent the ad said they would receive, so he phoned the agent, who assured him it was no mistake. The next day he flew to Alice, drove to Tennant, bought the block of units, and soon after a caravan park, and later a cafe.

'Tennant's a great place to invest,' Steve tells us, despite, or perhaps because of, the town's social issues. Barely a day goes by without a break-in but the number of public servants—health, education and social workers, mostly, there to combat the town's social problems—creates a two-tiered housing market that means strong return on investment.

While he was making a killing, Steve met his third wife, Jan, who was running an aviation fuel business. Much to her dismay, that's what started the Larrimah arm of their empire. Steve bought Larrimah's old Green Park in 2012 with the intention of restoring it as a fuel station. It was in a good position to benefit from fracking the Beetaloo Basin, but to say it needed some serious investment is an understatement. The old caravan park was a hellscape. It had been abandoned since the fire in 2008 and was a chaotic mess of asbestos sheets and overgrown scrub, with a ruined swimming pool and croc pens buried under the rubble. The only standing structure was an ablution block, which had done nothing but house snakes for the past decade.

Steve got to work. But four years later the NT government announced a moratorium on fracking of onshore unconventional reservoirs. His upgrades came to a halt and the hostile wilderness took over again until 2018, when the moratorium was lifted. Rather than cut his losses on an investment that had gone nowhere in six years, Steve turned around and bought the Larrimah Hotel. He couldn't even say he didn't know what he was in for—he'd stayed there quite a bit over the years of work at Green Park and was familiar with the difficulties Larrimah presented.

The town is not an attractive workplace and Steve has been through more managers than anyone can count, which means he's back and forth between Tennant Creek and Larrimah a lot more than he thought he would be.

He's done his best to sidestep the town in-fighting—everyone is welcome back at the pub now—but there are other challenges. Everyone wants a say in what will become of the town, Steve says, but no one's that keen to apply for grants or take ownership of initiatives. He's working on setting up another progress association. But everyone's getting on in age, the town's residents are plagued with health issues, and no one, except maybe Brent, has the same vested interest in the town's success because they don't have a business relying on tourists.

Nevertheless, Steve's confident he can get the place in shape. He doesn't even see Paddy's disappearance as a problem for business, however much it's a personal tragedy. 'If anything, it's marketing, isn't it?' he says. 'People do stop in because of it.'

'Do you want to see some of the plans?' Steve asks, and for the first time his face brightens with something other than business nous. Maybe Larrimah has crept under his skin a little, too.

He drags us back to a room behind the bar, where Barry used to let sort-of-pet wallabies take a snooze on his couch. We barely recognise it. 'The place was a mess. For the first six months we just cleaned and threw stuff away and sorted it,' Steve says. 'There was crap everywhere.'

He cracks open a laptop and shows us a mock-up of what the bar could look like if he's able to breathe new life into the Pink Panther. He's taught himself to use some kind of architectural design program so he can visualise it clearly. He'd like to knock out some walls and wrap a bar all the way around the side of the pub, maybe add a World War II–themed dining area. There could be murals, statues, themed menus. He'd grudgingly keep the Pink Panther theme.

'The pink, as much as I hate it, does work,' he says. 'And the panther thing. The souvenirs you sell are ridiculous.' As well as the hand-painted Pink Panther key hooks, there are new shirts, postcards, stubby holders, magnets, hats and hatpins.

But that's just the beginning. Steve knows he's competing with places like Daly Waters, the iconic pub down the road we're planning to visit tomorrow. If he wants to really put Larrimah on the map, he needs to think bigger than hatpins.

With alarming composure, Steve starts rattling off the world's largest outback to-do list. He's planning to get the fuel in at Green Park before the next wet season and upgrade the pub's hotel rooms. He's already extended the wi-fi coverage but the next step is getting Optus to provide mobile phone reception. They should be in town this week or next, he says, but then again, they were supposed to be here last week, too.

After that, he's applying for funds to put in a dump point over at Green Park, as that way he can offer free camping for tourists who'll likely repay the favour by eating at the pub.

But, really, a town like Larrimah needs an attraction, something that will keep people occupied longer than taking a photo with an oversized stubby. He talks about creating a sound and light show, like the ones in Uluru, or reviving the lost histories of Birdum and Gorrie. The bush is full of memorabilia, but it's all unrecognisable hunks of metal rusting in the elements, so he's been talking to an app designer about using augmented reality to bring the wartime civilisation to life, superimposed over the wreckage. Imagine it, he tells us. You could go out there and see Gorrie's now-disappeared aeroplanes and hangars and church and pub, all brought to life.

But we can't imagine it. It's not like we don't want to; it's just such a lot to resurrect from the dust.

The next morning, before we leave, we stop in at Karen and Mark's to drop off the mealworms. We hand them over with a sense of trepidation.

'They look pretty good,' Karen says, peering inside. 'Thanks!'

She takes us outside to see the enclosure she's building for Ray, the blind crocodile from the pub. 'So where are you heading, exactly?' Karen is standing in the shade of the shed's tin roof, but the glare still catches her full-force and it's impossible to make out her expression. We pause. It doesn't seem fair to tell one of Paddy's closest friends that a man we're calling the Bush Poet reckons the missing man is alive in Gulf Country somewhere. Not for the first time, it occurs to us that if somehow, against the odds, we did find Paddy alive we'd have to make some pretty difficult decisions. Is a man who does not want to be found entitled to his privacy, even if it's at the expense of the pain of the people who love him? Even if police have poured years into trying to find his killer?

We shuffle in the dust, which seeps between the cracks of our toes and brands our feet with an almost permanent orange thong-mark.

False hope can be poisonous, so we leave out the Bush Poet and tell Karen the rest. We're stepping back through all the eras of Paddy's life, we say: Daly Waters, Brunette Downs, Heartbreak Hotel. We're stopping in Tennant Creek, too, hoping we might even find his kids.

'That would be good, wouldn't it?' Karen says. 'Make sure you tell us all about it when you're back. And drive safe. Do you have plenty of water?'

On the way out of town we triple-check that we do, in fact, have plenty of water. We've strapped a tank of the stuff into the tray of the ute, along with a jerry can and an emergency position indicating radio beacon to send up a satellite SOS if we get lost or stuck.

After all our research, we're pretty much experts in terrifying ways to die in the bush. It's only an hour to Daly Waters, but we'll pass the unmarked sites of any number of historical misfortunes. In 1955, an English migrant on a bicycle perished, not far south of Larrimah. It took nineteen days for police and Aboriginal trackers to find his body under a tree. Police estimated he'd died three days and 15 kilometres into his journey, after becoming deranged and abandoning his bike, food and water. He is still buried out here, somewhere in this desolate countryside, under the tree with insufficient shade where he'd spent his final moments.

There are hundreds of these stories. Adventurers and drunks and bushies—the dead heart seems to claim them almost indiscriminately. It is a brutal thing, we now know, to die of thirst. In her book *The Great Australian Loneliness*, first published in 1937, writer Ernestine Hill describes how easily dehydration can happen. 'Too easy. A dozen do it every year at the end of the dry. Most of them are old hands, and heaven knows why, except that they follow the mirage.' Hill spent months trawling through old police diaries, in the process coming up with a description of death by exposure that is equal parts harrowing and exquisite; we think about it every time we hit the road.

So we check the water one last time and hit the remorseless road. First stop: Daly Waters, where Paddy lived before he moved to Larrimah. And where he was involved in another feud, with another neighbour.

26

A pub full of bras, a Super Mega Fugly stunt and a feed of beef and barra

If the Larrimah Hotel is deep in the trenches of a hangover, the Daly Waters Pub is its tenacious mate who drank its way through the boozy badlands of 3 am and is still partying hard well into the next day.

When we pull into the town's single, tiny street, it's a fiasco of caravans looking for a place to turn around, four-wheel drives lining up for fuel, and tourists lurching into the traffic, trying to get a photo that fits in all the building's rustic outbackness. It's easy to see why the place is so popular, especially if you look at the town in the context of its neighbours. There are plenty of travellers willing to hit the road in search of some Australian ideal, but the Northern Territory's outback is sometimes a little too outbacky. The next stops south of Daly Waters, places like Elliott and Tennant Creek, have plenty of red dirt and scenic loneliness, but they're also besieged with issues of racism, poverty, disadvantage and crime, the less-photogenic realities of outback living. Daly Waters, on the other hand, exists in a bubble. Apart from station workers, the place is entirely tourists; mostly grey nomads called Carol and Bruce.

We park in front of Paddy's old place. It's an elevated home that looks abandoned. But we can imagine Paddy there, on the verandah, looking over the road to the famous pub. Perhaps that's what drew him here in the first place: the world's easiest commute home from a night out drinking. Except the proximity and the trouble that came with it was also the thing that drove him away.

Barry Sharpe and Billy Lightcan had told us about Paddy's troubles with his neighbours in Daly Waters. He'd had a problem with the woman who owned the pub, they'd said. Used to scream abuse at her, just like he did to Fran. And she used to give it back, too.

After eighteen years behind the bar, Robyne Webster and Lindsay Carmichael sold the Daly Waters Hotel a few years ago, so before we left Darwin, we'd tracked them down in New South Wales where they were 'waiting for coronavirus to bugger off'. They were both there, on the line, but Lindsay did most of the talking. Between what he said and what we've heard from Paddy's mate Terry Taylor, who stayed with him here for a while, and Megan Ashley, who lived two doors up, a picture starts to emerge.

Lindsay and Robyne were living the dream. It was 1999 and Lindsay had bought a share of the Daly Waters Hotel with his mate Bruce; at first, Robyne was back and forth between there and her teaching job. The publican's life was good. Booze flowed, everyone was in a good mood, and there was always someone interesting around: tourists, crooks, bandits. Famous people like Slim Dusty and John Williamson called in all the time. But the couple hadn't been in Daly Waters long when things started to go sideways. In 2000, newly retired and fresh from a brief stint in Katherine, Paddy Moriarty bought the house across the road.

To begin with, it was friendly. The Irishman would come over for a drink and a chat and roll home when he'd had his fill of both. But Paddy stopped going to the pub. Then he started complaining that the pub was too noisy, writing letters, calling the cops and having outbursts. Paddy was angry about everything. Cantankerous. Opinionated. He complained incessantly. Lindsay wondered whether he was on drugs or whether he should have been on drugs, he wasn't sure which. And by then Paddy was drinking a lot. Before long, there was a not-unspoken agreement that Robyne and Lindsay would stay on their side of the street and Paddy would stay on his.

Something happened with the rest of the town, too. There were other disagreements with Robyne and Lindsay, petty things. It got to the stage where the couple banned most locals from the pub.

Over the road, Terry Taylor was staying with Paddy while he worked on renovations at the Hi-Way Inn. He had an uncomfortable front-row seat to Paddy yelling obscenities across the street at Robyne, usually at night. Terry didn't understand and didn't want anything to do with it. He tried to tell Paddy to stop, but he was unstoppable.

Two doors down, Megan was despairing, too—but she was on Paddy's side. She didn't blame him for his retaliations. She thought the Irishman was quite inventive, actually. Sometimes he'd get up first thing in the morning and point his speakers at the pub and play Kevin Bloody Wilson as loud as it could go. The insightful tunes, like 'Supa Mega Fugly' and 'Absolute Cunt of a Day', would go on all day, sometimes. 'I Knew The Bride (When She Used to Be a Moll)' was one of his favourites.

The turmoil went on for years—six, at least—and in the end, most people moved away. Including Paddy. On the day he packed up and left Daly Waters, Megan watched as all the pub staff lined up along the road and clapped his departure.

As we cross the road that once marked a battle line, we wonder what tourists who witnessed one of these stoushes would have made of it and whether Paddy's behaviour affected business. Inside the hotel, it's clear there's been no long-term fallout.

The pub is total chaos—charming chaos. Tourists are encouraged to leave their mark so hundreds of bras dangle from the ceiling, ID cards are tacked to every wall, hats, shirts, flags, boots all jostle for a space. People are lining up for beer, playing pool, ordering barista-made coffee and browsing the comprehensive collection of 'CU in the NT' merchandise.

The bar is staffed almost entirely by backpackers—the hotel employs about three dozen of them and they're all flat-out setting up for beef and barra night. Every night is beef and barra night; tonight they're expecting two hundred diners, and that's a number beaten down by COVID restrictions. A singer, wearing a dress fashioned from a 1989 Ken Done doona cover she says she stole from a washing line, starts playing 'On the Road Again' and the grey nomads go mental.

It's easy to see Daly Waters as Larrimah's *Sliding Doors* moment. Even a fraction of the nearby pub's success would turn things around in Larrimah. But the towns have more in common than you'd pick up with a surface glance. Although the media has pinned the word 'feud' to Larrimah as if it were exclusive to the place, here, at the next pub south, a remarkably similar thing happened. Small-town living is hard, and when you throw in isolation and unrelenting heat, it's even harder. It doesn't take much for tempers to fray and differences of opinions to turn into stand-offs. There's a bigger landscape of small, troubled towns with feuds that span generations of unrelated residents. So it starts to occur to us that maybe it isn't Larrimah's uniqueness that's drawn everyone into the story, after all. Perhaps it's familiarity.

'Who's camping here tonight?' the singer asks, and a show of hands replies. It's a participation-friendly crowd. While we're ordering some steaks at the counter, a tourist pays fifty dollars to hang his hat permanently on a taxidermy moose head behind the bar. It's the Aussie dream, and everyone wants to be part of it.

But memory is short here in this glam-outback bubble. The new owners have only been here a couple of years and there's no one else left who knew Paddy. We decide to move on. On the way out, we take a last look at Paddy's old house, the first home he'd owned. We've been told he bought it with the money from his mother's will, although we don't know whether that would have been his birth mother, Mary, or an adoptive or foster mother. We don't know for sure whether it's even true.

However he came to the house, there's no finding any shadow of him in the old building now. The raucous pub fades as we hit the road and we blast the air-conditioner and the radio to cover the silence. Maybe the whole trip will be like this—looking for the ghost of a man in places he can no longer haunt, uncovering things about him we wish we didn't know.

It's difficult to imagine what the owner of the Elliott Store was thinking as they placed a chocolate fountain on their stock order. Perhaps it was a mistake. Maybe sweat smudged the pen stroke on the order form and it leaked down into the wrong box. One look around Elliott and it's clear no one here is in the market for such an item.

Smack-bang between Darwin and Alice Springs, Elliott, or Kulumindini, is a puzzling place. It's all substandard housing, dead grass, blowflies and hopelessness. It hangs on because it's perched on the Stuart Highway but it looks like the town gave up years ago.

One of the reasons we're here is to meet Ray Aylett, one of Paddy's closest mates, in person. We interviewed him a while ago but haven't been able to get hold of him to set up a visit. Last time we tracked him down by phoning the store, so it seems as good a place to start as any.

'Ray's over in Queensland,' says the guy behind the counter, in between serving people who are not buying chocolate fountains. He gives us very detailed directions to Ray's place anyway, then tells us he can get a number for him if we need it.

We go back outside and sit on the back of the ute and throw together some lunch, as a party of peacocks gathers menacingly around us. We eat slowly, avoiding the real reason we're here. Maurice Darby—the guy who turned up to Paddy's inquest wearing very small shorts and gave a passionate but irrelevant speech about how Fran had been ripping off her customers. He was Fran's gardener before Owen, and he was Paddy's drinking buddy. For some reason at the inquest, Maurice gave his full address, so we'd written to him requesting an interview, but hadn't heard back. He knows the mess between Paddy and Fran better than anyone—he practically lived inside it—so we're planning to knock on his door anyway. It's hard to know who will answer. The few people we've asked about him have described him as a weird guy—but who knows what that means in this part of the world where everyone is eccentric.

The house is small and neat, with a spectacular garden, but the gate is closed and there is no car in the driveway. We call out a few times, but we aren't even sure if Maurice still lives here. Across the road, a strange, ageless girl-woman sits on her doorstep watching us, her savage dog begging us to come through her gate. From a distance we ask if this is where Maurice lives. Yes, she tells us, but offers nothing more.

We get in the car and briefly consider fleeing Elliott for good, but given how inappropriately helpful the guy at the store was, we guess he will know where Maurice is.

'Yep, the house with the really nice gardens,' the Elliott Oracle confirms. 'He's definitely home today. He parks his car around the back, you can't see it from the street. What time is it? Four o'clock? Yep, he's home. Definitely. Honk your horn, he'll come out.'

So we go back.

This time there is a shirtless man sitting on the verandah. We recognise him immediately. When we call out, he comes to the gate warily and there's an awkward interlude while we explain who we are and ask if he received our letter. He did not. Perhaps every town has a resident mail thief. We chat over the fence about Paddy for a bit.

'I'm happy to talk to you,' he says, looking tired. 'But not today. Can you come back tomorrow?'

We tell Maurice we're going to Tennant Creek for a few days. Could we stop in on our way back through?

'Sure,' he says. 'I'll be here every day.' Then: 'What are you doing in Tennant? Paddy never lived there.'

It's a fair point. We tell him we're looking for Paddy's children.

Maurice's eyebrows raise. 'Funny you should mention that,' he says mysteriously.

We lean over the fence in anticipation.

'I'll talk to you about it when you come back through.'

He shakes his head and bids us farewell, muttering under his breath as he walks back to the shade of his verandah. 'Funny you should mention that.'

His words ring in our ears for the next 250 kilometres, as we drive through barely existing places: Renner Springs, Banka Banka and Attack Creek.

Twenty-five kilometres north of Tennant we pass through Three-Ways, so-named for the options it presents for east, north or south travel. We look in dismay at the sign pointing to the Queensland border, where we had hoped to cross over to meet the Bush Poet. Right before we got to Larrimah, he'd phoned to say that despite his initial enthusiasm to speak in person and lead us to an apparently very-much alive Paddy, he wouldn't be able to make our rendezvous. We offered up a suite of different dates, but nothing was going to work.

'Just go up to Gulf Country, around the Calvert Road, Borroloola, Hell's Gate, Doomadgee. You're smart, you'll find him,' he'd told us. As if that's all there is to finding a man who is dead.

27

A burnt-down supermarket, a disgraced All Blacks player and another Moriarty

Just on dusk we reach Tennant Creek, or Jurnkkurakurr, pretty much the dead centre of the Territory. It's a hostile outlook: a struggling expanse of mallee scrubland, with fierce rocky ranges that hem in the highway. Why would anyone build a town here? we wonder. Were they blind? Or drunk? The answer to both is yes.

While Aboriginal people have lived across the Barkly for more than sixty-five thousand years, the town itself didn't spring up until the discovery of large gold deposits in the 1930s. Among those who had prospecting success were Jack Noble and Bill Weaber, who only had one working eye between them. It's said that Noble, blind in one eye, would look for gold and Weaber, completely blind, would feel for it. It was a system that worked. When they sold the lease to their mine it became Noble's Nob, which wound up the richest gold mine for its size in the world.

So that's the blind bit. As for the drink, by now we know that there is no town in Australia, until there is a pub. In Tennant Creek's case, legend has it that John Kilgariff chose the spot for a pub because his wagon broke down an inconvenient 12 kilometres from the watercourse. But with beer cheaper than clean water at the time and plenty of gold prospectors, he did a roaring trade there. It's a great yarn until we start digging into the story—turns out, Kilgariff bought the land before he arrived and there was no vehicle mishap of any sort. What is true, though, is that Tennant

Creek was built on a foundation of grog. It is not a legacy that has served it well.

Now with no gold but a bonanza of problems that come with alcohol consumption, the local tourism body has its work cut out for it. They've tried a few taglines, including 'Golden Heart of the Barkly Region' and 'A stopover full of surprises'. But Tennant Creek is mostly known for having a higher per capita murder rate than the United States.

The NT Police annual crime statistics (March 2020 to February 2021) show the number of alcohol-related assaults in Tennant Creek was up 60 per cent on the previous year. While the Territory rate of alcohol-related assaults sits at a startling 1688.4 per 100,000 people, Tennant Creek's rate is 8829.8 per 100,000. The stats for domestic violence are similar, and while the NT rate of crimes against property is 7396.3 per 100,000, in Tennant it's 27,819.8 per 100,000.

The town's reputation for crime is plastered along the main street: shop windows are barred or roller-doored from late afternoon, the bottle shops are only open Monday to Saturday between 4 pm and 7 pm, and the town's only supermarket is a blackened husk, burnt down by a bunch of kids a couple of weeks ago. One of the alleged arsonists was just eleven years old.

When he's not pouring money into a decrepit pink pub, Steve Baldwin runs a caravan park here. He told us it had been broken into or vandalised seventy-five times in the past twelve months. For some reason, we still agreed to stay there.

We survive the first night without incident and the next morning we go looking for a handful of men, all named Tony. To find them, we turn to Tennant Creek's own oracle: Jasmin Afianos.

If anyone should be writing a book, it's Jasmin.

Tennant Creek born and bred, her family ended up at this

outpost in the typical way—which is to say, her father was running from the law.

'He came to Australia as an illegal immigrant because he murdered someone in Greece,' she says, matter of factly. 'Actually, probably more than one person.'

Her mother came from Sydney and Jasmin isn't really sure why she ended up here—probably she was seeking an adventure in the north. 'Everyone comes to Tennant Creek for mysterious reasons,' she tells us. 'The rule in Tennant Creek is don't ask people where they come from. It's the height of rudeness.'

We dutifully drop our questions about Jasmin's parents' pasts and ask about their lives in Tennant instead. Jasmin's father arrived in the late 1950s, working in the gold mines and driving taxis, and her mother took over running the *Tennant and District Times* in 1983 after her father died. Following years of boarding school and travelling, Jasmin returned to her hometown when she was twenty-five, to work at the paper. Even though she's now based in Darwin, thirty years writing yarns means she knows everyone and everything Tennant.

We meet her early in the morning at the Top of the Town cafe, also owned by Steve Baldwin and the only shop in the main street that shows any sign of life. We order coffees and Jasmin tells us what she can about her hometown; it's a complicated place and writing news in a town that only has three thousand residents is more complicated still. In a larger community it's easier to write what you want, but here you're likely to run into the subjects of your stories in the main street. If you're not careful to respect the cultural sensitivities around death, for example, people will (rightfully) have something to say about it.

Despite the town's size, the issues Jasmin covered were big: the years-long battle over the proposal to use a tract of Aboriginal land at Muckaty Station as a dumping site for radioactive waste; the 2007 Intervention, when the federal government threw seventy-three communities across the Northern Territory into a bucket of dysfunction and seized control of Indigenous residents; and, most recently, in 2018 she broke the story of the two-year-old girl who was raped in her home. The child had to be put into an induced coma because her injuries were so horrific. That story sparked national outrage—soon after, Malcolm Turnbull became the first prime minister to visit the town in thirty-six years—but Jasmin doesn't think it resulted in any change.

'All it did was make Tennant Creek seem like a shithole,' she says sadly. 'It shocked people and made them realise what's going on, but a few months later it happened again, to a three-year-old. Stories go round and round, it's such a fucking mess. It annoys me Australians are so obsessed with frivolous stuff when this is going on. We had a one-month-old baby here die of cold because the parents fell asleep and didn't wrap the baby up properly. We had a husband murder his wife while their three kids were at home. This shit goes on all the time.'

Over the years, Jasmin's house here became an unofficial drop-in centre for kids having trouble at home, and she'll always find a blanket or some food if someone needs it. The personal stories that people shared with her as a journalist made the hardship of butting up against so much trauma worth it. Stockmen would turn up at the office and tell her their story, women would seek her out to confide secrets and she'd follow campaigns that affected the community, like land rights and fracking.

'Everything in Tennant Creek is hard,' Jasmin says. 'The climate is hard, the trees struggle to grow here, it's not easy for anyone. But if you look closely, and if you look at the right time, it's beautiful. The beauty that comes out of the bush is in the people, too.'

Given her wealth of outback knowledge, we put the theory that Paddy could be hiding out in some remote area in the Gulf to

Jasmin. Would it be possible for a person to disappear, in plain sight, if the town were small enough?

'No way.' She laughs and shakes her head. The Territory might be vast but its population clusters in small pods, she says, and word travels quickly between them. If Paddy were hiding out somewhere, we'd have found out by now. 'The smaller the community, the bigger the gossip,' is how she puts it.

Still, sometimes people manage it. Jasmin tells us about a man called Keith Murdoch. She knew him pretty well and he seemed like an ordinary guy. Friendly. Worked all across the Barkly for years. Then, in 2001 he was called as a key witness in a murder inquest. Jasmin turned up to report on the case to find the gallery packed with journalists from New Zealand. Turns out, says Jasmin, Keith was one of the best prop-forwards to ever play for the All Blacks, but he was sent home from the 1972 tour of the UK after he attacked a security guard in Cardiff on the night he scored the winning try against Wales. He was the first Kiwi player to ever be sent home in disgrace, and with his head hung with the shame of it, and knowing reporters would be waiting for him at the arrival gates in New Zealand, Keith jumped off the plane in Singapore and disappeared. It was a mystery the New Zealand media were obsessed with for thirty years. For most of those years, Murdoch had been living in Tennant. 'A lot of people here had known him for years, but we were all shocked he was so famous,' Jasmin says. 'He'd never mentioned a word of it to anyone.'

Jasmin picks up her car keys and says: 'We should head off soon if you want me to show you around.'

The coffee curdles inside us as we cruise silent streets lined with substandard housing, living conditions that evoke guilt and sadness in equal measure. It's too early to knock on doors, so Jasmin just drives by showing us where we need to go. She points out Tony Willy's place, as well as the home of a woman named

Shirley, whose family Jasmin says is from Brunette. We drive into one of the town camps, with its bare earth and overflowing homes and litter and skeletons of rusted-out cars.

Jasmin points out two houses that belong to more people who might be able to help. Then she points to another. 'That's where those kids who burnt down the supermarket live.'

There's time to kill before we start the awkward awfulness of knocking on strangers' doors, so we return to the caravan park. In the shop we meet Jan, Steve Baldwin's wife. She's busy serving people booking accommodation, buying cold drinks and food and petrol—it's been chaos here, since the supermarket fire. They're not as busy as the pop-up grocery store at the BP but it's still a constant stream of people desperately looking for bread and milk.

Jan bails up everyone on our behalf. 'Aren't you from Brunette way? Did you know that Paddy Moriarty bloke?'

We stand uncomfortably at the counter, as a parade of countrymen and cowboys apologise for not being able to help. Then a guy in a high-vis vest comes in. 'My brother would know him,' he tells us. 'Rossy. He's down at the polling booth.' The Northern Territory election is a week away and advance polling is important in places like Tennant, where many voters have to travel from outlying communities. 'Just go down there and look for the bloke in the canary yellow jumper.'

It's perfect timing. We've just arranged to meet Shirley, the woman Jasmin mentioned from Brunette. She's at the polling booth, too.

The voting station is at the Tennant Creek Civic Hall, and when we get out of our car it's like someone has fired a starting gun under the canvassers, gathered in orange and red clumps along party lines. While on the surface Tennant Creek looks utterly neglected by politicians, the truth is bush seats win elections. The air becomes thick with disappointment when we say we're not here to vote and they return to two small marquees, hopeless structures in the face of the sun's wrath. We quickly locate the canary mixing with the orange team.

'Rossy?'

He's a tall Aboriginal man with long curly hair and a big smile. When we explain ourselves, he says he's not our guy, but he rattles off a bunch of names we already know: Tony Willy, Tony Green. 'Oh, and Billy, he might know. He's like a historian. Tells a great story. I can take you over there if you like?'

We tell Rossy we have to find a woman called Shirley first, and he points her out, on the opposing red team. She's sitting with a baby, her grandson George, who she cares for. He is asleep in a pram, still sucking on his bottle.

'It's Uncle Tony you need to talk with,' she tells us.

Which Tony?

'Tony Cutter. I'll go see if he's home. Can you just watch George?'

She jumps into her car and disappears around the corner.

We pull up a couple of chairs beside sleeping George and watch uncomfortably as a couple of older Aboriginal men in big cowboy hats are mobbed by the canvassers. One party faithful is getting right up in their faces and the voting advice seems a bit coercive, more like instructions than options. Two people from the anti-fracking mob turn up and struggle to set up their stand in the fierce wind ripping through the car park.

About twenty minutes later, just as George's eyes start to flutter, Shirley returns. Tony Cutter's not home. Coincidentally, he's out cruising the streets with Tony Willy. She can't really say where we might find them, but suggests we go to Tony Cutter's house in an hour or so.

In the meantime, Rossy folds his large canary yellow frame into our car and directs us to Billy's.

We pull up out the front of a neat set of single-storey duplexes. There's an alcohol restriction sign on the gate, as there is on almost every gate here. It's difficult to tell if this is a 'bad part of town' in a place where no part of town looks great, but Rossy assures us it is. 'I call it the Bronx. Don't come here after 8 pm,' he advises, but he's cheerful enough about it, and easily a contender for the most obliging person in the outback.

He takes us to Billy's door, knocks for us. When there's no answer, Rossy realises today must be dialysis day—Billy won't be home until after 1 pm. So instead, he gives us a tour of Tennant, pointing out anyone who might be helpful—including some benches on the main street where the two Tonys hang out—and stopping to drop some keys off for a mate and to pop into the clinic for an appointment. Then he asks for a ride back to the polling booths. The plan suits us well because Shirley has texted to say she's thought of something.

Even from across the car park, we can't miss the look of joy that crosses her face when she sees us.

'Hey, I just had a message from someone. They reckon there's Moriarty mob up in Borroloola,' she says.

We start mentally mapping distances. We'd assumed that when Paddy said he'd had kids at Brunette Downs, it was with someone from the local community. But it's not that far to Borroloola from Brunette—four hours, which in outback terms is next door. And Borroloola is even closer to Heartbreak Hotel, where Paddy worked for years. If the child Megan remembered from Daly Waters was around eight, the timeline would fit.

'That Moriarty mob, they play football,' Shirley says, talking fast now. 'And John Moriarty, he played didgeridoo with U2 when they toured in Australia! My sister was at that concert. That must be his kids, hey?'

She's really excited now, having single-handedly solved our mystery, and it's a contagious emotion. We tell her about Paddy's house, which is sitting empty, under the care of the public trustee. Eventually, it will be sold off and the money will be held in trust until a relative is found, which may be never. If Paddy's kids are in Borroloola, they'd probably be entitled to something.

'That would be so good, hey,' Shirley says, beaming, and we get caught up in the idea that maybe we can help extract one good thing from the wreckage of all this. 'It's not about the money. But it would be nice for the kids to have something. Like the land, it's still country, you know?'

She gives us a hug and wishes us well as we head back to the car. 'You're going to make a lot of people really happy,' she calls.

And as we drive off, we imagine it: the happiness. It wouldn't make up for all the hurt—Paddy's, and Larrimah's, and the potential pain of the woman he was with and the children, who may not even know about his death and would likely have mixed feelings about it. But it would be something.

For the first time, we're close to something that looks like an answer. Moriarty isn't a common name in an Indigenous community. So what are the chances that an Indigenous mob of Moriartys, within spitting distance of where Paddy spent so many years, aren't related to him? It can't be a coincidence, can it?

It can.

We pull up in some patchy shade, a few blocks away. Google gets us to John Kundereri Moriarty quickly: the Yanyuwa man is a famous artist and former soccer player. But, just as quickly, we realise it's unlikely he is related to Paddy. John was born in 1938, making him older than Paddy, and his father arrived in the Territory at least three decades before Paddy came over in 1966 or 1967.

Our disappointment is palpable, but it's not complete. John Kundereri Moriarty's Irish dad was from County Kerry—right next door to the county Paddy was from. So, we reason, they would have to be at least distantly related. Perhaps John's father was the reason Paddy chose Australia and the Northern Territory? An uncle, perhaps. And even if both Moriarty men ending up here was a coincidence, even if they weren't related, John must at least know of Paddy. Two men with Irish roots, sharing the same last name, living in the same corner of Gulf Country—there's no way they wouldn't notice each other. If Paddy and John had met, maybe Paddy shared his elusive past with him?

But those questions will have to wait until we get to Borroloola. We were planning on going anyway; it's not far from Heartbreak and it's also one of the places the Bush Poet said Paddy might be hiding out.

In the meantime, we resume our search for Tonys. Two of our three Tonys live in Tennant Creek—Tony Willy and Tony Cutter. They both have connections to Brunette Downs and we're hoping they'll remember Paddy. Our third Tony, Tony Green, still works at Brunette so we'll catch up with him later in the trip.

We find Tony Cutter at home, his warm face shaded by a huge cowboy hat. He's legitimately confused by our arrival, but he still tries to help. He doesn't remember Paddy, though, doesn't know the guy. 'Try Tony Willy,' he says. 'Or Tony Green.'

So we swing by Tony Willy's again and find him behind the wheel of a car that's packed to the roof with suitcases and a couple of passengers. People have told us that he's the town's unofficial taxi and that it's probably good to bail him up for a chat—give him a rest from driving for a bit. But he's about to set out again, so we don't get a chance to ask about forced contraception at Brunette and the work he did for Indigenous women. It's the price we pay for not ringing ahead—but in some remote communities, where people don't always have phones or phone reception, and don't necessarily speak English as a first language, it's a common problem for journalists. And that's part of why so much gets missed out here.

We're also very aware that two white women lobbing up asking questions aren't entitled to answers. There is a good chance some of these people do know something but, for whatever reason, don't want to tell us. Given the history, we get it. But it doesn't feel like that at all. People couldn't be kinder. Tony Willy doesn't know anything about Paddy but he still tries to help. 'Try Tony Cutter,' he says. 'Or Tony Green. He still works out that way.'

Our last hope in Tennant Creek is Rossy's cousin, Billy Fitz, but when we finally track him down it turns out he never worked at Brunette and his link to the place is through his great-grandfather, Tom Nugent—a bushranger who sometimes stole cattle there. He doesn't know anything about Paddy, but we spend two hours in his daughter's living room, anyway, swept up in his stories.

By late afternoon, we're tired and sweaty. Tennant Creek's problems get under your skin and pulling leads from this mess is like trying to catch a handful of dust on the wind. All we have to show for our time here is a family of probably not-related Moriartys and a renewed interest in finding our third Tony. The evening stretches in front of us. There's not much to do. Except drink.

There are four pubs and three bottle shops to choose from. The bottle shop with the drive-through has a queue that stretches out along the main street, so we drive down the road to a small store with its windows blackened and barred. If it wasn't for the cop standing at the door, it would be easy to assume it's not open. She pays us no attention but, if she wanted, on the way out she could question us about where we're going to drink, and with whom. If she didn't like the answer, she could confiscate our alcohol. The point-of-sale interventions are part of the Northern Territory government's attempt to stem alcohol-related violence but critics say it's a measure that encourages racial profiling. You're only likely to be questioned if you're Indigenous.

We make our selection and hand over our IDs—another mandatory measure. Everyone is cross-checked with the Banned Drinker Register, a list that prevents people with court or police orders from buying takeaway grog. While the shop attendant scans our licences we stare at the blurry mural of drunks behind him: CCTV pictures of people who've been banned from the store.

Back at the caravan park, we sit outside our cabin, sipping slowly, staring out at the dry landscape. Steve Baldwin has covered up the drought by having an artist paint the park's dead trees in various themes, like the pink one in Larrimah. One is done up like the Australian flag, another the Aboriginal flag.

The day's heat fades until it's cold enough for jumpers and the sky turns a luminous orange. It's the shade that you see in outback paintings and assume is exaggerated, much like you assume Tennant Creek's felonious reputation is inflated. But the reality in both cases is startlingly accurate.

We'd always thought that if we could pull back the layers, we'd find the real Paddy, but now we're not so sure. The contradictions in a person don't cancel each other out; two things can be true at once. Tomorrow, we're heading back to see Maurice and we're bracing for more tangled logic. But for now, we drink. In the last of the light, Tennant looks beautiful. But then the darkness closes in again.

28

An abandoned Mardi Gras, $6000 in change and an accidental eavesdropping

'You could not have come on a worse day,' a voice calls out and we panic. We've backtracked several hundred kilometres up the Stuart Highway through sepia grasslands to interview Maurice Darby. Surely, he's not going to cancel on us?

He emerges from the courtyard wearing a green FILA jumper that's entirely too hot for the furnace we've returned ourselves to, even if it has been cut off at the elbows.

'It's terrible, just terrible, you really couldn't have picked a worse day. Come on, I'll show you,' he says.

He ushers us around the side of the house, refusing to accept any compliments on his garden. It's probably the only garden in town and his neatly trimmed row of bougainvillea bushes are a sharp, magenta contrast to the forsaken browns of the rest of Elliott. It must have taken an act of wizardry to keep things so neat and lush, we tell him.

'Well. It's normally much nicer,' he says. 'You'll see why.'

There is no sign of anything catastrophic. It's just a neat, single-storey house with a beautiful garden. Maurice stops and points across the fence, where a backhoe is kicking up great clouds of rusty earth.

'Isn't it terrible?' he laments. 'There's dust everywhere. I haven't been able to hang out my washing for weeks.'

Maurice, or Maurie—he's happy to be called either, 'as long as you don't call me late for dinner'—is bald, shiny and has a neat, white beard with the chin part shaved, so he looks a bit walrussy. But he's a kindly walrus. The sort who has a kitchen table with a lace table-runner, full bookshelves, a new gas stove and plans for a kitchen renovation.

He's part of a generation who spent the better part of their lives working itinerant jobs in far-flung places. In his case, he started out running pubs in Melbourne, then cooked in Tasmania, the Territory and on Thursday Island. It's a lifestyle that's full of adventure, possibility and exit strategies—if things aren't going well, there's always another seasonal gig to move on to. But it has the potential to age badly. Whether you're cooking, driving graders, working on stations or doing any of the dozens of other roles that tend to come up, room and board is usually included and, if a person isn't careful, they can end up drinking away a lifetime of wages, only to find that by the time they reach old age they have nowhere to live and no hope of ever retiring.

Maurie was determined not to be one of the many outback men working themselves into early graves. So, twenty years ago, he bought a house in Elliott. And then, because he likes the quiet, he bought the blocks on either side. Still, the rumble of the backhoe outside is proof that, on occasion, even an indirect neighbour can be too close.

'Okay, about Paddy's kids,' he says. 'What you said to me at the gate, that really stonkered me because I thought, "Jeez, I'm not the only one then that knows something." You're the only person who's ever brought that up. Not one soul ever mentioned children or a wife.'

We beg him to wait a moment, so we can set up the recorder. It's like he's been turning the memory over in his mind and now he can't wait to set it free.

'Okay, I know nothing or very little about any involvement

with a wife or child,' he says, taking a deep breath. 'But there was one night . . .'

━ ━

It was 2016, which was a good time to be pulling the world apart. Trump and Clinton were going head-to-head for the US presidency, and there was plenty for two blokes to comment on as they sat in a neat living room, watching the evening news. It was a habit they had fallen into. As dusk settled on the town and the highway started to quieten, Maurie would pop over the road to Paddy's, jump the fence and they'd open a beer or two and back-narrate the evening's viewing.

One Saturday, around half past six, they had settled into the usual routine when the telephone rang.

Paddy looked over at Maurie. 'Who's phoning up at this time of the night?'

Maurie shrugged. So Paddy got up and answered the call. There was a pause. Maurie heard Paddy's voice soften. 'Hello, love, how are you?'

It was enough to make anyone curious. Maurie and Paddy had been friends for some time. It was, perhaps, a weird friendship, given that Maurie worked for Fran, but Paddy was an easy listener who never interrupted and always had a good story to tell. It was good to have someone to drive to Katherine and do the shopping with. They even went on the occasional trip together.

But, as Maurie sat there, trying not to eavesdrop on Paddy's phone conversation, he looked around his mate's house and realised what a hard man Paddy was to get to know. Rover's bowl had already been washed up after dinner, resting upturned on the sink, and there were several hats lined up on one of the armchairs. Paddy's shoes, as always, were by the front door: boots on one side, thongs on the other. He was meticulous—the kind of bloke who covered his car mirrors with plastic bags so the birds wouldn't shit on them, and laid out fresh alfoil every time he used the oven. His house was orderly but it didn't reveal anything. There were bits and pieces around, but definitely no family photos.

'Yup, yeah, are the kids all right?' Paddy asked, between clips of Trump on the television. 'Yup, ohhhh, that's good, he's doing good, oh that's great, and you're well? Yup, yeah, she's doing terrific, oh, that's wonderful.'

Something about the way Paddy was speaking made Maurie think the caller was a woman, and that she was younger. A daughter maybe. He heard the word Borroloola and wondered if that's where she was from.

'Yup, well tell them to be careful,' Paddy went on. 'Yes, and you're all right? If you need anything, let me know and I'll send it down, okay? Ring me if you want anything.'

After he hung up, he returned to the lounge and the television. 'That was the wife and kids,' Paddy told Maurie. There was a moment between them, an opportunity to ask more. But Maurie didn't push it. It was a very personal matter. Paddy's past was his own. What right did he have to trespass into it?

For Maurie, moving to Larrimah was a bit like stepping into one mess inside another, and another. On one level, there was the spiderweb of resentment and anger that seemed to consume the whole town. Then there was the turmoil between Fran and Bill, whose break-up had been the catalyst for Maurie's arrival and whose bitter fights and petty acts of revenge added a weird texture to the otherwise indiscernible passing of days. And, of course, there was the business between Fran and Paddy, a less clear-cut hatred Maurie could never quite get to the bottom of. Years later, it's hard to know what's relevant to his friend's disappearance and what was, more simply, a strange interlude in Maurie's life.

A lot of things had surprised Maurie when he'd accepted a job as a live-in gardener and cook at the teahouse. He'd been surprised at how much a person could make selling pies from the middle of nowhere, and how delicious meat cooked in the early morning over fires in a couple of 44-gallon drums could taste. He'd been shocked to learn Fran was keeping her cash at the Bank of Karl Roth. And when Maurie suggested that was a bad idea and went to collect the money and help her deposit it at a more official financial institution, he was shocked again to find Fran had kept it in two .303 ammunition boxes. It took the credit union two days to count it all—he says she had almost $40,000, including $6000 in coins. He'd also been surprised by how nice the customers were, the nicest tourists in the country, even if Fran was liberal with the F-word or yelled abuse at anyone bringing in a dog.

In the end, Maurie stayed four and a half years and there's no getting to the bottom of how his teahouse tenure came to an end. Fran says she fired him; he insists he left on his own terms. Perhaps whatever happened has skewed his view of things.

Maurie has been through all this before, of course, with the police. He was living in Katherine when he heard the news about Paddy. It was the police who told him—at first, he assumed there'd been an accident or something. Paddy wasn't the sort of bloke to go missing.

'I said, "You've got to be kidding me, Paddy wouldn't stray far, a ball of string's about Paddy's length—you'd wind him in when it ran out because it's pub time or it's tucker time or his dog needs a drink of water."'

The police had questions, almost as many as Maurie. Was the door open, he wanted to know, because you could only open it from the inside, there wasn't even a handle outside? How many pairs of boots were at the house, because Paddy would have four and he'd never wear thongs to drive? Was his ute there? Had they checked his mobile and landline? What about his bank cards? Maurie and

Paddy had shopped together, banked together, sat together in the glow of the TV. There had to be some clue amid all of it.

He goes through it all again with us. It seems almost like he's relieved to finally have someone to tease it apart with. But every theory falls down when you look at it too closely. We run through a list of names of people who might have known Paddy, people we're trying to locate. He tells us they're all dead, or dying, one might not see out the week. The air in the kitchen suddenly seems heavy.

All we have is stories, so we fall back into them. Some yarns, Maurie tells us for no reason. They're not relevant to the case, he just thinks we should know. Because he knew someone who isn't here anymore, and it's important to mark the absence he's left, understand what kind of man he was. The way he stacked his groceries in the ute matters. So does the way he loved his dogs.

We wonder if Larrimah is a strange place for Maurie now, whether it's eerie to drive through on the way to Katherine, doing the shopping run alone.

'No,' Maurie says. 'It's not strange. Nothing's changed except Paddy's not there. There's no reason to go there. Barry's not there, either.'

When the stories run dry, we begin to pack up.

'I wish I could give you more,' he says, 'a bone to gnaw on.' But it's not his fault none of this makes sense. We've brought a stack of photos of Paddy with us, in the hope that they might aid us in the search for a probably dead man, and we offer one to Maurie.

'Yes, I'd like that,' he says. His thumb traces Paddy's image, the curve of his grin, the hat he never took off.

'I would like to find out he's alive and well,' he says. 'I'd prefer not to find out they've discovered some bones and they're not really sure. I'd sooner remember him gone missing. That's easier for me, at least.'

It's a fair position. The ambiguity is horrible, for everyone who cared about Paddy, but there are some answers worse than questions. Even still, Maurie makes us promise to call if we find anything and walks us to the gate.

If it's possible, the sun has grown hotter, and it's already unfor-givably late to be heading onward. Maurie looks down the street towards the highway and his town's own dying pub. Larrimah has the Pink Panther. Daly Waters has the glam-outback market cornered. Elliott used to be known for its gay and lesbian Mardi Gras—once a year, the dusty streets would fill with sequins and neon and fishnets, and the pub would be so full that people started spilling out the sides. But that's fallen by the wayside. The pub's only open three days a week now, from 4 pm to 7 pm, and it really only serves beer. For anything stronger, you're looking at a decent drive. It's one of the reasons so many people have moved away, Maurie says.

It's not just Larrimah that's on the brink. Australia is full of ghost towns, and ghost-towns-to-be, and towns hanging in the ghost-town balance. Places so small or remote or tied to resources or infrastructure that, at the whim of a bureaucratic pen or the drying up of a mine bed or the changing of alcohol laws or the shifting of a rail line, they could cease to exist, almost overnight.

Maurie is pragmatic about Elliott's decline. He doesn't mind that there's nothing to do on the weekend. That's kind of the point.

'All I need's here,' he says. 'And even Martin, on the backhoe,' he gestures towards the cloud of dust behind us. 'I went to Tennant Creek a few weeks ago for two nights and when I came back there's six cucumbers, two cabbages, two dozen eggs on the table.'

It's a sweet twist, but as we climb into the car, Maurie looks wistful again.

'I wish I could tell you more, I really do. I just keep thinking, all those nights we sat there and talked about Trump. Maybe I should have asked Paddy. Maybe I should have asked, the night of the phone call. But you don't know if it's going to upset someone, and what if he'd taken it the wrong way? Those things, wives, children, they're personal. You know?'

After hours of sameness on the Stuart, as soon as we turn onto the Carpentaria Highway, everything changes. The road narrows to one lane, heading dead straight, up and down hills of low scrub and bright yellow kapok flowers.

Gulf Country is a vast, mysterious land that straddles the border between the north of Queensland and the Territory. It's the world's largest intact savannah woodlands, interspersed with grasslands that stretch so far they bleed into the sky. It's a place that's huge enough to mean a lot of things, to a lot of different people. Barra fishing. Cattle country. Mining land—lead, zinc and silver—and all the testosterone and wealth and work and poisoned water that comes with it. The history of Gulf Country, especially on the Territory side, is terrible; it was the site of systematic killings of Indigenous Australians. Officially, there were at least fifty massacres through this region until as late as 1910. In the early days of colonisation, the government-sanctioned killings were carried out by British soldiers, then by police, settlers or a combination of both. Later, native police—a militia-style force under command of white officers—committed massacres. It's estimated that more than three thousand people were killed. But these are numbers that conceal the truth; historians say that, unofficially, there are many more unrecorded killings.

As the wide plains thicken into greener scrub and then woodland, the harsh light makes everything seem shadowy. We're venturing into a large haystack full of dark secrets, searching for an unspecified number of children who could be named anything and a man who is, more than likely, already dead.

29

Some booze-smuggling scumbags, a covert sausage sizzle and a lot of broken hearts

It is true, perhaps, that all outback pubs are lonely, but Heartbreak Hotel may be the loneliest because there is no town dragging its heels in the dust around it. There is nothing. It is just a pub with a caravan/camping area, a few dongas and some petrol bowsers. There's also a for sale sign pitched out the front, a real estate agent with neat hair smiling at us from someplace nowhere near here.

Heartbreak Hotel is plonked in a place called Cape Crawford, which isn't a cape and isn't on the coast. According to a laminated sign pinned to a pole in the bar and carrying the disclaimer that it may not be true, there are two rumours about how Heartbreak got its name. The first is that building the place took so long and was beset with such misfortune that eventually the crew realised how heartbreaking it had been for the owner and gave it the nickname. The second rumour is that the original owner and his wife split up just after Heartbreak opened. Now, legend has it that if you go to the hotel, you too will get your heart broken.

However the name came about, the pub has leaned into it. The front gate has a metal heart that breaks as you open it, and there are some bright pink 'Elvis' (men's) and 'Priscilla' (women's) toilets that seem like they'd be good for crying in.

But, out here, there are other kinds of heartbreak. We've arrived in a drought. Someone tells us that last year five hundred head of cattle died across the road from the hotel. The poor cows had come in looking for the last of the grass but then it rained and they all got bogged. It was horrific. Heartbreaking. Terrible to watch, and terrible to smell. Probably, it was terrible for business, too.

We've come here to meet Catherine Keating, a woman who ran the hotel for many of the years Paddy worked here. They became unlikely friends. When we phoned her a few weeks ago, she was busy serving customers, but even in her hurry, some memories of Paddy slipped out and we could feel her sad smile through the phone. We'd made a rough date to come here, so she's expecting us.

Is Catherine about? we ask the woman behind the bar.

'Nah, not here. She's gone to Darwin for a haircut.'

We set up our tent under some trees in the campground, grey nomads watching on smugly from under the awnings of their luxury caravans, and try to work out the best use of our time. Borroloola—one of the places the Bush Poet thinks Paddy could be hiding out, where Maurie thinks Paddy's children might be and where John Kundereri Moriarty is from—is just another 100 kilometres north-east.

This land is home to the Yanyuwa, Marra, Garrwa, Gudanji and Binbingka people. It's sometimes called saltwater country, because it takes in sweeping saltwater plains and the gulf coast and islands. But, since white settlement in this region, Borroloola has had a reputation for lawlessness. In the nineteenth century, it was a rum-smuggling base where, according to one then-resident: 'Drunkenness is epidemic and drunken men practise rifle and revolver shooting on the open roadways of the township at all hours of the day, whenever their sweet wills direct, to the constant danger of the rest of the inhabitants.' Criminals from all over Australia took refuge here in the late 1800s, all the 'Northern scum' who didn't dare go to Queensland or down the Telegraph line. Cattle-duffing, robbery, beatings and killings were common.

In Australia, for a lot of years, if you were on the run from anything, Borroloola was the place you came to hide. So, the next day, we head there too.

A barramundi can change colour to suit the environment around it—the fish grows dark and mottled as it moves through deeper waters, and in the glare of the sun its scales lighten into a silver so fierce it's almost white. As we drive deeper towards Borroloola, the possibility that Paddy has done the same rises to the surface in a way that turns every passing car and every sign to a cattle station into something weighted with impossible possibility. What would it take to disappear, without trace, in plain sight?

Paddy has been described, over and over, as a 'character', so much larger than life that chance encounters with him in the pub grew inside travellers' memories into something much more substantial. Even before his disappearance, he turned up in documentaries and TV shows, and every time he's the opposite of a wallflower. It's hard to imagine a place where he could make himself small enough to not be noticed.

When we reach the town we drive around wondering how to find a well-connected local who might know something about Paddy or his children, if they exist, until, eventually, we spot another polling booth and try our luck.

As evidence of the region's lawlessness, there is an illegal (or at least not COVID-sanctioned) sausage sizzle taking place. Nearby, a woman sitting in the shade takes pity on us. 'You'll have to go across town, to the camps,' she says, and points up the road. Then she gives us a couple of names. They'll know, she assures us.

Borroloola seems caught between two realities. There's a sweet little school and an oval so lush and green that it comes as a shock. A thriving Indigenous art gallery. Three supermarkets, a post office and a Chinese takeaway joint. But the two main town camps are enough to make our breath catch. Although some new building work happened in 2019 and there's more going on while we're here, it's not nearly enough. Decks and verandahs sag away from crumbling roofs. Paint peels on walls that show water damage. Dogs wander between houses, hot and hungry. Overcrowding is a pervasive issue because, as the older houses fall apart, people migrate into the newer ones, until there are no longer enough rooms. In the context of COVID, this density of living is even more dangerous. People still remember the deaths caused by the Hong Kong flu in Borroloola in the 1960s, and the Spanish flu before that. There are sites north of town, Ngangkarrdila and Wurrwurr, that are still avoided by the Yanyuwa people. They are Flu Dreaming places.

Our car crawls over dirt roads—we're unsure where to begin. At the edge of the camp, two boys swinging their feet off the edge of a verandah ask where we are going and cheerfully point us towards a huge house with a wide verandah.

As we get closer, we notice there's a crowd. A pair of long mats accommodate maybe two dozen people—kids, adults, elders—playing cards, with hundreds of dollars of cash between them. We've heard that some people in the community have been pressured into accessing their superannuation early, under the changed pandemic guidelines. It's going to be a generational disaster, people tell us.

One of the people we are looking for is sitting at the edge, her dark curls hanging over her green dress. We hand over the photo and ask if she knows Paddy Moriarty. Her soft face scrunches into a smile.

'Yes, I know him,' she says. 'Yes, he's a very nice man.'

We feel hope rising in our throats. Then it sinks, just as quickly.

'Paddy, yes, I knew him. I knew his mother.' But she's talking about the other Moriartys. John Kundereri Moriarty. She doesn't recognise Paddy, she's just being polite. But we're interested in finding John, too. We ask if he is around. No, she says. He runs a soccer program in town but he lives down south somewhere. We want to ask more, like how we can find him, but we're perched awkwardly on the edge of an illegal gambling situation and the language barrier is making it hard. So we thank her for her help and go looking for John online.

We find him through the Moriarty Foundation, which is part of the reason the Moriarty name is so well known in Borroloola. John Moriarty AM was the first Indigenous man selected to represent Australia in soccer. Now, he runs a youth soccer program that trains one thousand three hundred kids a week as part of a broader strategy to shift intergenerational disadvantage; the pilot program began in Borroloola.

John is also an artist. In 1994, Qantas commissioned the Yanyuwa man and his wife, Ros, to design artwork for the outside of five of their planes. And it was his son who had played didgeridoo for U2 in Sydney.

When we contact John over the phone, he's in Sydney and curious about Paddy Moriarty, but is pretty sure he's not related. John didn't know a lot about his father, an Irishman from County Kerry who came to Australia in 1921 to work in pubs run by other Irishmen.

John is part of the Stolen Generations and tells us he hasn't spent a lot of time in the area. He wasn't reunited with his mother, a Yanyuwa woman who lived at Borroloola, until he was fifteen, and he never saw his father again. He could never have met Paddy, could never have learned if they were somehow related, could never have become trapped in one of his long tales. Because like Allen Maroney, John was taken away when he was just four years old.

We pull in at the art gallery and caravan parks, accost a couple more strangers in the street, hang out at the supermarkets and hope.

But this is a fool's errand. In some naive dream we'd thought showing Paddy's picture around might be enough. Maybe someone would recognise him, or, if he is alive, maybe we'd stumble across him. It wouldn't be difficult to spot an old white man—there aren't too many of those in a place like this. Finally, we head back to Heartbreak.

It's late afternoon when we arrive, a time when the shadows start to pool on the impossibly green lawn. We buy some cold drinks, sit on the verandah and imagine Paddy here, on the ride-on mower.

With Catherine not due back from her 1700-kilometre haircut for a couple of days, we sit down with another man in a standard-issue blue singlet who knew Paddy but our conversations take place in disjointed snippets between drinks.

'Paddy came here a lot,' the guy tells us. 'He was here a few days before he disappeared, actually. Something else happened after he visited. It was weird—really spooked me.' But before he can tell us any more, someone calls out to him and he disappears into the fray of the bar.

We try a few times, but there's no getting any more out of the man tonight. He's too busy socialising with a work crew. We're leaving for Brunette Downs in the morning, but we have to drive back via Heartbreak. Can we catch up with him in a day or two? we ask.

'Yeah, maybe,' he says. Formal arrangements are futile out here. But there's a good chance he'll be here, in the same blue singlet, on the same barstool. Outback pubs are sticky places.

30

A pelican plague, two million cows and a poacher with a thorny devil

There are more than two million cattle in the Northern Territory. On the drive to Brunette Downs, it feels as though every one of them sashays in front of our car and casts a withering look in our direction, as if to say 'you don't belong here'. It's difficult not to take it personally.

We pass layers of mournful cows stacked high in a road train and are consumed by a choking cloud of dust. Bulldust. It encircles our car in a thick haze and creeps in through cracks, settling in our noses and eyes and over all our belongings. Parts of the road aren't sealed at all and we've been warned to look out for 'bulldust holes', pits of fine particles that form during long dry spells and sometimes trap unknowing cars in soft pools of powder. On some beef roads in central Australia, it's so bad trucks take 900-kilometre detours to avoid being bogged.

About 170 kilometres down the Tablelands Highway, a very generous term for the bumpy single-lane goat track we're driving on, we stop at a T-intersection heading east. 'Go out along the Calvert Road,' the Bush Poet had suggested. 'Paddy will be out along there somewhere.' Paused on the corner of nothing and nothing, the hopelessness of it strikes us again. If Paddy is alive, he's not just going to be standing on the side of the road we drive down, and it's not like we can call into every cattle station along the way. Even if we could, what would we do? Ask people if they're hiding a man everyone thinks is dead? Demand to search the premises?

We've left our plans for the night open to the possibility of following Calvert Road as far as it goes, then nicking over the border into Queensland, to Hell's Gate Roadhouse and around Doomadgee, those other places the Bush Poet mentioned. But sitting here, looking along this rough, secluded road, it begins to seem like a suicide mission. As we pull back onto the highway, we're still undecided. Either way, we realise we might not make it anywhere before dark if we stay too long at Brunette, so we start scoping out roadside stops, just in case we get caught up. They're all bleak, isolated, and out of reach of phone reception. Mostly, they just look like good places to get murdered.

After a few hours of blazing shadelessness, the Brunette Downs homestead appears. It feels as if we've stepped onto the set of *McLeod's Daughters*. There is almost an exact line around its perimeter, a border where the drought and beasts give way to quaint old buildings and people in cowboy hats so large they look like novelties won at a sideshow. Sprinklers *tch-tch-tch* across emerald lawns.

We follow a neat path, under an arbour drizzled in bright bougainvillea, up to the main office, where we're greeted by Rick Morrison, the operations manager. He's about thirty and his dress code and accent are pure cattle station.

'How's it going? I think someone mentioned some writers or something were coming,' he says, shaking our hands warmly for someone who obviously has no idea who we are. 'I'll go get MJ for you.'

MJ is Michael Johnson, Rick's boss. We follow both men and Rick's wife, Adelaide (Addy), who also works on the Brunette management team, to the staff dining room, leaving our dusty shoes outside. Inside is small, excruciatingly clean and noiseless. They tell us the food is excellent but almost always involves beef.

'I think we're the highest beef consumption per capita in the world just about,' MJ says.

It's great beef, Rick adds, some of the world's best. But he admits: 'Chicken night is exciting.'

Over cups of tea and fluffy homemade choc-chip biscuits, we get a 101 in cattle stations before we move on to the reason we're here. Paddy. We aren't certain how long he spent here—according to his Queensland friend Terry Taylor he came here straight from the boat in 1966 or 1967 and stayed twenty-seven years—but, like so many other things, Paddy's employment history is uncheckable. Some people have suggested he did a few stints at Brunette. Others say his time here was brief, that he bounced around to other cattle properties in the Barkly region, including Bauhinia Downs, Mittiebah Station and Balbarini Station.

'People who've worked on Brunette Downs always have a special link to it,' Rick says, when we explain that, even though we can't be sure when or for how long he worked here, it's the one place Paddy always talked about. 'Excuse my language, but she's such a big mean bitch, Brunette. And somehow, you love her. I don't know what it is.'

He thinks for a moment, then settles on an answer.

'I think most blokes, most people, want to be part of something tough. You just hate to be on the sidelines of hard times. You might complain about it, but you'd still rather be in it, helping, not sitting on the fence looking on.'

We've been told Paddy was either a ringer or the cowboy gardener. The latter sounds like a made-up position, but we're assured it's not. It's basically a yardman, and often it's a job given to the failed ringers, which tallies with something Paddy's mate Ray Aylett had said: Paddy couldn't shoe a horse or kill a beef, but he could mow a lawn.

There's a clear hierarchy on a station and ringers are at the top of it. A cowboy gardener is less prestigious but, the others tell us, the best thing about it—at least for us—is that they'd know everyone on the station. People would remember the cowboy gardener.

'Tony Green will know him,' MJ tells us confidently. 'He's been here forever.'

We ask how old Tony is so we can try to do the maths to see if he would have been here when Paddy was. They all shrug. No one really knows. Not even Tony.

It's easy to understand Rick's pride and affection for Brunette. At 3 million acres, the station is the biggest single pastoral lease in the Northern Territory, about third in Australia, MJ tells us.

'In volume and scale for a single operation, we probably run more cattle than anyone in the country, maybe the world.'

The homestead sits at the heart of the station. It's bigger than Larrimah, with more people. Because of the drought, it's running at part-capacity—thirty-five staff—but usually there are fifty, plus there are always contractors around, quite often a smattering of kids, sometimes a governess. Down the back, there's a cluster of charming high-set houses for couples or staff with families. The men's quarters adjoin the dining room and kitchen. There are also women's quarters, the manager's house, a guesthouse, a butcher, a fuel station, an airstrip, a hangar, offices, a tennis court, a footy field, a lagoon, work sheds and a little pub. When it's possible, the social club organises sporting competitions or water sports. It feels like a special kind of unpretentious luxury, unhitched from reality in a good way. But the last few years have been tough, the worst in thirty or forty years.

'There's been dry periods before, but last year was bad,' MJ tells us. 'I haven't talked to anyone who's seen it as dry as that.'

When we finally step back into the vengeful sunshine, we can still see vestiges of it. The homestead is a stubborn patch of green in a roughly 12,500 square kilometre patch of dust and Mitchell grass and cattle. It's one of the reasons the cowboy gardener job is so important, Addy says. You can't have teams out in the great brown nothingness, desperately tending to underfed cattle, and then welcome them back to more bitter browns. Out here, a nice garden means something. It means you're home.

We pull our boots back on; we're eager to meet Tony but Rick tells us he's out on a bore run and won't be back until after 4 pm.

It's not even midday and a 4 pm departure puts us firmly in having-to-stay-at-a-murder-rest-stop territory. Addy must notice our hesitation because she jumps in and offers us a room in the guesthouse.

'You should definitely stay,' she says. We protest, but it's half-hearted. 'Honestly, we like fresh company,' she continues, 'and with COVID we've hardly had any visitors this year.'

So we hoist our bags across the lawn, a couple of friendly work dogs scurrying after us. The guesthouse is stunning: cowhide rugs spread over polished wooden floors and vintage furnishings that instantly transport you back to a time when thank-you cards were common and towels always came with a matching washer.

'Help yourself to cold drinks from the fridge,' Addy says, leaving us to go through some old books and newsletters in the sitting room to see if we can spot Paddy. For the next couple of hours, we thumb through hundreds of pages of documents, squinting at every picture, just in case. There are other cowboy gardeners, and other men called Paddy. But the man we are looking for is nowhere.

The Queen of England, however, has signed the guest book.

'Sorry, the back seat is a bit dirty.'

Rick has to go out and check some stock and has offered us a ride-along. He's not exaggerating when he says the car's dirty—there is a literal pile of red earth on the seat behind the driver, as if someone has upturned a pot plant there.

'Funny story,' he says, scooping up the back-seat desert and chucking it out the door. 'I was at a noxious weeds conference last week and a ranger asked if I could drop a thorny devil they'd confiscated from a poacher back to its home country near Bark Hut. It made a bit of a mess.'

We nod, as if taking a thorny devil on a road trip is normal. In fairness, our barometer for normal has started to shift. So many strange things happen out here that we're starting to under-stand how people can be cavalier about the most extraordinary happenings.

When the back seat is clean-ish, we set off through the gates into the open plains. Rick grew up in the city but fell in love with the idea of the bush through Henry Lawson, Banjo Paterson and Slim Dusty. He's been on stations for around a decade now, the last three years in management. Before that he was a ringer. That's how he met Addy—they'd worked together at Morstone Downs in Queensland. Rick was in love, but there was something else competing for his affection: bull riding.

Rick travelled around the outback jumping on the backs of beasts who'd clearly prefer he didn't, winning some rodeo belts and shattering more bones than most people would consider healthy. He headed to North America to ride professionally, then used his winnings to buy Addy a ring. They've been at Brunette a couple of years now.

We cruise around on a canvas of cracked earth asking questions about cows for a couple of hours—a big part of Rick's role is checking on stock and infrastructure, trying to head off little problems before they become big problems. Obviously, the biggest problem at the moment is the dry, but often the opposite is an issue.

In the archives we found a story about a pelican plague at Brunette in the late 1970s, following extraordinary rains that put more than a million acres (4000 square kilometres) of the property under water. For a time, Brunette had fifty-six thousand head of cattle and half a million pelicans, which appeared out of nowhere. One minute it had all been dust, then the rain fell and little islands popped up in the flood for them to roost on and fish suddenly appeared to feed them.

Gazing out at the dry emptiness, it's difficult to imagine that kind of rainfall but Rick assures us the wet is spectacular.

'I love the Barkly,' he says. 'It sounds a bit spiritual, or maybe a bit silly, but it's almost magical your first wet season.' We're pulled up next to a paddock of Mitchell grass. There's nothing here, not even cattle. But Rick looks out at the endless carpet of blond stretched out before us and becomes poetic.

'In the wet, everything is new, everything looks happy. The cattle are all bouncing around, and there's this silver-green ocean of Mitchell grass, and as the wind hits it, it makes these beautiful waves that the sun catches and lights up. Out here, you get back some deep instinct for direction. On Brunette, I can always tell where north is, or the way back to the homestead. It's like that sensation is in you and when you come out here it finds its way back to the surface.'

There's something about the way that Rick talks now that reminds us of Paddy—the deep affection for a place that isn't yours. Staring out at the enormity of it, we wonder if Paddy had the same sense of Larrimah's direction and landscape. Everyone says there's no way he could get lost in a place he knew so well, but even bush-smarts have a limit.

As if to demonstrate this Rick pulls up high above a lake, where a memorial made from small stones is piled on a larger stone, a cattle guard encircling the structure. There's a plaque on the rusty fence that reads: 'Here lies Harry Redford alias Captain Starlight'.

In 1870, Redford pinched a thousand cattle from a station in Longreach, in western Queensland, and completed a 1200-kilometre cattle drive to around Mount Hopeless in South Australia. It's a feat that had killed Burke and Wills, who didn't have to worry about feeding a thousand cattle, and a jury was said to be so impressed by the sheer impossibility of what Redford had done that they didn't convict him. Actually, it's those skills that earned him the gig droving the first mob of three thousand cattle to Brunette in 1883.

'He's supposed to have drowned here,' Rick tells us. He was crossing a flooded creek, some say with a horse in tow. 'But I dunno. People question it. He knew what he was doing, he shouldn't have drowned. Then again, horses aren't predictable. A kick in the head, maybe he got knocked out—who knows?'

It wouldn't be the first time a highly skilled person met their end in a place they, of all people, should have been safe. In years of wrestling crocodiles, it's preposterous that a stingray killed Steve Irwin. Grizzly Man Timothy Treadwell lived with bears for years, claiming he had gained their trust. Then they ate him. These things do happen.

Doubt is a powerful thing and, looking at the lonely little grave, we feel it catch us, too. Maybe Paddy did get lost. Maybe we're underestimating the power of nature.

Tony Green is sitting outside the Saddler's Arms, the little bar run by the station. He's wearing a green collared shirt and a huge cowboy hat. His face is crinkled, friendly. He looks like the type of person who has stored up some good yarns over his indeterminate years, but when we approach him, he doesn't want to talk.

'Maybe I'll talk to you tomorrow morning,' he says, tired and intent on enjoying his knock-off beers.

But the day starts at 5 am here, so it feels like a long shot that any of us will feel like talking any more then than we do now.

We go inside, disheartened, and buy ourselves a round of beers. The staff all take turns bartending, and tonight is Addy's shift. She chats with her co-workers, handing over two beers at a time, which is the limit.

'You might find Paddy in one of those,' she suggests, pointing at the photographs lining the walls of the small room, which was once the saddlery. We start at opposite ends of the room, leaning in and inspecting group photos of staff, posed like school class photos, trying to make out the smiling faces squinting into the sun. They're all date-marked and stretch back to the 1980s, though the fashions don't change. There are families, children, young people and old, stockmen and women, domestic staff, managers and governesses. By the time we meet in the middle, we're certain of one thing: Paddy is not in any of these photos. We've spent over a year trying to fill in the thirty-year gap in Paddy's history, but the more we unpick it, the more Paddy's past starts to fray—apart from his stories, there's no tangible evidence he ever worked at Brunette at all. A dread settles over both of us.

We whisper our fears to one another and try to force down the panic with beer. What if we drove all the way out here and had these kind cowboys put us up for the night for no reason? And, worse, what if nothing Paddy told people was true? How can we get to the bottom of what happened to a man with no verifiable past?

'Any luck with the photos?' MJ asks. We try to rearrange our expressions into nonchalance and join him at a bar table. Some homemade jerky is doing the rounds, and the general consensus is it's too sweet. A few people ask who we are and MJ tells them about Paddy. We sit there quietly, sweating and feeling foolish. Then Tony Green comes in for another round.

'Tony, can you help these girls?' MJ explains our plight and we hand over a photo of Paddy. Suddenly Tony breaks into a smile.

He speaks fast, huskily, with a heavy accent that sometimes slips into pidgin. 'Paddy, yeah, I know him. He was my friend. My best friend,' he says. He forgets the plan to talk to us at some ungodly hour tomorrow, grabs his two beers and ushers us over to a table in the undercover area outside, away from the throng. He's effusive about Paddy, he clearly knew him. He even coincidentally drove through Larrimah a few days after Paddy went missing. The police pulled him over and asked some questions. It wasn't until later that Tony realised he knew the person they were looking for.

We begin to relax. Paddy had been here. We weren't victims of a tall tale, after all. Then Tony adds: 'I knew him so well from Heartbreak.'

We can't disguise the desperation in our voices. But he was here too, right? Before Heartbreak. Tony looks confused, then his brow furrows as if he's flicking back in the archives of his mind, trying to locate Paddy in the file on the early days of Brunette. 'Yeah . . .' he says. It's not convincing, but then we ask if he can remember when Paddy was here and he gains some confidence. 'From 1972, I think. I can't remember for how long. My memory's not so good. Maybe from 1974.'

This falls somewhere in the middle of that huge cavity of years we had thought Paddy was here, but if Tony's memory holds up, it doesn't explain where he was before that.

Tony says Paddy was employed as a jack of all trades. Cowboy gardener fits with that, at least. He thinks Paddy worked on other stations around the area, too. He gives us a few names of people to follow up and advises us to go to Borroloola—everyone there knew Paddy, he says. We tell him we've already tried.

He sips his XXXX Gold—the same beer of choice as Paddy—then he calls out to two other men sitting outside. 'Hey, you mob, get over here.' They slip into language when talking among themselves, each trying to prompt a memory, then seamlessly return to English when they address us. The other two men remember

Paddy too, but from Heartbreak, not Brunette. They weren't here back then, or they were too young to remember.

We put the question of children to them, tell them we heard Paddy may have had children with a woman from the old Aboriginal community here, back when it was located next to the Brunette homestead. As we ask, we feel some of the weight of it—this beautiful station, built on the back of the terrible conditions its Indigenous staff worked and lived in, on land that was taken from them. It's not just Brunette—it's the story of almost every Australian cattle station.

'He didn't tell me if he had a son or a daughter, I didn't ask him anything about that,' Tony replies. Then he backtracks. 'But I'm sure he must have had a daughter.' He can't say why he thinks that, just that he does.

Suddenly a loud bell sounds and everyone is on their feet. 'Last drinks!' says Tony, downing the end of his can. We thank him for chatting with us and he stops and looks sad for a moment. 'I miss him,' he says. 'He was a good bloke. We would drink together. He was my best mate.'

Back inside the bar everyone is scrambling for final beers and we get caught chatting to another young cowboy. He mentions he once worked on a station in western Queensland, around the same area the Bush Poet works. We casually drop his real name, without the context or what he's told us.

The young cowboy's head jolts. 'How do you know *him*?' He sounds a bit panicked.

The Bush Poet knew Paddy, we tell him. They were mates. But the look of horror on the man's face remains. He shakes his head. It's like he wants to say something but can't find the words. So we decide to run the Bush Poet's name by one of the other guys at the bar. The reaction is almost identical.

'Be careful,' he says. 'He's a nice guy. But he's also the kind of guy who would tell you anything, just for his own amusement.'

We sit through dinner—beef—with the words roaring in our heads. It's impossible to shake an image of the Bush Poet sitting at his local pub, laughing to his mates about how he duped a couple of gullible journalists.

As tempting as the idea of Paddy being alive was, we had always had a healthy level of doubt about it. What we had stopped doubting, though, after those few phone calls, was that the Bush Poet believed it. His conviction was part of what made the idea interesting, especially since he'd known Paddy for more than thirty years and claimed to have seen him not long before he disappeared.

After dinner, we go back to our cosy outback palace and strike Queensland off our itinerary. The move isn't entirely based on the less-than-flattering character assessments of the Bush Poet. It's also because we're running out of time. We've had a taste of the vastness of this country, and even if we believed the Bush Poet, we simply don't know where to start finding a person who doesn't want to be found, somewhere in a plain of Mitchell grass so wide and flat you can see the curve of the earth.

In the morning, we farewell our gracious hosts and head back into the dust. We have one last shot at excavating Paddy's Brunette past.

Back when Paddy would have been here—if he ever were— the Wambaya people lived a couple of hundred metres from the homestead. But in the 1990s, a previous owner of Brunette Downs offered them a 16–square kilometre excision at Corella Creek, about forty-five minutes north of the homestead. 'Excision' seems such a precise and formal word for returning country to its traditional owners. Not to mention the injustice of being 'given' only a small tract of land that already belonged to you. But some of those traditional owners moved to the new site and we've been told that Tony's wife, Kathleen, is somewhat of a local historian, who lived in the community when it was still near Brunette homestead, and she's apparently chatty. She might be able to help.

We drive about 90 kilometres back up the Tablelands Highway. There's a huge tin sign on the way into Corella, welcoming us, but when we pull in, the community is entirely silent. Clothes hang on lines and cars are parked outside the dozen or so houses but, except for some lazy-looking camp dogs, there is no sign of movement. The modern little school is deserted. A generator whirs, but that's the only sound.

We don't know which house Kathleen lives in, so we stop the car in the middle of the dirt street and cast around, hopelessly, for signs of life, finally spotting a teenager in a yard. We edge the car closer, get out and ask if someone can point us in the right direction. This is Kathleen's house, it turns out, so the teenager leaves us in the sun by the gate and eventually, an older lady comes out. We tell her what we're looking for.

'My husband, Tony, knew Paddy from Heartbreak,' she says. 'Talk to him.' She turns and walks back into the house, closing the door behind her.

If it's possible, the Corella Creek community looks even more forlorn on the way out. The whole place seems such feeble compensation for what was once a wide, rich existence on this land. The same reasons that have made Brunette so well suited to cattle had also made it a good place to live and hunt for the Wambaya people. The lakes and the Mitchell grass attracted emus, kangaroos and birdlife. But the cattle edged the native animals out, and the station edged the traditional owners out. In a much less brutal and unjust way, there are forces edging out station life as we know it, too.

Yesterday, we'd been chatting to Rick about Brunette—how pretty it is, how much we'd loved it, how we'd live there if we could. There's something so familiar about it all, like some lost sense of Australiana we didn't know we had.

Rick had smiled, maybe recognising something of himself in our enthusiasm. 'The young ones, they love it too,' he'd said. But it's all changing. Even though the ringers love the weeks out at the stock camp, eating and sleeping under the stars, when they come back the first thing they do is log on to the internet.

'Young people now want to be more like 50 Cent than Slim Dusty,' is how Rick had put it. It's hard for stations to recruit. In the past they'd only needed to provide staff with food and water, now wi-fi is considered an essential, too. It's a shame, Rick had said. He used to think he wanted to keep the bush the bush. But he could also see that stations have to evolve.

We're a long way from Larrimah, but our thoughts drift back there as we hurtle north again. There's a whole ecosystem of outback settlements and stations that help keep towns like Larrimah afloat, providing a steady stream of people dropping in for beers or picking up their mail. Towns rely on them for income and news and fresh gossip. But it's precarious. Brunette has sidestepped most of the idiocy of civilisation. But civilisation is increasingly mobile. It can't stay unhitched forever.

31

A lost city, a miraculously green lawn and an endangered pygmy hippopotamus

The drive back to Heartbreak is long, and when we arrive, the afternoon is longer. This whole trip we've been struck by how hours on the road can fold in on themselves; days either race by or stutter along in spurts. A slow rush. But at Heartbreak, as we wait to talk to Catherine, time just stretches. We find ourselves with nothing to do but watch the sun move across the sky. It's too hot to walk and there's nowhere to walk to, anyway. It's too hot to sit still. The pool sparkles under the fierce sun—just looking at it is enough to give you third-degree sunburn, and the grey nomad floating there is decidedly pink. There's a huge sign out front advertising helicopter flights over the Lost City, underneath a picture of a sandstone formation behind a gorge. But the picture is not, in fact, the Lost City—the graphic designer has simply ripped off a generic gorge picture and presented it as local. Plus, however beautiful the real Lost City sounds, it's too far. By the time we got anywhere, we'd have to turn around and come back.

The thing is, Catherine is here. She's just not back at work yet. When we find her on the back verandah where staff sit for breaks, she'd already knocked back a few drinks on the charter plane home, and is keen to stretch her last day of holiday out as long as possible. 'Tomorrow morning, before you go,' she tells us. So we return to the tourist part of the verandah and sit it out in the heat. In a few hours, the road workers will start coming back, covered

341

in a thick film of orange dust. The grey nomads will emerge from day trips and afternoon naps for happy hour, taking photos of the occasional wallaby on their iPads and drinking sweating glasses of chardonnay. The gap between afternoon and evening widens. We order a beer, then another. It would be nice to have more, but that feels like slipping off the precipice, and so many people slip off the precipice. They pack eskies full of beer to go to work. They drive drunk, they build roads drunk, they sit on verandahs and tell stories, drunk. Everything out here is done drunk, someone tells us. It's so hot and time is so brutal. It's almost like people don't have a choice.

The next morning, Catherine joins us outside with a mug of herbal tea almost the size of her head, but certainly not larger than the hangover she's nursing. She admits, cheerfully, to being a bit stonk-ered last night.

Sliding into one of the picnic-style tables across from us, she wraps her ring-covered fingers around the tea.

'I'm the worst person to talk to about memory,' she admits, upfront. 'I've just been so busy all my life that I forgot to have children and everything.'

She laughs, even though the context isn't that funny. 'I did. I was spewing. I was over forty and I tried IVF and it was too late. Shit, hey? I just got so busy with everything, it was just a whirlwind.'

She has a soft way of speaking that smooths out all the hard consonants, so even though she's trigger-happy with an F-bomb, it feels somehow lyrical. 'Especially this mongrel place. It's a beautiful place but there's so much work.' We look around. It's obvious how much work is being done here; it's also obvious how much needs to be done.

Catherine is glamorous—a word that we haven't had much occasion to use on the road. We look thoroughly haggard by the elements but, even hungover, Catherine's blonde hair is shiny and her smile is warm and even. She first came to Heartbreak in about 1996, when the hotel was an unconventional jewel in the crown of a motley empire of businesses—three cattle stations, a fattening property and a Darwin-based limousine—owned by a man called Don Logan.

As is the way of these outback outposts, it didn't take long for Heartbreak to get under Catherine's skin. She eventually based herself between here and Darwin, managing the whole portfolio of businesses, and got her pilot's licence so she could travel between the properties and ventures.

She still remembers the first time she flew into Heartbreak. The grass was so green it felt like a mirage and there, on the ride-on mower, sporting a hat and a grin, was Paddy.

'It was better than schmick, mate, it was fucking awesome. Paddy would go round over the wet season and literally hand-pick all the prickles. Unbelievable. He never stopped. Just go all day, we'd have like twelve sprinklers a day going, and it was magic, as he used to call it. Magic.'

Catherine does a good impression of their first encounter, including an Irish accent that was strong in those days. '"G'day folks,"' she says, in imitation of Paddy greeting them from the mower. And then she laughs. 'Fuck, he laughed all the time, didn't he?'

There were plenty of things to laugh about, back then. It was an era characterised by mischief and wonder—the sort of thing that, in retrospect, might feel like a life so fantastical it belonged to someone else altogether.

There was the time Catherine flew Paddy into the Tipperary Station wildlife sanctuary, which was kind of like an outback Jurassic Park, if you replaced the dinosaurs with rare African animals and then plopped it down in the midst of a working cattle station. It was the pet project of millionaire property developer Warren Anderson, who somehow got his hands on more than two thousand exotic animals: fallow deer, ostriches, blackbucks, zebras, nilgais, greater kudu antelope, Congo buffalo, cheetahs, chitals, scimitar-horned oryx and South American tapir.

None of it was open to the public (though, apparently, a number of former prime ministers used to holiday there), but Catherine was friends with someone who'd invited them to visit. She remembers flying in with Paddy in the back, green and sweating, because he hated aeroplanes. But even he admitted it was worth it to spend the afternoon looking at giraffes and watching zebra wander in paddocks next to the cattle. Hippos and rhinos and hundreds of birds.

Another time, Catherine flew everyone to Mt Isa for the rodeo, but the accommodation was all booked out, so there were nine of them staying in two beds.

And on slow afternoons at Heartbreak, when they were feeling a little mischievous, they'd wait for a tourist bus to pull in and Paddy would duck out the back and tie a hanky over his mouth. Then he'd leap onto the tour bus, brandishing a toy gun, and tell everyone it was a hold-up. The tourists loved it. They thought he was fantastic.

Catherine is patient with us, as we try to fact-check a series of tall stories from Paddy's time at Heartbreak. Most of them have come to us third-hand, and the years (plus all the beers that no doubt accompanied the tellings) have stretched them in unexpected directions.

Was there a shootout, we ask, trying not to mention the recent shooting because it's going through court. The shootout we're talking about would have been in the 1980s or 1990s. Paddy was supposed to be there, loading the gun, cheering on the shooters.

'We did have one night with a couple of guys who had guns,' Catherine says, though it takes a little while before she can call it back. It was a racist attack on an Aboriginal family. A man was beaten so badly with a wheel brace that he lost the use of his arm, and the staff had to shelter his wife and children behind the freezers.

'Paddy would have been talking about that, probably,' Catherine says, though the fjord between the two stories is so wide that it makes us squirm. Maybe he'd been talking about the fake tourist-bus hold-ups? We move on.

And what about escorts? we wonder. Did the hotel ever run escorts, and did Paddy look after the girls? We've heard it from so many people who spent time out here, people who knew Paddy and people who didn't. It's information that has often been delivered unprompted. 'Those escort girls used to work out there. They'd work the bar, then at the end of the night, they'd be doing other things,' an old rodeo clown who stopped in at Heartbreak each year told us. 'Don Logan would fly them in from Cairns or Townsville or something.' At least three others have told us the same.

Catherine laughs at the suggestion. 'That was all shit. That's all fucking shit. Paddy and Donny used to start all that rot. I said to the pair of them, "Shut your fucking mouth", otherwise they all thought I was a bloody escort as well . . . Cheeky buggers. Never had one escort here in our lives. Would have made a fortune if we did. There were just men everywhere.'

The rumours started in the days when the boys from McArthur River Mine used to be able to stay for a few days of big drinking, she tells us. Sometimes, if they didn't get up in time to drive back, Catherine would drop them back in the chopper.

It's a credible denial, and Catherine says it good-naturedly, without defensiveness. But the way everyone tells it, Heartbreak has always been a place of exaggeration and shit-talking so it's hard to know what to believe. The story about the guy with a station full of exotic animals sounds far-fetched but it's absolutely true. And what came after is even more extraordinary. When Tipperary's owner went broke, the animals were sold off, mostly to zoos, but there are rumours that a couple of deals fell through and now at least half the Territory is convinced there's the occasional lion or rhino wandering through the outback. They're probably right. In 2009, a cattle station manager shot what he thought was a wild pig. Turned out, he'd killed an endangered pygmy hippopotamus.

We spend the rest of the time at Heartbreak hearing things we don't know what to do with.

First, someone else tells us that even though Paddy is remembered fondly around here, he left on bad terms. It was a bit of a scandal, they say. He ran off in the night with a young girl, about eighteen, legal but only just. Probably, this is the same girlfriend Terry Taylor told us about, the woman who lived with Paddy for a spell at Daly Waters. Terry had said she was young, but we hadn't known quite how young. There would have been about thirty-five years between them.

Then we spy the guy who saw Paddy, right before he went missing. He's smoking on the verandah, wearing the same blue singlet, and this time, he's happy to tell us the whole story. 'It still creeps me out,' he says. 'It was real weird.'

What the man says happened is this: A few days—or maybe it was a few weeks—before he disappeared, Paddy had stopped at Heartbreak. Paddy popped in a lot, and there was nothing remarkable about their encounter, but a few days later, a strange couple showed up at the hotel looking for work. The guy was in his sixties, big belly, not Irish but not Australian. Maybe Dutch. The woman seemed submissive, their relationship a bit off. And one of the things they asked about was Paddy.

'He told me his dad was supposed to be on the boat out to Australia back in the 1960s, but Paddy took his place. He seemed angry. Really angry. You know, like his resentment had been building for fifty years.'

The man tells us the whole thing made him uncomfortable. The couple hung around for a few days, then took off. But shortly after Paddy disappeared, their car came through again, heading down the Tablelands Highway. The man passed all the information on to the cops. They checked it out and came up with nothing. But as the media around the case built, so did his sense of unease—he still thinks about it, often.

It makes us uneasy, too. We came here chasing Paddy's past, and now it feels like that past is chasing us. Time is a wily thing, especially out here. We'd always thought the rumours that Paddy was wrapped up in something back in Ireland were far-fetched. But five decades of anger is a powerful thing, a long time to nurse a grudge. And we never did find Paddy's name on those shipping manifests.

We fuel up and take one last look at the heartbreakingly green oasis in the desolation, wondering what we'll tell Paddy's friends about what we've found here. We'd come expecting stories of prostitutes and shootouts but it turns out Paddy wasn't loading a gun to defend the outpost. He was dressing up as a bushranger and holding up busloads of tourists with a fake gun. Running away with a barely legal woman. Maybe even dodging a long-ago past, hiding from something bigger. It's hard to say what's a lie, and what's just reality that has been worn and torn over the years, soaked in booze and withered by bad memories and heat and time.

It takes us back to that quote we got stuck on, when we first started writing about Larrimah. It was the Mark Twain line about how a lie can gallop halfway round the world before the truth can even pull its britches on. Back then, it seemed to capture the idea that the myth of Larrimah and Paddy's disappearance grew to the point that the truth couldn't possibly compete.

Except, it turns out, the quote is a lie, too. Mark Twain never said it. Twain was dead by the time it was linked to him and now no one can agree who wrote it. Jonathan Swift? Thomas Jefferson? Winston Churchill? Terry Pratchett? It's a mess of names, and even the saying varies. People can't decide what article of clothing the truth is pulling on while the lie takes off with a head start: maybe a pair of britches, maybe a set of boots. Sometimes, the lie gallops around the world, sometimes it flies. In every version, though, the truth is slower.

We know how it feels to limp after a lie. We're weary, and the further we get into this, the less we have to go on. We're three years deep and less sure than when we started.

And so we find ourselves speeding out of Gulf Country, haunted by questions for which there are no answers, trying to see what we can sift out from stories that don't add up to anything. We'd hoped that understanding the kind of man Paddy was would help us understand what could have happened to him, but the answer is so much more complicated. He's a larrikin, is what so many people told us, but that is not the whole story. He is, apparently, the kind of guy who'd give you his last dollar. A man you could laugh with. And a man you could be quiet with. A man who held a grudge. A shit-stirrer. A bloke who didn't always understand the world. A drinker. A drunk. A liar, perhaps. Someone with a sink-hole past. Someone with secrets. Someone with trauma. An abusive neighbour. A great storyteller. A dog-lover. A loner. An absent friend, without whom nothing is the same.

When we list them off, there's no way to reconcile the contradictions or make them add up to any coherent whole, but maybe that's the point. Maybe nobody is any one kind of person.

The bright kapok flowers give way to sepia. Scrub crowds the Stuart Highway, closing in, as we turn back towards the Never

Never, 'that elusive land with an elusive name', says Jeannie Gunn, she of the Mataranka park full of statues. '[A] land of dangers and hardships and privations yet loved as few lands are loved—a land that bewitches her people with strange spells and mysteries, until they call sweet bitter, and bitter sweet.' As we drive, we catch ourselves thinking about how close together bitter and sweet can be.

32

A vegan dog, a stuffed panda and thirteen death adders in a jar

It's strange to approach Larrimah from the south for a change—it's like someone has flipped the whole landscape upside down and sent us through the looking glass. But, aside from being a mirror image, Larrimah looks the same no matter which side you enter from. A few signs bearing ill-proportioned Pink Panthers that look twisted by the heat. Hand-painted invites to Fran's teahouse. And the huge police poster, printed on corflute, with Paddy's face and a number to call with information. The one at this end of town has been shredded by the elements, though. What's left flaps sadly in the wake of road trains.

There's no change, here, just slow decay. And yet, this time the town really does appear like an oasis on the horizon. Maybe it's that the sports field is lush and green. Or maybe it's the sense of homecoming we allow ourselves to have, for a moment, for a town that does not belong to us.

'I won't hug you, I'm too sweaty,' Karen says, beaming. Behind her is what can only be described as a crocodile palace.

After termite-proofing everything, Karen and Mark have excavated a huge hole and then sunk a water tank, chopped in half unevenly to make two adjoining pools, one deeper than the other. Karen has concreted in a series of steps, so sightless Ray-Ray can always find his way out, and the whole thing is enclosed with solid fencing. There's a shade cloth over half the pond, plus space for an undercover garden so he can lie in the cool during the worst parts of the day.

'There will be water plants, of course,' Karen says. 'We'll get it looking really nice.' Eventually, they might even put in a sound system, so Ray-Ray can listen to the nature noise soundtracks he apparently enjoys.

'He's going to love it,' Karen says. Then, she points out the fenced viewing platform they've erected, presumably so she and Mark can have a beer or a cup of tea while admiring the world's happiest blind crocodile.

'It's been a lot of work, though,' she admits. There's a bit more to do, but she's running out of time. Work keeps calling wondering when she'll be back in again, and she needs to book in a ranger to come and move the saltie over from the pub.

'You here for a couple of days?' Karen asks. We are, so we make plans to have dinner at the pub tomorrow night and leave her and Mark to start filling the croc ponds with water.

The next day, our second last in Larrimah, we pull up outside Paddy's place. It's a strange home, when you think of it, living in the husk of a long-closed roadhouse, next to a burnt-out caravan park. The grass is almost shoulder high and the shade cloth flaps forlornly. But when he first moved in, Paddy told people he'd found his forever home.

'This is me done,' he'd told his mate Ray Aylett. 'This is where I'll die. This is where they'll plant me.'

It's eerie now, to think of how right—and wrong—he might have been.

We drive around the back along his fence line and let the car crawl down the road Paddy and Kellie walked every day to the dump. It's not a pretty walk and the dump is not a welcoming destination. There's no recycling plant or waste management system—towns like this don't get facilities like that. It's just a clearing with carcasses of old cars, household refuse and industrial waste.

It's too hot to get out, but even from inside the air-conditioned vehicle, it's clear there's no way Paddy would've ventured far off the path on purpose. Larrimah is an against-the-odds place, stubbornly beating back the wilderness that's closing in. Anyone sane would cling to the roads and dirt tracks.

When we first set out to tell this story, we were struck by how contained it was. Twelve people, one of them gone. Roughly 800 metres end to end. Someone must know what happened here, we thought, drawing a line around it all, with no idea how the story would explode, taking in almost every great outback yarn this country has ever told.

But now, at the end of it all, the fate of a man, his dog, and the town he loved are wrapped up together so tightly, there's no way to prise them apart. And we realise: it all begins and ends with Larrimah. Because, whatever happened, it happened here. Or at least, it happened *because* of here. And none of it is really that original. In this town of echoes, everything has happened before. A man and his dog dead in the bush. Pub owners banning residents. Pranks. Drunks. Crime. Death. It's like the town is constantly screening reruns.

The crunch of the coarse gravel is harsh as we trudge across town, under the wide, fierce sky towards Lenny's shed. It's our final tour of Larrimah and we're struck, all over again, by the conspicuousness of it all: the way sound travels in the emptiness, how exposed it's possible to feel in a town bereft of landmarks. A person can hide in a city, but the paradox of Larrimah is that, although everyone comes here for privacy and isolation, the town is too small for either of those things. It's a place of open space and open ears, where an argument or a dog barking or a car revving travels straight into a neighbour's lounge room. The geography of Larrimah conspires to expose things.

Of everything that doesn't add up about Paddy's disappearance, the most puzzling element is the lack of a witness. Whatever happened—an attack, an accident, a medical episode—someone should have seen something. An unfamiliar car. The hovering birds of prey. A neighbour acting strangely. And someone should have heard something, because even whispers carry.

A secret shouldn't survive, out here. And yet, the town is full of them.

In many ways, it's the mysteriousness of it all that has brought so many people to Paddy's story. The seduction of a puzzle that cannot be solved. It's not like we'd expected to solve the case. Looking back, we suppose we were trying to find Paddy another way—by recording him, wrangling the person from the myth. But at this point, we're not sure whether we're looking for answers or clutching at ghosts, trying to record something that's already half-gone.

Lenny is shirtless, sucking a blackcurrant Zooper Dooper, sitting in the detritus of his shed. He half-heartedly tells us to make ourselves comfortable but there's nowhere to sit and it's the kind of heat that would tempt you to snatch a half-melted ice block out of an old man's hand. As if sensing this, Lenny folds the top of the packet and deposits the small puddle of purple safely in the freezer.

'Those biscuits you brought were pretty good,' he says, of the home-baked shortbread we'd given out on the way down. It seems such a long time ago, now. 'I mean, they were a bit tasteless, and a bit crumbly. There was something missing. Did you forget to add something? Like some flavour? It needed more flavour.'

We laugh it off, but the review of our baking is a little galling, given that Lenny's got two teeth, is sitting beside a camp stove where he's been using an enamel plate as a frypan and the only thing in his fridge and freezer is the half Zooper Dooper.

Lenny points out the crack in the floor that tripped him up a few weeks ago. 'Got me good, hey,' he says, gesturing to the cut on his forehead, which has healed a little since we were last in town but still doesn't look great. We think back to Judy's comment about Lenny needing a will and wonder who this mess will fall to when he dies.

'They're trying to get me to go to a retirement home, but what would I do with all this?' He gestures around at his collections. 'And anyway, I hate those places. You go in and the only way you come out is feet-first, in a box. I told them that at the clinic, and they didn't like that.' Lenny grins and we try not to think of Barry and his own final days in Larrimah, clinging on to the freedom he'd spent his life enjoying, only to find it had become its own terrible prison.

'Anyway,' Lenny goes on, glib as ever, 'my parents both lived to be eighty-five, so I'm hoping to at least outlast them.'

We ask how old Lenny is.

'Eighty-four,' he replies. 'My birthday's next month.'

There's a long silence. We don't know what to say, so we suggest a cup of tea at Cookie's place next door, and Lenny says he'll come too. On the way, we pass one of Lenny's eight cars. There's a swag in the back with a three-foot plush panda on top of it.

'I picked that up at the dump,' he tells us. 'There were heaps of stuffed toys there, all in really good condition. I'm going to sell them.'

Cookie ushers us in, wearing pants this time, and immediately offers up cups of tea, apologising that he hasn't baked recently. His house is still up for sale and he hasn't had any takers, which he thinks is more to do with COVID than the fact that his house is in a town where, if buyers are interested in 'location, location, location', he's striking out on every front. He finds the pandemic baffling—he only just slipped back into the Territory after visiting his girlfriend in Tasmania before the state border closed. Then he got into an argument with staff at the clinic about whether he needed to be in isolation and eventually they called the police on him. Not because he should've been in isolation, apparently, but because of his language. 'They said I was swearing and stuff, I wasn't swearing, I just said, "This is bullshit." That's not friggin' swearing.'

The afternoon passes, talking about everything and nothing. We try but there's not much they can say about Paddy, or the town— neither of these blokes are sentimental. Things just are the way they are. Even though we're enjoying their company, we wonder what it is we are doing here.

At some point Cookie produces some black-and-white pictures of terrifying men that his sister found when she did the family tree. The first photo is a face that quite simply cannot be described. It's just terrifying. Flat-out maniacal. We can't even pretend to be polite about it. Cookie, we say, you're descended from a lunatic.

'He's a brute, isn't he?' Cookie says, laughing. 'Look at him. Can you believe it? And as for those two, they're no better.'

He points at the second picture, which looks to be a mugshot and is split down the middle. On the left, a man is staring out at the camera. There's a definite murdery vibe. On the right, he's in profile, equally murdery. But it's definitely one person.

'The pair of them, what a sight. Imagine finding out you're related to them.'

There's no way to tell someone that a single-person mugshot is not, in fact, a set of twins. So we return the photos and change the subject by asking about a framed picture on the wall.

'That's k.d. lang,' he says, pointing to a smug, fluffy-eared face, probably a King Charles spaniel. 'Isn't she gorgeous?'

Doggy k.d. lang is photoshopped onto a poster with two other pups, and they all seem to be floating against some kind of whimsical forest. Cookie explains they are all dead, but that they were good dogs, especially k.d. lang.

As he and Lenny run through all of the dead dogs in their lives, it finally occurs to us why we are here: it's for this. Cookie and Lenny don't know what happened to Paddy. They don't give a shit about the town's history. What they want to share is their own stories. Yarns about home renovations and long-distance love; train derailments by termite mound and the sudden joy of a stuffed panda at the tip. We've been so caught up in all the things that have been lost here: the war history, the rail legacy, the pub, Barry, Paddy. But here, right in front of us is history in the making, not yet lost.

⌣⌣

Eventually, Cookie tells us he's got to get going. He has to shift some stuff out the back because he thinks it will attract death adders, then he's got Mark coming over to help him out with some welding. 'Me shoulders are buggered; I need a knee replacement. Fuck me dead, they should shoot me like a horse.'

We wish him well with the upcoming operation, and with the house. He's trapped here until he can find a buyer and it must be hard on him and his girlfriend.

'When I sell this place, I hope it's a family that buys it because the wildlife you see around here, kangaroos and that, kids love that kind of thing, you know? They go crazy over kangaroos.'

We're not sure what kind of family is looking to relocate to

Larrimah, but we agree. A kid would love a garden full of kanga-roos. As long as they don't find out about all the taipans waiting to shut down your nervous system and hoe into you.

Having unearthed a genuine purpose for the collection of weird-ness we've been accumulating, we feel a little lighter as we walk to Karl and Bobbie's. We call out over the soft tinkle of the wind chimes, and Bobbie appears in the driveway. Every time we're back here we're shocked at how effortlessly elegant she is for someone in her eighties and living a million miles from the nearest shop. Her long hair is twisted back into a knot and she's in oversized jeans and a blouse, despite the heat. She was going to wash her hair, she says, but she'll put the kettle on instead.

'Sit down, make yourselves comfy,' she tells us, and leaves to call Karl, then returns with a tray of teacups and a packet of lamingtons. She apologises that they're not home-baked, even though we're the ones who turned up uninvited. 'Those shortbreads you brought were lovely, though, very nice.'

We laugh and say that Lenny's review was less than glowing. Bobbie shakes her head—Cookie has the same problem, she says. Apparently, he makes dinner for Lenny a couple of times a week, to make sure the poor guy eats something, but it's always too bland or too spicy—there's no pleasing Lenny. 'Cookie calls me, beside himself, asking for recipes,' she says. He can't read, so she has to dictate everything down the phone, which takes ages. She was trying to teach him to read for a while but he got sick of all the beginner books she'd got to get him started, so she told him to pick something he wanted to read. He returned from the library with something the size and complexity of *War and Peace*. Cookie is nothing if not an optimist.

Karl joins us, with a little shadow at his feet.

'This is Bob,' he says, smiling down at the black-and-white scrap of a dog, a scruffy thing with cute raccoon eyes, who leaps onto Karl's lap the second he sits down.

'Karl was in hospital in Darwin, for surgery,' Bobbie says, and then they slide into that habit of co-narration that's so endearing. 'And I told him that when he was better, we could think about getting a dog.'

But Karl moved quickly. The day after the operation, Bobbie got a call to say her husband was awake and, somehow, he'd already adopted a six-week-old puppy.

'I got it from a vegan and it demands to be hand-fed,' Karl says, scratching Bob's head. He complains about walking him, too, the way someone who is over the moon complains.

'Have a lamington,' Bobbie urges, 'I've only got the plastic on so the birds don't get them.'

It's a security measure that turns out to be necessary, because before long a crow they call Adelaide turns up demanding a feed, then a mob of bush chooks and a lovely black bird with a blue neck. Every time, Karl obliges, to the soundtrack of his own half-hearted complaints. It's like he can't stop adopting things and caring for them, even things he speaks ill of.

The Roths are still taking care of the town, too, in a way. Every night when Karl walks Bob over to the museum, to lock it up for the night, he checks out the situation in the Pink Panther. There's a nice young backpacker working there and he worries about her— the pub's been selling a lot of takeaway booze and it gets rough some nights, so he looks in every few hours, makes sure she's not alone with the till.

'We do lock our doors now,' Bobbie says.

Really? we ask.

'After the disappearance, we changed all the locks,' Karl agrees. 'I guess it's changed the town. I'd like to know what happened to Paddy. Partly it's curiosity, but you look at people differently because of it. It would be good to know what happened.'

It's a perfectly logical response to the disappearance of a neighbour but we're shocked because Karl and Bobbie have always seemed so self-contained and unaffected by it all. We ask again what they think happened to Paddy.

'I reckon it's the IRA,' Karl says. He's the first person who doesn't make the theory seem far-fetched. The past has a way of unearthing itself, and if there was any kind of personal secret that might wait decades to catch up with you, perhaps involvement in The Troubles would be it.

Of course, Karl's ideas have shifted over the years. Ours have, too. It's such a hard case to pin down. It's like trying to see the outline of something through moving water.

⌣⌣

At one point, Karl disappears. We assume he's gone to the bathroom but he returns with a jar, which he plonks down on the table, next to the lamingtons.

'Thirteen death adders,' he says. 'Just caught the last one the other day out here on the road.' He's keeping them for the museum.

The gesture sparks a series of reptile anecdotes, the best of which happened about a year or so ago. Bobbie became convinced their backyard pond must have had a hole in it because all their goldfish kept disappearing. She asked Karl to check, and when he parted the lilies he discovered a 2-metre freshwater crocodile.

'Someone must have put it there as a joke,' Karl says. Probably a couple of drunks at the pub. Karl says the pub *had* owned a freshie that mysteriously went missing years ago. But it must have been in the fishpond a long time, if it was the same croc, because now it was four times the size.

What did you do with it? we ask.

'I caught it, then called Parks and Wildlife and told them to come pick it up,' Karl says. 'But they reckoned they were busy and couldn't get here for a while. We had to go out, so I told them I'd tie it up on a dog leash in the driveway with the sprinkler going.'

It's an only-in-Larrimah story, the kind of yarn that reminds us that we can't disentangle Paddy's story from Larrimah's.

It says something about Paddy, that he chose Larrimah. It says something about everyone that they took this town as their own. We're outsiders, so it's hard to pinpoint what it means, exactly. But, against the odds, it has got under our skin, too.

Any life is shaped by the place in which it's lived—the wind and the earth and the sound. And in this wide, harsh, featureless landscape, it's almost impossible not to build an expansive life, one that's full of tall tales and true absurdities and reptile anecdotes. In most places, if two strangers knocked on the door asking for a story, people would be surprised and cagey, and often they'd come up empty. Out here, people put on the kettle, as if to say: finally, someone has come to hear the stories spilling over in me.

But we haven't heard them all yet. Fran's twenty-six-year-old grandson Brent Cilia moved here from Melbourne two years ago. He's living on the edge of this dying town and we've heard he's been weaving dreamcatchers. We're eager to sit down with him properly. Making dreamcatchers in a place where, historically, dreams have come to die is the kind of heady optimism the outback is built on.

33

A space mural, some fluffy scones and the town dreamer

We find the teahouse gates open and some indie folk playing. At first, we're hit by a sense of familiarity, but as we get closer, we can see there are a few changes. The signs (banning dogs, bicycles and people asking to use the toilet and EFTPOS) are noticeably absent and there's a spray-painted mural of a space scene on the wall of the old bungalow where Owen used to live.

'It's changed because Nan's not here,' Brent tells us. 'People walk in and they go, "Where's Fran?" and I'm like, "Well, I'm Fran now. I've had a face lift."'

He laughs, high-pitched and contagious. Brent is a good deal taller than his grandmother and has his Maltese father's dark eyes, but there's still a reflection of Fran in his face. He directs us to the new menu—another change, plus he's added clear and affordable prices—and tries to talk us into trying his signature spaghetti bolognese pies. It's only 8 am, though, and neither of us has eaten breakfast so we settle on tea and scones. After he puts plates in front of us, there's a nervous silence while we take the first bite.

'Are they okay?' he asks, suddenly shy.

They're delicious. Soft, fluffy and fresh. The CWA would approve.

Fran's breast cancer recovery is going well, and in the meantime Brent's done his best to honour her history and quirky aesthetic while modernising things. Last week he took the gallery of broken toys to the dump.

'Don't tell Nan,' he laughs, and of course we wouldn't. We also won't tell Lenny, whose Larrimah dump stuffed-toy windfall suddenly makes sense.

We've got a lot of questions for Brent, but there are two at the top of our list. How the hell did he end up here? And what does he think of the accusations that his nan might have been involved in Paddy's disappearance?

The post had come up in Brent's Facebook feed: MISSING PERSON—LARRIMAH. Brent knew a little about Paddy, enough to recognise him as the bloke who lived near his grandma. At first, he assumed the old guy had been bitten by a snake or something, but then he read some of the comments on the article. Shit. They were blaming his nan for it.

He and his mum jumped on the phone. Why hadn't Fran told them?

'I didn't want to stress youse out,' she said. 'They'll find him.'

Brent wasn't so sure. It was just like his nan to underplay something serious, she was always a little bit oblivious. So they kept in touch as the police search escalated into a murder investigation. Not long after, Fran told them she'd found a lump in her breast, which they urged her to get checked; cancer ran in the family.

'I'll get it sorted when they find Paddy,' she assured them.

Days stretched into months. The inquest was looming and there was no sign of Paddy. Fran finally got the lump checked—it was cancer. Stage four. Behind her heart.

Brent made the promise in a teary instant. 'I'll come up. You're going to need help.'

It would only be his third time in Larrimah. He knew it wouldn't be an easy place to live, but moving here for a while wasn't a hard promise to make to his nan.

Brent was the youngest in a noisy single-parent house of eight kids. His mum raised and protected them, and made ends meet, but hardship seemed to follow them around. Through it all, his nan was there for them. Even when Fran and Brent's mum weren't on good terms, she sent the kids boxes of jerky and things she had knitted for them, called to ask about them, offered to take them in for a while.

So, reading through the comments people were making about Fran online, Brent was struck by the unfairness of it all—people were calling her a murderer, saying she'd baked Paddy into pies. Someone had graffitied the teahouse signs, calling them 'Sweeney Todd Pies'. Fran wasn't some crazy old lonely weirdo, she was someone's grandma and great-grandma. She was his nan.

So Brent left his boyfriend and dog and went to help. His mum came too.

When Brent first arrived, the murder accusations made the prospect of going into town an unpleasant one. From the teahouse kitchen, he could see the pub and his pop's caravan a few hundred metres away (technically Bill is his step-pop, but Brent's never thought of it that way), but it took six months and his brother coming to visit to work up the courage to go to the Pink Panther.

The day the pair of them went to the pub, there was a tense moment as they walked up to the tall counter and ordered a beer and a Vodka Cruiser. Karen took the order. She was in the middle of a short stint working back at the pub to help Steve out, and Brent recognised her from the news.

'That will be seventeen dollars,' she said. Brent recoiled. So this was it, he thought: he wasn't welcome in the pub.

The next day, Brent called Steve to tell him he'd been ripped off. Only, it turned out he hadn't been. Brent wasn't the target of a passive-aggressive personalised pricing gouge, just a victim of bush pricing.

'I'll put you on local discount,' Steve said. 'And tell your grandmother to come and get her mail. It's been sitting here for years.'

And so the town settled into a truce. Brent did the rounds, explained who he was and how he didn't want any trouble, he just wanted to help care for his nan. It was awkward but it worked.

And Fran did need help—Brent was shocked at her condition. Some days, he had to dress her. One morning he heard a thump and ran in to find her lying on the kitchen floor, unable to get up. She was forgetting things, too, and getting confused. There was talk of her going back to Melbourne with Brent's mum.

At that point, Owen was still living in the bungalow. Brent hadn't spoken to him much. He was a quiet man, the kind of person who seemed like he'd had a hard life. Brent understood why Owen didn't want to speak to the media. But the inquest had received a lot of attention.

So eventually, Owen was asked to go. His exit from town was as quiet as his arrival, almost a year earlier. Then Fran went to Melbourne and Brent was left in the teahouse alone.

The evenings are especially dark in Larrimah. The nightly show of stars—a sky so full that you can see the way the earth curves—is beautiful but it's deep and impenetrable, too. It can make the town feel far away from everything.

'There's a part of living here that's scary,' Brent admits. 'I worry about . . . like last night I was doing my washing and coming back in the dark with my torch, making sure I can see everything before I walk, looking for snakes. I'm petrified of snakes actually; I'm not used to this stuff. You don't get a snake in your house down in Melbourne, you know what I mean?'

Brent laughs—he knows he's a fish out of water.

But other worries are larger. Some days Paddy's disappearance seems like it happened somewhere else, to some other group of people, but there are nights it keeps him awake.

'I found bones in the garden once, and I freaked out,' he tells us. 'I called the police. They turned out just to be animal bones, but they hadn't searched the garden properly because it was a new garden so I got them to come back. I said, "Dig deep, rip the plants out, go hard, if someone's going to be in there you've got to do it." It actually helped me because now I know he's not there.'

The question of his nan's involvement doesn't haunt him, though. 'I know that I couldn't kill anyone, I know Nan couldn't kill anyone. I just know. It's like Karen said she knew something had happened to Paddy when she went to the house and it's the same thing for me, knowing my nan is innocent.'

Brent's a long way from Melbourne now, a long way from his pets and family. But he isn't alone in Larrimah anymore. His pop, Bill, is looking frailer by the day and has moved back into the bungalow so Brent can keep an eye on him.

In the fragile and short-lived cool of the mornings, Brent and his pop have a cup of coffee together. After so many years of bad blood between Bill and Fran, Brent likes hearing stories about better times. Like how Bill and Fran planted a boab stick together when they first moved in, a hopeful gesture that has grown into a huge tree, even if the relationship didn't last. Lately, Fran and Bill have softened towards each other. They call each other 'darl' on the phone now.

Across town, other tensions have softened, too. Maybe it's Fran's absence and Barry's death, or maybe it's having someone young to look after and rely on. Whatever it is, the town has come together a bit. Brent helps where he can—lifting things, checking on people. He adores Karen and Mark, would help them with anything—like moving a crocodile, if they needed. He says Karl and Bobbie are great people; they drove Bill to hospital last week when he took a turn.

'From the media stuff it's like everyone hates each other, but it's not like that,' Brent says. At first we think he's being naive, but he actually means something much more complex.

'Deep down people didn't hate each other. They couldn't have,' he says. The problem was they never really knew each other—most of the residents hadn't spoken to Fran for years. They'd based their opinions of her on outdated ideas and suspicions they never crossed the road to check out. And they filled in gaps with wild stories about roadkill and pies.

'I asked Nanna, "Where's this pie war?" She's sick of pies. She hates the word pie now.'

Brent is an optimist—we weren't wrong about the dream-catchers. They're garish, feathered things, entirely unironic, as earnest and hopeful as he is. So when he talks about the town, he looks forwards. He hopes Larrimah can have a more peaceful future and that he can be part of building it.

'That's what we should be about, like family. I'm the youngest of eight and there's about that many people in town, and I'm the youngest here, too. It's like living with my family, in that one house, we're all in this one town. So I know how it's gotta work. You've all gotta be there for one another. Even if you do fight, you put that aside and help each other.'

34

A graveyard of barrels, a drink-driving cowboy and a final bittersweet beer

It's early evening and the pub is quiet. Despite Steve's sprucing, the Pink Panther looks all of its sixty-eight years—tired, ready for retirement, but pushing through the fatigue.

A young blonde Czech woman is behind the bar, the girl Karl worries for when the pub gets rowdy. She and her boyfriend have been here a few months and we ask if they're COVID refugees, but she says they're here by choice. They love Larrimah.

We're shocked, but then again, we've fallen for this strange place, too. We've sat on this verandah so many times over the past three years, talking to Barry and Richard and Karen and Mark, eating pub dinners, drinking beer, watching TV, that now we slump comfortably in the chairs as if in our own homes.

We catch Karl and Bill in the dying light of the day. They're drinking beer and speaking quietly. It's nice to see Karl at the pub—he's a semi-regular these days. Bill's rake-thin, but he smiles when he sees us.

'I'm all right,' he assures us when we ask after his health. 'I'm on the mend.'

When nobody is looking, he pulls a slice of stale bread from the pocket of his too-large shorts and throws it to the water fowl pecking around on the floor. 'Here you go, mate,' Bill says. That same bird turns up every year, Karl tells us. Always on his own.

We tell them we're keen to go to Gorrie, the old airfield north of Larrimah, on our way out of town tomorrow. They insist it's impossible to get lost out there, but we ask them to draw a map on a scrap of paper anyway.

'You can borrow the radio, if you want,' Karl says. 'We'll come out for you if you don't come back.'

The conversation turns to other things—the pranks truckies used to play on each other and the treasure fields of war relics that might be buried out at Gorrie. Beyond the pool of light from the pub, trucks rumble past like dragons, lighting up the otherwise black highway. Paddy's corner sits empty but it's still his—his name's high up, near the bird clock and the backwards Coopers sign. It's easy to be part of something in Larrimah. Whatever side of the rift you're on, you're part of it. There's an object or a sign for pretty much everyone, hidden among the memorabilia in the pub. It's almost like Steve has started pre-memorialising the other long-term residents. One of the new additions is a series of signs, for Bill and Lenny and Karl and Bobbie. 'Karl x Bobbie were here. Here they were. Were they here? Course they were.'

But while we're staring at it, we notice another sign, hidden in plain sight above the too-tall bar, which isn't the highest anything. 'Welcome to the Pink Panther Pub,' it says, 'where the beer is cold and the bull shit is free.' It's a shame, really, that we didn't see it earlier.

Karen and Mark arrive and we order dinner and beers and pull up a table. There's some small talk, about the weather, the addition of pizza to the pub's menu. We fill them in on our trip—the queen signing the guest book at Brunette, the search for the three Tonys, the chocolate fountain in Elliott. We all have a good laugh, they ask questions, we buy more beers. Then there's a moment of silence as we all prepare for what's coming: 'So, what did you find out?'

Like everyone else, Karen and Mark still hold out hope that something will turn up. And it might. The government recently earmarked Larrimah for an agricultural precinct—5712 hectares with potential for citrus, mango, melons, more cattle. If anyone takes it up, it could increase the chances of someone out planting or ploughing or building a fence stumbling across Paddy's remains. It's happened before, a contractor jolted out of hard labour by a jumble of bones. But even having a body doesn't guarantee a resolution.

Together we rehash the possibilities. Paddy might well have been murdered. He might well have had an out-of-town enemy. He might have fallen into a sinkhole. He might have had a heart attack. The past might have caught up with him. We tell them the story about the diviner and get caught up, again, in how specific all the details are. But since we left Batchelor, we asked a local contact to walk by the address where Paul told us Kellie was now living and check for a kelpie. They've been past several times and there's no dog matching her description. There are almost infinite possibilities. Some scenarios are more likely than others. But it's impossible to rule any of them out for sure.

So eventually, we turn back to the other stories. Karen and Mark crack up when we tell them about the fake hold-ups on the tourist buses out at Heartbreak.

'That's just like Paddy,' Karen says.

And we realise that we've answered the wrong question. They're not just asking about the case, they want to know *everything* we've found out. So we lay down all the contradictions and snippets and stories—all the pieces of their friend we've found along the way. For a while Paddy's memory is alive in the corner of the pub he loved so much. And then we get back to talking about sprinkler-crocodiles and how many times Lenny has derailed the train.

At one point, a young ringer from a nearby station saunters in, dressed in boots, jeans and a cowboy hat. Karen and Mark know him, and after he's had a feed, he brings his beer over to our table.

We chat and laugh and drink a little more. Life carries on as normal. As if your mate didn't go missing. As if you didn't accidentally find yourself in the centre of a murder case that has the whole world talking. It's nice and it's normal and it's all you can do.

The second hand of the bird clock twitches without moving on, but we know it's getting late, so we start saying our goodbyes. The young ringer is pulling up stumps, too. Even though the station he works on is 'nearby', it's still about a 100-kilometre drive. He finishes up telling Mark how he's lost his licence for drink-driving, again, then goes to his ute in the car park, an open tinnie in his hand and at least four beers under his belt, and drives off into the night.

Leaving Larrimah always feels bittersweet. The rush of the air-conditioning as the car hits 130 kilometres per hour on the highway and the prospect of having mobile phone reception soon is comforting, and the sight of scraggly stringybarks and blood-woods whirling past the windows feels, somehow, as if you are escaping something. But there is always a moment of doubt where we wonder: what will be here when we come back?

The last thing we pass on the way out is Paddy's place. It's full of ghostly reminders, like the basket of XXXX Gold cans that never got recycled or cashed in, and the marble tombstone that marks Rover's final resting place in the patch of sun he always lay in. The dignified burial the border collie's owner and canine successor, Kellie, never received.

Unlike the World War II staging camp at Larrimah, Gorrie was not a build-your-own-bed-from-saplings kind of operation. It was an aircraft and vehicle maintenance site for six thousand Australian and North American air force personnel, baffling in how well established it was for a place that was always destined for a short life. There was a huge recreation hall that seated hundreds of people in front of an elaborate art-deco stage. A pretty chapel where men on dozens of neatly lined-up pews could sweat through Sunday service. A two thousand-person outdoor cinema. Gorrie had a bar, a hospital, a boxing ring, four tennis courts, a cricket pitch and a football field. And, of course, there were the aircraft hangars, workshops, depots, fuel stores, bomb dump and the runway.

It's hard to imagine any of that now, though.

We turn off the highway and make our way down a red dirt track, through a couple of gates and over cattle grates. But then the road forks and forks again. Four, five, six featureless roads disappear into an insanity of sameness. We have a UHF radio, the mud map Karl and Bill have drawn us and some extra water. We're only a few hundred metres from the Stuart and already our presence feels precarious, like we could slip off the edge of civilisation and get lost forever.

Someone—we've been told it was Paddy—has tied a metal bin lid to a tree and painted a few arrows on it. It's the only way to navigate the nothingness, and it's not enough, not without the mud map—there's no sense of where the arrows might lead. We choose a road to follow, driving slowly to avoid ant beds and fallen branches. And then, all at once, the track opens up onto the airfield—a wide, hopeless scar on the bush, both sudden and surprising in its scale, littered with scraps of metal. Skeleton trees twist around it, as if in warning. Don't go too far. Don't go so far you can't find your way back.

We park. Our footsteps are sticky as we creep into the bush, careful to keep the car in sight. We're not hunting for treasures—somehow, even being here feels enough like trespassing—but we want to know what was here.

There is a graveyard of barrels, half-full of tar. The skeletons of cars. Concrete slabs where buildings used to stand, now littered with glass and rubble and fragments of metal that have been honeycombed by the elements. It's a good reminder that nothing can be truly settled out here, only borrowed.

Over the last few years, we've thought a lot about what makes a town die and what keeps it alive. But there's no logic to these things. A thriving town can be erased with the swipe of a bureaucratic pen. Maybe the mistake is trying to impose reason on this unsound landscape.

There are mounds everywhere, places that look like they might conceal a lottery load of war vehicles—and there are holes, too, evidence of deep digging. It's hard to say what's true or possible. This is a country full of buried things—treasures and secrets, layered in bulldust. It has swallowed whole settlements, eras and dreams. And it has almost certainly swallowed a man, his dog, and the story of what happened to them.

All that remains is the myth.

Epilogue

From time to time we catch ourselves thinking of Paddy in present tense.

He's in Gulf Country, somewhere so wild and weird and remote that it's not on the map yet. There's not much there but there is a pub—there is always, always a pub. He's shaved his moustache, replaced his hat with a cap, renamed Kellie something near-enough-but-different. He has a new name, too, someone else's, and he's filled out a backstory with details that don't lead to questions. It isn't hard—after all, he's done it before. 'What was Ireland like?' people will ask, and he'll reply: 'Potatoes, potatoes, potatoes.' There'll be a laugh, and that will be the end of it. The conversation will drift into other territories.

And if we could only stumble into this one-pub town, we'd find him: keeping the seat warm as the hot afternoon melts into evening and the stars begin to crowd the sky, telling stories to anyone who'll listen. The stories will be wild, almost familiar, but the details will be twisted into something unrecognisable. And the whole time Paddy's talking, his eyes will be crinkling with the story he cannot tell. The one about the bloke who disappeared with his dog and pulled the wool over the whole world's eyes.

Of course, it's impossible. We know that. But it's tempting to think of Paddy alive—easier to imagine that this whole murky tangle of facts and lies and half-truths and unverifiable rumours is the site of some kind of elaborate hoax, the greatest story ever not told. Nicer than what it really looks to be—the site of some terrible, violent trauma.

We feel the possibility tug at us. Perhaps, however slim, there is a chance.

After all, a man can shoot a pig and later find it's an endangered pygmy hippopotamus, a Russian spy can turn up in a remote town pretending to be a bird watcher, an old man in a caravan behind an emu enclosure can hold the secret to the mystery of an elusive gold reef. A pink pub can struggle on, populated mostly by ill-proportioned Pink Panthers. Impossibility is part of the very fabric of reality out here, in this landscape of shifting stories. So who can say?

Postscript

On 25 February 2021, Northern Territory Police announced a
$250,000 reward for information relating to Paddy Moriarty's
disappearance.

In a pre-recorded video, Detective Sergeant Matt Allen said: 'It's
hard to keep a secret. Someone out there knows what happened.
We want them to come forward and help us to solve a murder.'

Acknowledgements

This whole thing started because of a bloke named Andrew McMillan. Andrew was a writer who spent a lot of time in Larrimah and penned some terrific books there (we recommend *Strict Rules*—the story of Midnight Oil touring the outback with the Warumpi Band in the 1980s—and his short feature about Larrimah, *We're All Eccentrics Here!*, published in Griffith Review). When he passed away his estate, in conjunction with the NT Writers' Centre, started an annual writing retreat to his beloved outback town. Kylie was the inaugural recipient and that's when this obsession began, over beers with Barry and Paddy at the Larrimah Hotel in 2016. Even though it took over our lives for five years, we do profusely thank Andrew, his mother Lorna, his estate and the NT Writers' Centre for introducing us to this extraordinary town and these extraordinary people.

Before this was a book it was a podcast called *Lost in Larrimah*, and we have barrels of gratitude for everyone who made that happen, including Siobhan McHugh, Liz Trevaskis and Hamish Robertson, for their early encouragement; Ellie Turner for her court liaising; Krista Mathis for being the best stage mum/beach-walk-sounding-board/interview transcriber and friend; and student researchers Cloe Read, Emily Bradfield, Dinushka Gunasekara and Eliza Reilly. We're indebted to Bond University, especially Cath Webber and Professor Tim Brailsford, who backed an unfinished podcast that used the phrase 'donkey dick pies' in the first 30 seconds; the Faculty of Society and Design (for support, time and recording space/equipment); and Caro's eternally supportive and enthusiastic colleagues, especially Donna Henson, Jennifer St George, Rob Layton, Jeff Brand, Marilyn Mitchell, Taryn Mathis, Mark Dinnen, Roger Patching, Michael Sergi and Darren Fisher. We reserve the biggest barrels of thanks for Gemma Jones at *The Australian,* who believed in the story from the start and fought to have it made, and Eric George, who used his magic to turn our not-always-good recordings into something great. Without Gemma and Eric, we would not have made any podcast, let alone one that won a Walkley Award. Thank you also to the *Weekend Australian* for commissioning the feature on Paddy's Last Hurrah, which we draw on in Chapter 17.

When this project morphed into a book, we fell in love with the outback spirit. Every stranger we phoned was up for a yarn or prepared to pass on a bunch of contacts, particularly Elliot McAdam and Jasmin Afianos, whose Territory networks are extensive. For expert advice, we're grateful to: Allen Maroney, chairperson of the Wubalawun Aboriginal Corporation and traditional owner; Dr Paul Luckin; criminologist Terry Goldsworthy; and ABC Amateur Race Club secretary Linda Blackwood. We also thank the professionals who helped us locate the scattered bits of Larrimah's history: everyone at the NT Library and Archives, especially Katherine Hamilton and Emily Prichard, the Australian Institute of Aboriginal and Torres Strait Islander Studies, the State Records of South Australia, the National Archives, the Australian War Memorial, the librarian at Darwin Languages Centre who found Clem Coady for us, and the late Trevor Horman, whose North Australian train trivia was unmatched.

We've drawn on and learned from so many books it's impossible to list them all, but some of the lesser-known titles that deserve mention include *Larrimah Connections* by Stanley G. Breynard (the most comprehensive personal account of the war years); *Birdum or Bust!* by Bob Foster (which served to inspire some of the trucking legends in Chapter 22); and everything ever written by or about Ernestine Hill. We also gained a lot from Peter Dermoudy's survey of Larrimah and Birdum's historical sites, and the late Ann Kanters' filing cabinet of research.

It is impossible to write about the history of the Territory without including the stories of First Nations Australians and we've tried to do so sensitively. We'd like to acknowledge that there are gaps in our writing and knowledge and that the true crime genre, broadly, fails to consider the ways government and police have participated in the frontier massacres of Indigenous Australians—a fact that still undermines and complicates the relationship so many people have with our justice system. Heartfelt thanks to Maddee Clark for his expertise and advice on this and other issues.

Writing a book is really, really hard, and so we owe much to the excellent writers we are lucky to call friends: Jennifer Pinkerton, Kate Wild, Miranda Tetlow, Johanna Bell and Matt Garrick. We've also had some great readers and thought-givers: last-minute sub-editor Karen Stevenson; Paul Dyer, who is a human back-catalogue of strange Territory news stories; Tara Goedjen, the queen of uncanny stories and a one-woman cheer squad; the thoughtful and savvy Shady Cosgrove; the dear, smart and thorough Michele and Jamie Clark; and our go-to Irishman Conor Byrne. Thanks to all our journo friends who've shared knowledge and incredulity, particularly Anna Henderson, who has always encouraged us.

To the amazing team at Allen & Unwin, thank you for loving Larrimah as much as we do and making sure the town and its history doesn't disappear. Particular thanks to Kelly Fagan, Tom Gilliatt, Tom Bailey-Smith, Deonie Fiford, Isabelle O'Brien and Sarah Barrett. Huge thanks to Jeff Kleinman and Erin Harris from Folio Literary Management, who are so generous and astute, and to Grace Heifetz at Left Bank Literary, who encouraged us to write a book and has been an outstanding advocate from the very beginning. Also, sorry/not sorry for the drunk text from Outback Spectacular.

Our friends and family have put up with a lot. None more than Kylie's husband Michael Usher. Not many people would willingly spend their annual leave in Larrimah, but Mick did—and cared for their five-month-old son Eddie while there. There is no thanks great enough for this selfless act—and we're very sorry that your birthday coincided with this Larrimah trip, and that all we bought you was a pair of headphones, which we immediately borrowed to make a podcast. We're the worst. We're also grateful to Alec Piovesan, for supporting and believing in this for so many years. We are fortunate to have the best families, who support our bonkers writing endeavours: much love and thanks to Karen and Garry Stevenson, who have flown to the other end of the country to help out on deadlines; David, Shelagh, Alex and Jenni Graham for their ongoing support; and the extended, hilarious and generally delightful Gorfunkle clan. And to Ali Taylor: love and thank you for the peanut butter toast, pep talks and sad pancaking necessary to get the book over the finish line. If Caro had two 'Good Egg' badges she'd give both to you.

We never would have made it to the final chapter without Kylie's wonderful neighbours and friends Tahnee Badrock and Mark Houston, who regularly provided a quiet space in which to work; Kim Stephens, who let Caro live at her house, drink her coffee and play with her kitten; and everyone else who offered us support, childcare, desk space and living space. And to all of our long-suffering friends and family who have listened to us talk about Larrimah for years. Sorry.

Finally, thank you to everyone who trusted us with their stories. We hope we've done them justice. MJ, Rick and Addy, we'll never forget the hospitality offered to us at Brunette Downs, an oasis on a long, rough roadtrip; Paddy's friends, who shared endless anecdotes; and Paddy's Irish relatives. Special mention must go to Ethel Webb, the daughter of Bill Jacobsen, who was murdered in Birdum in 1936. We tried for years to find Ethel and were so excited (and utterly surprised) when we finally did. Big thanks to Peter Cooke, Ethel's son-in-law, who not only connected us with Ethel but also sent on home videos of the family reunion in Larrimah, a precious family book, letters and documents to help us tell the family's story.

And most of all, to the residents of Larrimah. Cookie, Lennie and Bill: you never seem to run out of amusing stories to tell us. Fran and Brent: thank you for trusting us, and for the delicious scones. Karl and Bobbie: just when we think we've heard it all, you pair come out with a cracker story about finding a croc in your fish pond. We have truly enjoyed all our times sitting under your carport, sipping tea, eating lamingtons and hearing all your wild Territory yarns. Thank you also for loaning us a radio and offering to rescue us if we came into strife in the Larrimah wilderness. Karen and Mark: you've been enduringly kind and patient and are always doing something surprising—who else spends their annual leave building a croc enclosure? You've also been such wonderful advocates for Paddy. We'll never be able to repay all the times you've taken us out bush or met us at the pub for a drink or been on the end of a phone line to answer our questions. And to the late Barry Sharpe: Larrimah isn't the same without you.

Last, but most definitely not least, we thank Naomi at the Daly Waters pub, who loaned us her tent so we did not have to sleep in the dirt with the snakes. Naomi, you are (possibly) the reason we lived to tell this tale.